FURTHER PRAISE FOR **BLACK DAHLIA, RED ROSE**

(UK) Book of the Year

UK Crime Writers' Association
er Award for Nonfiction

"Black Dahlia, Red Rose by Piu Eatwell provides fresh evidence that we can never get enough of our favorite pin-up corpse. . . . [A] juicy page-turner. . . . [Captures] both the allure and the perils of the dream factory that promised riches and fame to star-struck young women from tired little towns all over war-weary America and who, even today, find themselves at the mercy of predatory men."
—*New York Times Book Review*

"Black Dahlia, Red Rose . . . [puts] Elizabeth Short at the center of her own story, while still managing to read like a classic noir tale. Eatwell's extensive research pays off in the narrative, which is impressively detailed. . . . Fascinating."   —*Bustle*

"After decades of cultural appropriation by journalists, novelists and filmmakers, Eatwell has finally offered Short a type of belated justice. Her book reads like a thriller, but it never loses sight of the real woman whose life was so savagely extinguished."
—*Sunday Times* (UK)

"Piu Eatwell is hot on the trail of one of the twentieth century's most famous cold cases—the Black Dahlia murder—and she takes us along for the ride . . . back to Los Angeles in the winter of 1947, back to the wealth of evidence assembled by the cops, by the tabloids and news dailies, by a 1949 grand jury. The ride is well worth taking, especially when she hones in on a plausible and previously neglected suspect in the case." —Jon Lewis, author of *Hard-Boiled Hollywo͏͏ ͏* *Crime and Punishment in Postwar Los Ang͏*

"Not since James Ellroy has an author stepped back and taken such an objective look at the Black Dahlia case. Everything about Eatwell's research is meticulously detailed, giving the reader a fine-tuned insight into the smoky suburbs of LA at a time when police work was gritty and the onslaught of journalists vying for a story was raw and untamed."

—*Real Crime Magazine*

"A meticulously researched work that is delivered with all the punch, pace and suspense of the finest noir thrillers."   —*Irish Times*

"A thoroughly researched look at the crime. . . . The investigative materials provide a solid foundation for Eatwell's film noir–style narrative; a first purchase where true crime titles circulate widely."

—*Library Journal*

"Eatwell pursues her suspect to the nightmarish end, uncovering corruption of every kind, and offers a convincing solution. Her book could also be read as a critique of an era in which emotional devastation and exploitation were inevitable byproducts of a system capitalizing on desire."   —*Mail on Sunday* (UK)

BLACK
DAHLIA,
RED
ROSE

ALSO BY PIU EATWELL

The Dead Duke, His Secret Wife, and the Missing Corpse:
An Extraordinary Edwardian Case of Deception and Intrigue

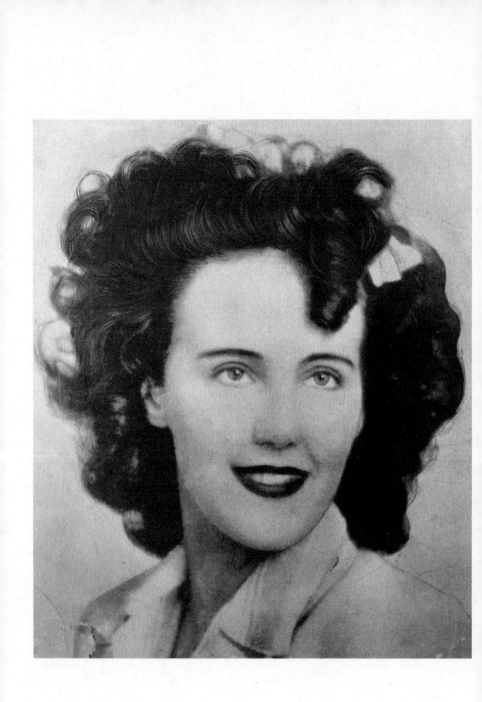

BLACK DAHLIA, RED ROSE

The Crime, Corruption, and Cover-Up of America's Greatest Unsolved Murder

PIU EATWELL

LIVERIGHT

LIVERIGHT PUBLISHING CORPORATION

A DIVISION OF W. W. NORTON & COMPANY

INDEPENDENT PUBLISHERS SINCE 1923

NEW YORK · LONDON

For information about permission to reproduce selections from this book,
write to Permissions, Liveright Publishing Corporation, a division of
W. W. Norton & Company, Inc., 500 Fifth Avenue, New York, NY 10110

For information about special discounts for bulk purchases, please contact
W. W. Norton Special Sales at specialsales@wwnorton.com or 800-233-4830

Manufacturing by LSC Communications, Harrisonburg
Book design by Lisa Buckley
Production manager: Anna Oler

Library of Congress Cataloging-in-Publication Data

Names: Eatwell, Piu Marie, author.
Title: Black Dahlia, Red Rose : the crime, corruption, and cover-up of America's greatest
    unsolved murder / Piu Eatwell.
Description: First edition. | New York : Liveright Publishing Corporation, [2017] |
    Includes bibliographical references and index.
Identifiers: LCCN 2017035228 | ISBN 9781631492266 (hardcover)
Subjects: LCSH: Short, Elizabeth, 1924–1947. | Murder—California—Los Angeles—
    Case studies. | Murder—Investigation—California—Los Angeles—Case studies.
Classification: LCC HV6534.L67 E23 2017 | DDC 364.152/30979494—dc23
LC record available at https://lccn.loc.gov/2017035228

ISBN 978-1-63149-493-2 pbk.

Liveright Publishing Corporation
500 Fifth Avenue, New York, N.Y. 10110
www.wwnorton.com

W. W. Norton & Company Ltd.
15 Carlisle Street, London W1D 3BS

2 3 4 5 6 7 8 9 0

This book is dedicated to
Donald and Patty Freed

CONTENTS

PREFACE

This is the story of one of the most notorious unsolved murders in California history—probably in American history. The story of the murder of a twenty-two-year-old girl, whose bisected body was found in the grass beside a sidewalk in a Los Angeles suburb in January 1947. Perhaps, if the newspapers had not come up with the name, the case would have languished in obscurity along with the hundreds of others marked "unsolved" in the basement of the Los Angeles Police Department. But the moniker "Black Dahlia"—evocative of an exotic flower, of desire both toxic and intoxicating—has ensured that the case remains forever imprinted in the public consciousness, a potent symbol of the dark side of Hollywood, and, by extension, of the American dream.

This book is part detective story and part history. Partly, it is also a snapshot of a great American city and its police department as they stood at a specific moment in time. This era is commonly visualized through the movies, as the era of film noir: a time of corrupt cops and gun-toting gangsters, cynical heroes, and bottle blondes doling out deadpan one-liners. But the slick film noir repartee belied the brutal inequalities of reality. In truth, it was a tough time after a tough war in a tough world. The Black Dahlia case tapped into both the imagery and the issues. As such, it became a real-life noir story, acquiring its own mythic dimensions as fact and fiction became hard to disentangle.

In the following pages I tell the story of this extraordinary case. However, despite its narrative form, this is not a work of fiction. Anything between quotation marks comes from a letter, memoir, or other written document. If I describe the weather on a particular day, it is because I checked the contemporary weather reports. The action takes place almost exclusively in Los Angeles, but I must beg forgiveness for a wide sweep across the decades from postwar to the present. Such a range is necessary to present the story in its entirety. I hope the reader will also allow for a change of narrative voice at the end of the story. This is necessary to broaden the scope of the account, from a historical retelling of the tale to the context of a modern-day investigation. Readers who find the chapter headings evocative of film noir movie titles of the 1940s and '50s would be absolutely correct.

An especially challenging aspect of investigating this particular case is that the Los Angeles Police Department has consistently refused to release the crime scene photographs and the full autopsy report. In addition, various key items of evidence—in particular, physical evidence such as the victim's purse, shoes, and letters—are no longer available or have disappeared. The main source of contemporary evidence remains the important cache of papers related to the case collated for a grand jury investigation in 1949, and recently released by the Los Angeles district attorney. While it is highly probable that some items of contemporary evidence were suppressed by certain members of the police department at the time, it should be emphasized that police practices in general and the conduct of the LAPD as described in this book are limited to the period of the historical events discussed. There is no evidence whatsoever that today's LAPD was involved in any "cover-up," or indeed has any idea whether these items of evidence actually exist, or, if they exist, where they are.

In the end, this is a story about truth: the search for truth and its suppression. The sixteenth-century English philosopher Francis Bacon has said that truth is the child of time. If this is the case, then I offer this book as the offspring of the years, which, like Moses in the cradle, has finally come to rest in the bulrushes of the Nile (or, in this case, the Mississippi).

Piu Eatwell, 2017

KEY DRAMATIS PERSONAE

(A full list of dramatis personae begins on pp 275.)

THE COPS

Chief of the LAPD
Clemence B. Horrall (until summer 1949)
William A. Worton (after summer 1949)

Assistant Chief of the LAPD
Joe Reed (until summer 1949)

LAPD Chief of Detectives
Thaddeus Franklin "Thad" Brown (from summer 1949); elder brother
  of Finis Brown

LAPD Homicide Division
Head of Homicide:
Captain Jack Donahoe (until September 1947)
Captain Francis Kearney (after September 1947)

Homicide Detectives Assigned to the Dahlia Case:
Lieutenant Harry "the Hat" Hansen
Sergeant Finis Albania Brown; younger brother of Thad Brown

LAPD Gangster Squad

Head of Gangster Squad:
William "Willie" Burns (until late 1949)

Gangster Squad Detectives Assigned to the Dahlia Case:
John J. "JJ" O'Mara
Archie Case
James Ahern
Loren K. Waggoner
Con Keller

LAPD psychiatrist

Dr. Paul De River—police psychiatrist to LAPD from 1937 to 1950
Fred Witman—private investigator and close friend of Dr. De River

THE JOURNALISTS

James Hugh "Jimmy" Richardson—city editor for the *Los Angeles Examiner*, Hearst newspaper
Agness "Aggie" Underwood—city editor for the *Los Angeles Evening Herald & Express*, another Hearst newspaper and rival of the *Examiner*

THE VICTIM

Elizabeth Short—the "Black Dahlia," victim of a gruesome murder in January 1947
Phoebe Mae Short—mother of the victim
Mark Hansen—Danish nightclub owner and Hollywood business-man, close friend of Short; no relation to Harry "the Hat" Hansen of the LAPD
Ann Toth—Hollywood bit player, close friend of Short
Marjorie Graham—girlfriend of Short
Lynn Martin—nightclub singer, girlfriend of Short

Dorothy and Elvera French—cinema assistant and her mother who
housed Short briefly in San Diego in December/January 1947–48

THE SUPPECTS

George Hodel—celebrity Hollywood doctor

Leslie Duane Dillon—twenty-seven-year-old drifter and hotel bellhop

Corporal Joseph Dumais—one of over five hundred "confessing
Sams" who claimed to have committed the murder

PART 1

FALLEN ANGEL

"This is a rotten town with a lot of
rotten people in it."

—*A MAN ALONE* (1955)

FAREWELL MY LOVELY

S unrise was at 6:58 a.m. in Los Angeles on the morning of Wednesday, January 15, 1947. The month had been an unusually bleak one for Southern California. Dense fog had descended on the coastal towns of Long Beach and Redondo. The sea fog was accompanied by a razor-edged wind that whipped up the Pacific rollers and sent raw blasts through the boulevards of a city more accustomed to the hot, dry, dusty winter gusts of the Santa Ana winds.

The previous night had been a rare one in Los Angeles because there had been a hard frost on the ground. Black smoke trailed across the sky from the smudge pots lit to protect the orange groves that, in those days, still carpeted the slopes of the San Fernando Valley. A slice of waning moon hung over the orange trees, their pale blossoms and fragile perfume already in the process of being obliterated by rows of white concrete grid housing. Farther south from San Fernando, in Hollywood and downtown Los Angeles, trolley cars shuttled their late-night cargo of drunks, streetwalkers, and transients around the city, seemingly oblivious to their impending annihilation even as they rattled along in the shadow of the construction work on the latest phase of the Hollywood Freeway. In just a few years, the freeway would become the major road linking northern suburbia with Tinseltown. The old central tramway would be demolished as part of a lofty plan to transform the City of Angels into, in actor Bob Hope's words, "the biggest parking lot in the world."*

Like much of Los Angeles, Leimert Park in the south of the city was the planned master community of an ambitious property developer. When Walter H. Leimert† began his dream project in 1927, he envisaged a model community of homes in the newly fashionable Spanish Colonial Revival style, which would give white middle-income families their piece of the American dream. Sandwiched between Jefferson Park to the north, Hyde Park to the south, and Baldwin Hills to the west, the residential district boasted its own town square, movie theater, and shopping malls. Even more impressive, it was designed by the firm Olmsted and Olmsted, sons of Frederick Law Olmsted, the man who landscaped New York's Central Park.

In the 1940s, Leimert Park was the perfect place for young, white married couples to start a family. So it was for John and Betty Bersinger, who in 1945 had purchased a bungalow with a neat garden and wrought-iron grilles in the 3700 block of Norton Avenue—one of a series of narrow ribbon-roads to the north of Leimert. As elsewhere, the war had stopped housing development on their block, and the lots one block south were covered with weeds: stiff horseweed, yellow mustard, and stinging nettles in the spring and summer; clumps of wiry grass, ranging Mexican oleander, and hard, black earth in the winter. Nothing stood on the vacant scrub other than a row of electricity pylons, a line of black masts linked with skimming wires that leaped and ducked to the horizon.

Despite the unfinished housing developments, sidewalks had been put in along the vacant lots, and this part of the park was a

---

* The Hollywood Freeway—the primary shortcut spanning the Cahuenga Pass to link the San Fernando Valley with the Los Angeles Basin—was completed in three stages in 1940, 1954, and 1968.

† Walter H. Leimert (1877–1970) was born in Oakland, California. The son of German emigrants, he was to become a significant Los Angeles property developer.

popular recreation area for mothers and children. It was also where Ringling Bros. and Barnum & Bailey sometimes had their circus. So it was that, at 10:00 a.m. on the clear, cold morning of Wednesday, January 15, 1947, Betty Bersinger packed her three-year-old daughter, Anne, into her stroller and headed out south across the vacant lots, making for a repair shop to pick up her husband's shoes. The crunch of broken glass underfoot at the 3800 block of Norton caught the young housewife's attention as she tried to steer the stroller clear of the shards scattered on the sidewalk.

Then, glancing up, Betty saw the flies. There was a big black cloud of them buzzing low over something. Squinting, the young mother could just about make out what appeared to be a white shop mannequin sprawled on the rough grass by the sidewalk. Bizarrely, it appeared to have been cut in half. "My goodness, it was so white," said Betty, many years later. "It didn't look like anything more than perhaps an artificial model. It was so white, and separated in the middle. I noticed the dark hair and this white, white form." The presence of the palely glinting object, in a place where children played, was troubling. "It just didn't seem right to me," said Betty. "I could see these kids on their bicycles, and I thought, maybe it will scare those kids if they ride to school and see this, so I'd better call somebody to come along at least and have a look, and see what it is." The thought that what she had seen was anything other than a broken store dummy barely entered Betty's head.

Hurrying past the vacant lots, Betty tried the doorbell of the first house on the next block. There was nobody home. At the second house, however, a woman opened the door. Betty explained that she had seen something strange a block back. She asked to use the telephone. When the call was answered at the police station, she briefly outlined what she had seen and told them someone should come check it out. Then—having triggered what was to become one of the biggest manhunts in the history of modern America—Mrs. Bersinger trundled on her way with her buggy and her child to the shopping mall.

—

The call came through to the police complaint board at 10:55 a.m.
A shrill-voiced female—who hung up abruptly without identifying
herself—complained that there was an unsightly object off the sidewalk in the vacant lot on Norton Avenue between Thirty-ninth Street
and Coliseum, in the middle of the block on the west side, and could
someone please take care of it. At 11:07 a.m. a radio car was dispatched to the scene, with uniformed patrolmen Frank Perkins and
Will Fitzgerald of the University Division. Accustomed, as regular
flatfeet, to booking the streetwalkers, dope peddlers, and drunks
who were the usual detritus of Skid Row, Perkins and Fitzgerald were
ill-prepared for the sight that awaited them. They immediately radioed in to the Homicide Division.

By 11:30 a.m., word of there being a "man down" on Norton
between Thirty-ninth Street and Coliseum had spread through
town. A throng of newspapermen with heavy camera equipment and
phosphorescent flashbulbs gathered to join Sergeant Finis A. Brown
and Lieutenant Harry L. Hansen, the Homicide Division detectives
who had been dispatched to the scene. "'A 390W–415 down' meant a
female drunk passed out sans clothes," recalled Los Angeles journalist Will Fowler, twenty-four years old at the time. Fowler had never
had his picture taken with a dead body before, so he cut a deal with
news photographer Felix Paegel to split a bottle of bourbon if Paegel
took a photograph of him kneeling beside the corpse. A circle of
fedoras, jabbing fingers, and smoking flashbulbs soon surrounded the
form with its cluster of buzzing flies.

One of the first to arrive on the scene was Agness Underwood,
veteran crime reporter of the *Los Angeles Evening Herald-Express*.
Agness, known to all as "Aggie," had been born in San Francisco
in 1902. Her mother had died when she was six years old. She had
subsequently been dumped by her itinerant, glass-blower father into
a series of charity homes and foster families around the country.
Finally, abandoned as a teenager in Los Angeles by a relative who
had tried unsuccessfully to get her into the movies as a child actress,

Aggie had managed to find her way to a Salvation Army hostel downtown. She had worked as a waitress and married a young soda jerk, Harry Underwood, for fear of being turned over to the authorities for living on her own underage. The pair had settled in Ocean Park in 1920, running a soda fountain lunch counter. Aggie was a housewife in Los Angeles when she applied for her first newspaper job, working vacation relief on a metropolitan switchboard. She later claimed she only wanted the job to buy new silk stockings, which her husband told her they couldn't afford.*

By January 1947, Aggie had worked her way up from switchboard operator to the *Herald-Express*'s premier crime beat reporter. She was forty-four years old, a short, sturdy woman with a square jaw, pugnacious appearance, and a ready grin. "She should have been a man," said the *Herald-Express* managing editor, J. B. T. Campbell. She was "a rip-snorting, gogettum reporter that goes through fire lines, trails killers, weeps with divorcees and rides anything from airplanes to mules to reach the spot that in newspapers is usually marked with an arrow or an x." Aggie took great pains to distance herself from the sob-sister line of reporting that was the traditional beat for female journalists. "To hell with that. I'd rather have a fistful—an armload— of good, solid facts," she said. Underwood wrote like a man, cussed like a man, and joined in her male colleagues' pranks. Once, she slapped the city editor in the face with a fish that had been brought to the office in a tank. She dressed in the shabby, slapdash fashion of the male journalists: rumpled and unremarkable dresses, no makeup, low-heeled shoes. Colleagues recalled that her hair often looked as if it had been combed by an electric mixer. "She was a raggedy-looking woman," said Jack Smith, a high-profile columnist who worked with Aggie. But Aggie could also work her gender to advantage, when it suited her. She sewed back the wayward buttons of her male col-

---

* Aggie added the distinctive double *s* to her name on her second marriage in 1920, to the same man. Her husband, Harry, persuaded her to marry him again, because a dance hall was running a promotion that was paying couples $100 to tie the knot. Aggie was reluctant to do so, but Harry assured her there was no illegality in marrying the same person twice.

leagues' shirts, invited them home for spaghetti dinners, and brought her kids into the office to hand out gifts at Christmas. From the very beginning, she saw the big picture: skillfully mapping out a strategy where she would be seen as an exceptional journalist who just happened to be a woman. Within two years, she was to become the city editor of the *Herald-Express*, one of the first women to be appointed to the position on a U.S. national newspaper.

It was a matter of great pride to Aggie that she was tougher than any man when it came to covering gruesome crime stories. "I was no sissy in my control of my reaction to blood and guts," she said. Once, when police discovered two rotting corpses on a living room sofa, male officers and newspapermen waited outside for the room to air. Aggie marched straight in, climbed over the corpses, retrieved their IDs, and phoned in her story. Afterward, she sent her brown dress to the cleaners, but complained that "the odor persisted."

But even Aggie was shocked at what she saw on Norton Avenue the morning of January 15, 1947.

The body—wreathed in smoke from dozens of flashbulbs—was unquestionably female. It lay amid sparse weeds a couple of feet from the sidewalk. The arms were bent in right angles at the elbows and raised above the shoulders: in supplication, it seemed in death, in reality, the consequence of having been strung up by the wrists when alive. The legs were spread apart. There were bruises and cuts on the forehead. The face had been severely beaten. The hair was blood-matted. The eyes, which were closed, seemed strangely peaceful in contrast to the mouth, which had been slashed from ear to ear in a satanic smile. Most shockingly of all, the body had been cut in half through the abdomen, under the ribs. The two sections were ten or twelve inches apart. The liver hung out of the torso. A deep, gaping slit had been cut from the pubic area to just under the navel. It was, as one eyewitness was later to recall, as though "two hunks of human flesh had been laid down like two sides of beef."

In the city of Los Angeles in the 1940s, homicide detectives encountered a killing every two or three days. The department listed 131 murders in 1946, and 119 in 1947. Only a few blocks west, in the Baldwin Hills—as those who gazed at the grisly spectacle were all too aware—was the spot where ten years beforehand Albert Dyer, a WPA street-crossing guard, had assaulted, garroted, and tossed aside the bodies of three little girls, the "Babes of Inglewood."* But this was the most grotesque murder that those hard-nosed cops and newshounds had witnessed. The scene, Aggie said later, "showed sadism at its most frenzied—the worst butcher murder I was ever assigned." The male policemen and reporters thought the woman was about thirty-six years old. But Aggie, with her sharp eyes and personal experience, noticed the "youthful condition of the breasts and the smooth thighs." She knew the girl was much younger—early twenties, probably. Later that morning, the gruesome remains of "Jane Doe #1"—as the corpse had been christened—were sealed in an aluminum coffin with screw-clamps and taken by Black Maria† to the Los Angeles city morgue.

The Hall of Justice in downtown Los Angeles had rats as big as cats. They scampered and squealed down the drafty corridors of the massive fifteen-story building, which towered grim-faced over the city's civic center. The hall had been built in 1925 from Sierra granite, and its squat Corinthian columns were inspired by the Mausoleum at Helicarnassus, one of the Seven Wonders of the Ancient World. This was all the more fitting in that the building—which housed the district attorney's and the sheriff's offices—also happened to house the city morgue, deep within the vaults of the basement floor. The rear basement entry to the morgue was much like that of a wholesale grocery receiving entrance. Here it was that the two pieces of the corpse of Jane Doe #1 were unloaded and weighed on a set of black floor-level scales. "When they were told that the body was cut in

---

* Albert Dyer and the Babes of Inglewood case are discussed in detail on pages 84–86.
† Black Maria: Contemporary term for the coroner's truck.

half," recalled news photographer Felix Paegel, "the Coroner said the autopsy would be performed right after lunch."

Later on Thursday, January 16, the body was placed on a hard porcelain mortuary table. Above it hovered Dr. Frederick D. Newbarr, M.D., chief autopsy surgeon for Los Angeles County. Dr. Newbarr was dressed in a white autopsy gown, rubber apron, rubber gloves, and white galoshes. The table upon which the corpse lay was one in a row of several in the room. Each table had a corpse laid out on its gleaming surface, the head propped up on a wooden block. The room was infused with the stench of disinfectant, masking the unmistakable odor of decay.

The saying went that dead men told no tales, but Dr. Newbarr knew this was not true. Of the many dozen corpses that passed under his scalpel each week, every single one told a story, compelling to those who could read it. They spoke of empty lives in glamorous Hollywood villas, violence behind the mock-Tudor façades of the mansions of oil magnates, secrets in the basements of ranches in the forested canyons. There were the torn and broken fingernails of the woman who had clawed her attacker's face in a last bid for her life; the grip marks on the shoulders of the "accidentally" drowned child; the hesitation scars and cuts on the wrists of the youth who had committed suicide rather than face a court-martial for desertion. For Newbarr, toiling in his basement morgue, every single body presented a new and coded message to crack.

The body found in Leimert Park was a challenge for even the most experienced of forensic pathologists. Yet, by meticulous examination and assessment, Dr. Newbarr succeeded in itemizing the many horrific mutilations inflicted on the victim. His final report, with its staccato-like scientific terminology, made chilling reading. The body, Newbarr noted, was that of a female, about fifteen to twenty years of age, measuring five feet five inches in height and weighing 115 pounds. There were multiple lacerations to the face, inflicted by a sharp knife: in particular, a deep laceration over three inches long, which extended from the corners of the mouth. The teeth were in an advanced state of decay: the two upper central incisors were loose, and one lower incisor. The rest of the teeth showed cavities. The head showed evidence of severe blows, although the skull had not been fractured. Depressed ridges in the wrists suggested the girl had been strung up by the wrists and tortured. The blows to the head and lacerations to the mouth had been delivered while the victim was alive. It was these, Newbarr decided, that had probably killed her. The rest of the lacerations had been inflicted upon her when dead, including a distinctive network of crisscrossed slashes to parts of the body and across the pubic region, where the hair had been cut off and removed. There was no evidence of strangulation or suffocation. The grass upon which the body was laid had been wet with dew, suggesting that it had been placed there before dawn. Newbarr was of the view that death had occurred twenty-four hours previously, probably less.

A square of tissue had been removed from the right breast; and there were multiple scratches on the surface of the left. Healed scars on the chest suggested an old operation on the lungs. This was corroborated by the fact that, while the left lung was healthy, the right had pleural adhesions. Both arms were covered in cuts and scratches. Her nails were very short, and bitten to the quick. The palms of her hands were roughened, but not with calluses. The hair was dark brown but had been hennaed, with the original dark strands beginning to grow out. On each foot, the big toenail was painted bright red.*

The trunk was completely severed, by an incision that cut through the intestine and the soft disc between the vertebrae. It appeared that a very sharp, long-bladed butcher's or carving knife had been used to sever the body, and that the killer might have used a straight razor to inflict torture before death. The organs of the abdomen were entirely exposed, with lacerations of the intestines and both kid-

---

* While the hair had been hennaed, it had the overall appearance of the original dark brown, as the hair was growing out: as evidenced by the dead body report and morgue photographs.

neys. There was no evidence of pregnancy, and the uterus was small. There was, however, evidence of what Newbarr delicately described as "female trouble." This was later explained as a cyst on the Bartholin gland.* There was also a gaping laceration four and a quarter inches long, extending down from the navel to just above the pubis. A latticework of cuts had been made on both sides of this laceration, above the pubic bone. There was also a square pattern of lacerations in the skin of the right hip, and an irregular shape of flesh that had been removed from the front of the left thigh.† While the vaginal canal remained intact, the anal opening was markedly dilated with multiple abrasions, indicating insertion of a foreign object. The soles of the feet were stained brown, and the stomach was filled with feces and unidentifiable particles. All smears for spermatozoa were negative. The corpse was completely clean and drained of blood, indicating that the killing had been accomplished at a different location from which the body was found. Fibers from what appeared to be a stiff brush revealed that the body had been thoroughly scrubbed, particularly in the pubic region and points of mutilation. The fibers were sent to the FBI for analysis. They were found to be of coconut hair, probably from a cheap scrubbing brush. They were of no assistance to a possible identification.

Dr. Newbarr's report made it clear that the majority of gruesome mutilations had been performed on the dead woman's body after her death. They suggested necrophilia and a fetishism with knives. The blows to the head and lacerations to the face, on the other hand, had been performed when the victim was still alive. They were the hallmarks of a sadistic lust murderer. There was much discussion about the "clean" nature of the bisection of the body, and the fact that the corpse had been professionally drained of blood. It was speculated that the killer either had medical training or experience with

---

* Bartholin's cyst: a small, fluid-filled sac inside the opening of a woman's vagina, which if inflamed can cause an abscess and resultant discomfort during sexual intercourse.
† The removal of the flesh from the left thigh was particularly significant and is discussed in later chapters.

handling corpses in a mortuary. While the possibility that the killer was a doctor was entertained, this was not a requisite. The famous LAPD detective "Jigsaw John" St. John, who was to inherit the case many years later, stated that while "the perpetrator may have had some knowledge of anatomy . . . he wasn't necessarily in the medical profession." Of greater significance was the manifest fascination of the killer with death.

Two key items of information relating to the mutilations were withheld from public disclosure. These were to be kept secret, as an aid in interviewing potential suspects. They were facts that only the killer would know.

For the moment also, only the killer knew a third fact. Who was Jane Doe #1?

A DOUBLE LIFE

The news flash came through to the offices of the *Los Angeles Examiner* on the morning of January 15 from its police reporter, Bill Zelinsky. When it did, the city editor, Jimmy Richardson, shot every newspaperman and photographer in the office out on it. The staff of the *Los Angeles Examiner* called Jimmy the "last of the terrible men." He had been born in Windsor, Ontario, in 1894. His father was a Detroit horse-drawn carriage retailer put out of business by Henry Ford. Jimmy had started his career as a reporter in Winnipeg in 1912, after being expelled from school. The following year he moved to Los Angeles, to work at the *Los Angeles Evening Herald*, the *Post Record*, the *Daily News*, and finally the *Los Angeles Examiner*.

By 1947, Jimmy—a recovered alcoholic now hitting his fifties, scrawny, balding, and bespectacled—had worked virtually every big story that had come out of L.A. in the last thirty-five years. In the 1930s, he had single-handedly waged war against the gangster Bugsy Siegel. Jimmy was tough as boots, but there was just the tiniest chink in his hard-boiled armory: a predilection for quoting the poetry of G. K. Chesterton.*

---

* Jimmy Richardson's hard-drinking and hard-living newspaperman's life story was retold in fictional form in the novel *Come, Fill the Cup* (1952) by Harlan Ware, later to be dramatized in a film starring James Cagney.

Jimmy knew, from years in the newspaper game, that the way for a city editor to jump on a story was to "shoot the works at it." Then you waited, with your "blood pounding and your insides churning."

The *Examiner* reporter Sid Hughes was the first to call in on the story.

"It's a pip," he told Jimmy.

"Who is she?"

"Don't know. Can't find a thing to identify her. Nothing on the body. Good looking gal."

"Pictures?"

"Plenty but you can't print them. She's all cut up. Face and everything. I can give you detailed description, hair, eyes, height, weight and all that stuff. That's all there is to go on."

When Sid called the story in, the huge city room in the *Examiner* offices at Eleventh and Broadway was just waking up. The photo editor hurried up to Jimmy with a dripping eight-by-ten blowup of the bisected body. The reporters gathered around and stared. Richardson dispatched a man from the art department to make a sketch of the girl as she probably looked in life. He set the photographers working on printable crime scene photos that showed the nude corpse decorously covered by an airbrushed blanket. The *Examiner*'s January 15 Extra edition came out with the headline "Fiend Tortures, Kills Girl." It sold more copies than the edition that had covered the bombing of Pearl Harbor. The only edition to beat it was the one that came out on V-J Day. The writer Arthur James Pegler had said that "a Hearst newspaper is like a screaming woman running down the street with her throat cut." For once, nobody accused the newspaper of exaggeration.

Bill Zelinsky called in that the girl's fingerprints didn't match any on file at the police department or sheriff's office. "They're airmailing them to the FBI in Washington," he said. Warden Woolard, the assistant managing editor, then came up with the idea that was to give the *Examiner* its first big lead on the story: the jump that, in Jimmy's words, "made it our story from then on." That night, a couple of Homicide Division detectives came to the *Examiner* offices and asked if they could have their artist's drawing of the girl. Warden lambasted them for airmailing the prints to the FBI in Washington. There was going to be a big storm in the Midwest and the East, and all planes were to be grounded.

"That's tough," said one of the detectives.

"Not as tough as you think," said Warden. "We can send those fingerprints by Soundphoto.* We can send them tonight right now, and have the answer within a few hours."

Warden called Ray Richards, head of the Washington Bureau of the Hearst newspapers. Richards called the FBI and arranged for the prints, once wired to the *Examiner*'s Washington office by Soundphoto, to be delivered personally to Quinn Tann, the inspector in charge of fingerprint identification at the FBI. The first transmission over the telephone wires failed. The prints were indistinct. Russ Lapp, a photographer at the *Examiner*'s news bureau, then had the idea of blowing each fingerprint up and sending them one by one, as eight-by-tens. The prints reached the FBI at 11:00 a.m. But the images wired by Soundphoto, even when enlarged, were defective: two of the eight fingerprints were missing entirely, and three others badly blurred. Quinn Tann doubted that they could be used for identification. Nevertheless, dozens of assistants searched the fingerprint records by hand, leafing through card indexes under the glare of electric arc lights in the vast FBI vault. By 2:50 p.m., the prints had been identified.

She was Elizabeth Short, twenty-two years old, from Medford, Massachusetts. The fingerprints used for the identification had been filed with the FBI some years back by the Santa Barbara police. They had been taken on September 23, 1943, when the girl had been arrested for underage drinking with soldiers in a restaurant in the Mission Valley. At that point, she had been living with another girl in a bun-

---

* Soundphoto: an early form of fax machine.

galow court at West Cabrillo Beach. Soon a second matching print was traced with the help of the first: a national defense print submitted by the Services of Supply at the U.S. Army's Camp Cooke, Lompoc, California. It transpired that the girl had been working as a clerk at the Camp Cooke post exchange when she was arrested.

The Santa Barbara police mug shot showed a sallow, sulky-faced girl with an upturned nose, a shock of raven-black hair, and eyes with strangely pale, glassy irises. She had a look that went straight through you. The pressmen, habituated to writing up all "tomatoes as stunners," were for once not lying. Nobody had expected her to be so sullenly beautiful.

It transpired that after her arrest for underage drinking and while awaiting trial in Santa Barbara, the girl had been looked after by a local policewoman, Mary H. Unkefer. Officer Unkefer had befriended her and taken her into her home.

"She had the blackest hair I ever saw," Unkefer told the swarm of reporters who descended on the Santa Barbara Police Station. "I noticed that she was a very nice girl and was most neat about her person and clothes." Unkefer also mentioned that the girl had a rose tattooed on her upper left leg. "She loved to sit so that it would show," she said. The killer had cut out the rose tattoo.* Eventually, Unkefer said, the juvenile court at Santa Barbara had released the girl on probation. Officer Unkefer had accompanied her to the bus station and put her on a bus home to Medford. The Santa Barbara Neighborhood House gave the girl $10 in expense money for food and Cokes on the six-day return trip.

---

* Among the many mutilations of the body of Elizabeth Short, Dr. Newbarr noted in his autopsy report: *"There is an irregular opening in the skin on the anterior surface of the left thigh with tissue loss. The opening measures 3½" transversely at the base and 4" from the base longitudinally to the upper back. The laceration extends into the subcutaneous soft tissue and muscle."* This was in fact a reference to the incision that was made by the killer in order to remove the rose tattoo. The cutting out of the tattoo was never revealed in the press, but it was hinted at in a *Herald-Express* report on the discovery of the body: "A piece of flesh was gouged out of the left thigh, leading to the belief her murderer may have removed it to conceal an identifying mark" (*Herald-Express*, January 16, 1947).

It was the first time in history that fingerprints in a criminal case had been identified by Soundphoto. Jimmy Richardson took some time to crow about it before he sent Sid Hughes racing out to Lompoc to check out records at Camp Cooke. Sid prowled about the Army camp for a day or two. Soon he resurfaced with the information that the girl's mother was Mrs. Phoebe Mae Short of Medford, Massachusetts.

Jimmy called in his reporter Wain Sutton, who was writing up the story. He told Wain to get on the telephone to the murdered girl's mother.

"Now I want you to be careful," Jimmy told Wain. "She probably doesn't know her daughter has been murdered. So, find out everything you can about the girl without saying anything about her being dead. If you tell her at the start she'll probably throw a wing ding and you won't get anything."

"What if she asks what it's all about?" Wain asked.

"Stall her. Just keep asking questions. When you've got all you can then break the news to her."

Wain gave Jimmy a look. "What a sweet guy you are," he said, with deep sarcasm. But he proceeded to dial the number. Soon he had Phoebe Mae Short on the line. The mother was blissfully unaware of her daughter's recent fate.

"Well Mrs. Short," said Wain, "your daughter has won a beauty contest and we want to know all about her."

Richardson was whooping inwardly. "Wain might have been sad-eyed," he wrote later, "but he sure had come up with a daisy."

After scribbling furiously for some time, Wain looked imploringly at his boss.

"Do I have to tell her? She's so damn happy about the beauty contest."

"Tell her."*

---

* Richardson recalls this episode with some pride in his 1954 memoir *For the Life of Me* (New York: Putnam, pp. 299–300).

And that was how Mrs. Phoebe Mae Short heard the news that her twenty-two-year-old daughter Elizabeth had been murdered and left on a sidewalk three thousand miles from the family home.

When Jimmy Richardson got back to his desk, Sid Hughes came up and told him that the girl had won the Camp Cooke "Cutie of the Week" contest during her brief spell at the Lompoc Army Base in 1943.

"Tell all this to Wain," Richardson said dryly. "He'll be glad to hear about her winning that contest."

Wain, in the meantime, had extracted more facts from the mother. It transpired that Elizabeth was the third of five girls, born into a single-parent family in a working-class Boston suburb. She had no fixed address or job. She had lived at various times in Florida, Long Beach, Los Angeles, and Chicago, and had been staying, only ten days previously, at an address in Pacific Beach, San Diego. Jimmy called Tommy Devlin, his top crime reporter, to his desk. Tommy had been working on the Mocambo heist,* in which arrests were being made. Jimmy ordered Tommy to drop everything and hightail it to San Diego to dig up what he could.

Up until now, the newspaper reports had focused on the victim as a pathetic ingénue, a New England beauty who had been drawn to the dark lights of Hollywood like a moth to a flame. Elizabeth's former boss at Camp Cooke, a Mrs. Inez Keeling, said that she first met Elizabeth in the spring of 1943. "I was won over all at once by her almost childlike charm and beauty. She was one of the loveliest girls I had ever seen—and the most shy." Mrs. Keeling said that Elizabeth suffered from an acute bronchial condition: the doctors back home were afraid that she might have tuberculosis. "That is why her parents allowed her to room in California alone. She was just 18 then." Most of the girls at the PXs used to date the servicemen. "But not Eliza-

---

* Mocambo heist: a holdup of the Mocambo Nightclub on the Sunset Strip, for which several local gangsters were rounded up and arrested in January 1947.

beth," said Mrs. Keeling. "She never visited over the counter with any of the boys, and always refused to date them. She was one of the few girls in my employ who didn't smoke or occasionally take a drink. She lived in the camp and never went out nights." In 1943 Elizabeth left her job, but she came to see Mrs. Keeling for the next few weeks. Then the girl suddenly dropped out of her life, and she never saw her again. The rumor was that Elizabeth had been assaulted by a sergeant at the Army base, known as "Sergeant Chuck," whom she had been dating. The sergeant had been court-martialed and left the base. Elizabeth left shortly afterward.

But as the weeks passed, the image of the victim began, subtly, to change. There were incoming reports of many and various boy-friends; a rootless and drifting existence; and there had been the arrest for underage drinking in Santa Barbara. While it was clear that Elizabeth Short was no prostitute, equally she could no longer be characterized as an innocent. "This victim knew at least fifty men at the time of her death and at least twenty-five men had been seen with her in the sixty days preceding her death," noted a police report. "She was not a prostitute. She was known as a teaser of men. She would ride with them, chisel a place to sleep, clothes and money, but she would then refuse to have sexual intercourse by telling them she was a virgin or that she was engaged or married. She has been known to see as many as four men in one day chiseling a ride, dinner money or a place to stay, and would then brush them off with a fabricated line of conversation."

And so, slowly but surely, the public image of the murder victim began to change from that of a violated beauty into a "man crazy delinquent," a temptress prowling the rain-soaked streets of an urban film noir. The society columnist on the *Herald-Express*, Caroline Walker, saw in Elizabeth's fate a warning to the young women of postwar America:

"Two girls," wrote Walker, "with the innocent curve of babyhood still rounding their young cheeks, walk down this or that boulevard. There is no innocence in the knowing eyes of these girls." For such young women, wrote Walker, an evening of bar-hopping would end in a cheap hotel. Or the girls might go home: "home" being an apartment meant for two, crowded with bunk beds for eight. What, opined Walker, did these girls think of at night? Did they remember Sunday mornings, and a white steepled church in a little town? Perhaps, until the rush of excitement when the night returned, and they felt the same urge to prowl the streets like "animals in the jungle." Such women, concluded Walker, were accusations against society, against parents, and against the American home, "as stark as the handwriting on the walls in Biblical days."

Walker's diatribe tapped directly into a wider social anxiety about Los Angeles' "girl problem." Southern California had always been sold as a destination for white American males seeking to escape the influx of "ignorant, hopelessly un-American" foreigners flooding into the eastern cities. But lately—largely due to the movie industry—the region had become a target for a new type of female immigrant. The movies portrayed heroines with thrilling life experiences, liberated from the restraints of work and family. The golden life they promised stimulated a wave of women in the massive wash of emigrants that deluged Southern California in the early twentieth century. By 1900, female migrants outpaced male, effecting a stunning reversal in western migration patterns. "There are more women in Los Angeles than any other city in the world and it's the movies that bring them," said a shopkeeper in 1918. The figures supported the claim. In 1920, Los Angeles became the only western city in which women outnumbered men. The "extra girls" were everywhere: "girls—tall girls and short girls, curly-haired girls and girls with their hair drawn sleekly back over their brows, girls who suggest mignonettes and girls who suggest tuberoses; girls in aprons and girls in evening gowns—girls by the score, their faces all grease paint, waiting in little chattering groups for their big moment of the day."

The uncontrollable tide of youthful female flesh let loose on the West Coast created a moral panic. As the journalist Walter Lippmann put it, "external control of the chastity of women is becoming impossible." The dangers facing girls who left the white clapboard houses of home to venture into Sin City were starkly highlighted in books such as Edgar Rice Burroughs's *The Girl from Hollywood* (1922). Written at his Tarzana ranch in the San Fernando Valley (where Burroughs penned his more famous *Tarzan of the Apes*), *The Girl from Hollywood* features two heroines, neither of whom, with telling irony, actually comes from Hollywood. Seeking fame and fortune, the girls wind up drug-addicted, pregnant, and—in the case of one—dead; a telling parable of the dangers of a city whose sinister temptations were all the more insidious in that they took place under a blazing azure sky. Those girls with the "Bohemian bacillus" in their system, warned the film producer Benjamin Hampton, were in danger of reaching the "end of their journey" in a store, a restaurant, or the morgue.

Elizabeth Short—the dead extra girl from Massachusetts—made even better preaching material than any heroine of Edgar Rice Burroughs. She was real. But the murdered girl now required a new, headline-grabbing moniker to fit her new image. The newspapers found one. It came from a pharmacist in Long Beach, where, in the summer of 1946, the girl had drifted for a few months. The druggist, Arnold Landers, Sr., recalled her hanging around the soda fountain. "She'd come to our drug store frequently. She'd usually wear a two-piece beach costume which left her midriff bare. She'd wear the black lacey things. Her hair was jet black, and she liked to wear it high. She was popular with the men who came in here, and they got to calling her *The Black Dahlia*."

The Black Dahlia. It was the moniker of the decade. Jimmy Richardson said it was the brainchild of one of his reporters. Aggie Underwood claimed it as her own. Whoever first printed the name, it must have been inspired by the 1946 film *The Blue Dahlia*, a hard-boiled noir movie scripted by Raymond Chandler, featuring Alan Ladd and Veronica Lake. Floral names were fashionable for murders in those days. There had already been the "Red Hibiscus" and the

"White Gardenia" killings.* The "Black Dahlia" fit right in the box, although—as Aggie Underwood speculated—a "red rose" murder might be even better, as it would sound like "class as well as homicide." Aggie herself was a pro when it came to floral murder tags. Once she had dropped a white carnation on the body of a waitress who had been stabbed to death, dubbing the killing the "white carnation murder." When a cop objected to her taking a picture of her creation, Aggie smacked him with her purse.

Within weeks, the "Black Dahlia" sobriquet had established itself as an integral part of what was swiftly becoming a Hollywood legend. For many—including Lieutenant Harry Hansen, one of the lead LAPD detectives on the case—it was the reason for the legend. Hansen recalled that there had been many other crimes that year, at least as horrific and with victims at least as attractive. But not one got the same attention. It was the name "Black Dahlia" that sparked a national obsession.

Beneath the smoldering gaze and the lacy black chiffon outfits of the Black Dahlia legend, however, the reality of the victim's life was more prosaic. Jimmy Richardson summed it up best of all. "She was a pitiful wanderer, ricocheting from one cheap job to another and from one cheap man to another in a sad search for a good husband and a home and happiness. Not bad. Not good. Just lost and trying to find a way out. Every big city has hundreds just like her."

"We're hotter than a firecracker," Tommy Devlin told Jimmy Richardson upon his return from San Diego. "Just listen to this." The letter that Elizabeth had sent to her mother from San Diego had been writ-

---

* The Red Hibiscus murder: name given by the press to the killing of Naomi Tullis Cook, who was found beaten to death with a bolt and left in a clump of bushes in Lincoln Park in 1946. The White Gardenia murder: moniker for the murder of forty-two-year-old Ora Murray, whose partially nude body was found on the Fox Hill Golf Course in West Los Angeles in 1943. The killer had carefully placed a white gardenia under her right shoulder.

ten while she was staying at the home of a Mrs. Elvera French on Camino Padera Drive in Pacific Beach. Mrs. French's daughter, Dorothy, was a cashier at the Aztec Theatre downtown. The Aztec was an all-night movie theater where the homeless would crash. Dorothy had found Elizabeth asleep in the theater on the night of December 8, 1946, and had offered to take her to her home. Elizabeth had only been meant to stay a night with the French family. In the end, she lived there for a month.

"She left the French place about six o'clock on the evening of January 8 with a man known as Red," Tommy reported. "This Red sent her a telegram from Huntington Park saying that he would pick her up the next day. She told Mrs. French and Dorothy he was taking her to Los Angeles." Red was apparently a tall, red-haired, freckled man in his twenties.

"Good going, Tommy," said Jimmy. "Call me in an hour. Have we got this all alone? Have you told the Frenches not to talk? If it takes dough to shut them up give it to them."

"They're shut up," said Tommy, "I've seen to that."

The urgent task now was to track down "Red," the mysterious man who had collected Elizabeth on January 8. He must have been one of the last people to see Elizabeth alive. Jimmy sent a crew tearing down to Huntington Park to trace the telegram to which Tommy had referred. They found it. It read: BE THERE TOMORROW AFTERNOON LATE WOULD LIKE TO SEE YOU, RED. But there was no address.

Jimmy told Tommy to keep searching the records of motels at Pacific Beach for any trace of Elizabeth and Red. It was, he well knew, the time when a city editor sweats it out: the moment when he needs those little white pills. These were tough times for city editors. The City of Angels had, at this point, more than its fair share of newspapers in a cutthroat fight for a piece of the market. They included the staid and sober *Los Angeles Times*, the bastion of the conservative establishment, steered by the latest scion of the Chandler dynasty, real estate billionaire Harry Chandler; the shoot-'em-up and go-get-'em papers owned by Chandler's rival press magnate, William Randolph Hearst, the *Herald-Express* and the *Los Angeles Examiner*; and the ever-struggling *Daily News*, run on a shoestring by the Democrat-supporting Manchester Boddy. Everybody knew it was the Chandler and Hearst interests that ran the show. While very different men, Harry Chandler and William Randolph Hearst were united in their implacable animosity to the unions, organized labor, nonwhite "foreigners," and the "hot bed of Communism" which Hollywood was alleged to have become. But their approach to the threat differed. While the *Times* remained aloof and overtly allied to WASP establishment and business interests, the Hearst newspapers entered the fray with hysterical forays into yellow journalism to keep working-class readers entertained and well distracted from the issues that most affected them. The writer F. Scott Fitzgerald, blacklisted by the Hearst establishment for his alcoholism, was one of many to mock the typical Hearst headlines of the day. "Mickey Mouse Murdered! Randolph Hearst Declares War on China!" shouts a newsboy in Fitzgerald's 1941 novel *The Last Tycoon*. The difference in editorial approach between the media moguls at Los Feliz and San Simeon partly explained the difference in the attitude toward the Dahlia case taken by their respective newspapers. Chandler's *Times*, on the whole, did its best to ignore the sordid story as beneath its dignity. Hearst's *Examiner* and *Herald-Express*, on the other hand, flogged it within inches of death.

Of all the newspapermen on the street, Jimmy Richardson's were the most aggressive. They had huge expense accounts, bankrolled by the old man, who still barked out orders from his monolithic castle at San Simeon. Other newspapers, Jimmy knew, did not stand a chance in competition. Not that they didn't try. The *Daily News* had two reporters assigned to the Dahlia case to the *Examiner*'s twenty. In a desperate attempt to get more copy, the *News* sent a rookie reporter, Roy Ringer, into the *Examiner* offices in the early days of the story, posing as a copyboy. Ringer went to the spike where the proofs were ready for the next day, grabbed a bunch of them, and returned to the *Daily News* office. The next day, the *Daily News* ran the same "exclusives" as the *Examiner*. On Ringer's third visit, he felt a tap on his shoulder from behind. It was Jimmy Richardson. "Nice try, but don't try it again."

All through the night and day, Jimmy waited for word from Tommy. When it arrived, he could have kissed him.

"I've got it," said Tommy. "I've found the motel where Red stayed when he was down there and where he stayed with the Dahlia the night they left the Frenches."

Tommy had gotten the license-plate number of the car from the owner of the motel at Pacific Beach where Red had stayed with Elizabeth Short the night of January 8. Red and Elizabeth had checked out of the motel at 12:30 p.m. on January 9. That meant they would have arrived in Los Angeles later that afternoon.

It took no time to run down the license. The owner of the car—a 1939 Studebaker coupe—was a twenty-five-year-old pipe clamp salesman called Robert M. Manley. He had been a musician in the Army and had a psychiatric discharge from the service. He resided on Mountain View Avenue in Huntington Park.

Jimmy ordered two crews of reporters and photographers to hightail it over to Huntington Park. He'd be damned if he wasn't the first newspaperman to get an interview with "Red," the prime suspect in the Dahlia case.

3

THE CAPTURE

n the end it wasn't one of Jimmy's boys who got the first interview with Red. It was Aggie Underwood.

Red wasn't home when Jimmy Richardson's team arrived at the house in Huntington Park. He was on a trip to San Francisco with his boss. Jimmy's men had to make do with Red's wife, Harriette, a pretty young woman who came to the door with the couple's four-month-old baby in her arms. Mrs. Manley was adamant that her husband had come straight home on the evening of January 9. He had been at work all day and home every night since, until he left for San Francisco. She wouldn't believe he'd been with another girl unless she heard it from his own lips. He was faithful and good to her and the baby and his home. She loved him no matter what happened to him and would stand by him. Harriette posed for pictures with the baby and gave the reporters pictures of Red. "Gad, what a woman!" sighed an *Examiner* newspaperman. "Beautiful and forgiving. Why can't I find somebody like that?"

Red was arrested on the night of Sunday, January 19, returning from San Francisco to his boss's house in Eagle Rock. Detectives and journalists lay in wait together in the garden and bushes of the suburban home. As the headlights of the returning automobile cut through the blackness to light up the garage doors, a gaggle of police and pressmen shrank back into the shadows. No sooner had the tall figure, clad in pin-striped suit and gray fedora, emerged from the vehicle than he was immediately pounced upon and frisked from behind by one of the detectives. "I know why you're here, but I didn't do it," he told the waiting newspapermen. Within minutes, Red was bundled into a waiting police car. The vehicle sped up Santa Fe Avenue to the police station at Hollenbeck, cleverly avoiding the swarm of pressmen and photographers who had gathered outside Central.

At the Hollenbeck Police Station detectives grilled Manley for most of the night. By the time Aggie Underwood got there early Monday morning, both Red and the interviewing officers were exhausted, and Manley had clammed up.

Aggie sized up the suspect. She was ready to talk sympathetically about hangovers, and this guy "looked like the kind who would strike up a decent conversation in a bar." Even after a night of being given the third degree by the cops, he was still dapper and dandy, with his slicked-back hair.

"You look as if you've been on a drunk." Aggie said to Red.

"This is worse than any I've ever been on."

Perry Fowler, Aggie's photographer, took his cue and helpfully handed Manley a cigarette.

"Look, fella," said Aggie chummily. "You're in one hell of a spot. You're in a jam and it's no secret. If you're innocent as you say you are, tell the whole story; and if you haven't anything to hide, people can't help knowing you're telling the truth. That way, you'll get it over with all at once and it won't be kicking around to cause you more trouble."

"She's right," said homicide detective Harry S. Fremont, who immediately spotted the opportunity. In a mean police department, Harry Fremont was one of the meanest cops in town. Once, he had nearly beaten a prisoner to death at the Seventy-seventh Street sub-station. The journalist Gene Fowler was convinced that Fremont had

killed a number of criminals in back alleys.* But Harry was smart
enough to see that a woman's touch might accomplish more than a
beating in this case. "Tell her everything that happened. I've known
this lady for a long time, on lots of big cases, and I can tell you she
won't do you wrong."

So Robert "Red" Manley told his story. First to Aggie, and then
to the cops—many times over in the ensuing months. What he had
to say was straightforward, and barely differed through the many
times he was to tell it. The first time he had met Elizabeth Short,
Red said, was when he picked up the pale, black-haired girl at a San
Diego street corner on a business trip, sometime around December
16, 1946. She was such a "pretty gal," he said, he had to stop and rake
up a conversation with her.

Red and his wife had just had a baby. They were, in his words,
going "through an adjustment period." They had lots to iron out—
"nothing important, just little things." So when he saw the black-
haired girl on the street corner, he decided to pick her up and make
a test for himself, to see if he still loved Harriette. "I asked her if she
wanted to ride. She turned her head and wouldn't look at me. I talked
some more. I told her who I was. And what I did and so forth. Finally,
she turned around and asked me if I didn't think it was wrong to ask
a girl on a corner to get into my car. I said 'Yes, but I'd like to take you
home,' so she got into the car." She told him she was staying tempo-
rarily with a family called French in Pacific Beach and was working
at Western Airlines.

Red was adamant that he and the girl "didn't do anything." They
just rode around and talked, had a dance and dinner, and he dropped

---

* Gene Fowler also claimed to have been eyewitness to an incident when Harry Fremont
interrogated a man who had just shot and killed Fremont's partner. The man was lying on a
bed in a hospital. Fremont, according to Fowler, told the man to get off the bed and run for
it, and as he did so, he put six shots into the man's back. There was no investigation. Harry
Fremont was one of the police officers later indicted for the "Bloody Christmas" beatings of
Chicano prison inmates in 1951. (See page 218.)

her back where she was staying with the French family. "No, I didn't ask her to stop at my room. We did sit in the car and talk for a short time, and I kissed her a couple of times, but she was kind of cold, I would say." Red told the girl he was married and she told him she had been, too, to a "Major Matt somebody." He told her he would wire her if he came back again San Diego way.

When Red had to make another trip to San Diego a few weeks later in January 1947, he sent the girl the telegram. He arrived in San Diego on Wednesday, January 8, and headed to the Western Airlines office, where he waited for her to come out. But she never showed up, and the folks there had never heard of her. He doubted she really worked there. He then went to the French house, where the girl was there to greet him. She asked him to drive her to Los Angeles. Red agreed, but said he could only do so the next day. She left the Frenches' house with him that night. They checked into a motel at Pacific Beach and went to the Hacienda Club in Mission Valley, where she threw herself into the music. She really loved dancing: at one point, she danced with the singer of the band. "We danced several times and had several drinks. She was gay and happy and seemed to be having a swell time," Red recalled.

But once they got back to their motel room, it was as though all the light went out of the girl. She became sullen and silent. She took a blanket off the bed and propped her legs up against the wall by the heater, shivering. Red asked her what was the matter. She said she didn't feel well, to please leave her alone. It was her time of the month. So Red didn't interfere with her. All that long night she acted very cold. She didn't want to even talk about sex. He didn't know what was the matter with her. In fact, he was beginning to think he'd be glad to get rid of her.

The next morning, January 9, Red gave the girl a dollar to go get some breakfast and told her that he would collect her around noon. He had some business to attend to in the morning, so he came back after that and they set off. They stopped at the beach city of Encinitas en route because he had business there with a water company. They stayed about an hour and a half there, a time during which she might have made some calls, but as far as he was concerned she was waiting in his car. She mentioned that a couple of fellows on bicycles talked to her while she was waiting. They had a hamburger at Encinitas, which she ate with relish. After Encinitas, he made a couple more stops before they got to Los Angeles—one at Oceanside, then one at Laguna Beach, for gas, at around 5:00 p.m.

All along the road to Los Angeles, the girl seemed anxious. She would strain her head and look at cars that overtook them and cars they overtook, as if she were worried about being tailed. Every time they passed a car, she would turn her head and take a look at the occupants. That seemed funny to Red. She was pretty much silent all the way back. Red remembered remarking to her, "Don't like my company?" She replied, "It's not that."

When they arrived in Los Angeles, the girl told Red that she was going to meet her sister from Berkeley at the lobby of the downtown Biltmore Hotel. Then, she said, she intended to go back to her home in Boston. She suggested checking her baggage into the Greyhound bus depot: her sister might not be at the Biltmore right away, and she didn't want to have her baggage at the hotel. She seemed happy for Red to leave her there at the bus depot. But Red said no: it was a bad part of town. He insisted on dropping her at the Biltmore. It was, the girl said, her first time in L.A.

When they got to the Biltmore the girl went to the restroom to freshen up. Red went to check at the desk to see if her sister had arrived, but she hadn't. He left Beth at the Biltmore about 6:30 p.m., as it was late and he was anxious to be getting home. That was the last he saw of her. The doorman at the Biltmore was later to corroborate Red's story. According to him, Beth spent several hours alone in the lobby of the Biltmore after Manley had left. She made some telephone calls. Finally, she left the hotel via the Olive Street exit about 10:00 p.m. The doorman saw her figure retreating into the fog, southward down Olive. It was the last reported sighting of Elizabeth Short to be confirmed, before her bisected body was found in the vacant lot at Leimert Park.*

Red could recall very little about the girl's conversation. It seemed there wasn't much between them in the way of communication. He remembered that she had a little address book in which she noted people's names and addresses, and that she kept harping on about some fellow named Gordon, or something like that, whom she claimed she had married. She had shown him a picture of the guy. He described the clothes she was wearing when she left Pacific Beach, the last outfit in which she had been seen: a black tailored jacket and skirt, white frilly blouse, white gloves, black suede open-toed high-heeled shoes, and "her last pair of nylons." She carried a beige camel-hair coat over her arm and gripped a black clutch purse in her hand, but wore no hat or jewelry of any kind. Above all, Red remembered the strange and distinctive perfume that she wore: heavy, musky, and sweet. It enveloped her like a pall.

Robert "Red" Manley's sensational interview—carried in the *Herald-Express* in boldface quotes under Aggie's byline—established his innocence. As Aggie said, nobody could doubt that "there was the resonance of truthfulness in what he had to say." Manley's Studebaker coupe was thoroughly investigated for bloodstains by LAPD chemist Raymond Pinker. The results were negative. His wife and friends swore to his alibi, that he was playing cards with them on the night of the killing. Harriette was a rock throughout. "The whole idea that Red had anything to do with this case is absurd," she told the newspapermen. "He'd faint if he merely saw blood." After undergoing two grueling lie-detector tests and passing with flying colors, Red was released clear of suspicion. According to Aggie, he "eliminated himself by his own

---

* There were (unconfirmed) reports by the bartender and two other witnesses at the Crown Jewel Cocktail Lounge on Eighth and Olive that Elizabeth had been seen there later on the night of January 9.

straightforwardness, and the police got him out of their hair." Manley told Aggie, "I'll swear on a stack of Bibles and tell my minister, too, that [Thursday, January 9] was the last time I ever saw Betty Short. I did not kill her. But, brother, I'll never cheat on my wife again."*

Aggie had barely finished celebrating her victory with the Manley exclusive when she got the biggest shock of her life. She was—suddenly and inexplicably—pulled off the Dahlia case.

At first, Aggie was stunned. Then, so as "not to take the thing lying down," she defiantly came to the office brandishing an enormous embroidery hoop. She sat down wordlessly and busied herself with her needle. Soon there were snickers around the bullpen. Aggie bent down over her fancy work undeterred. While the entire office rocked with laughter, Aggie kept her needle going until quitting hour.

"What do you think of that?" Aggie's fellow reporter, Caroline Walker, said with a snigger. "Here's the best reporter on the *Herald*, on the biggest day of one of the best stories in years—sitting in the office doing fancy work!"

The city editor kept his head down.

Early the next morning, the assistant city editor called Aggie over. He told her that the city editor had changed his mind overnight. He had reassigned her to the Dahlia case. All resumed as before. Then, once again, Aggie was pulled off the case. This time, however, she was not kicked off, but kicked upstairs. She was appointed the new city editor of the *Herald-Express*.

Aggie, a woman of the world with a family to provide for, was not of a mind to refuse promotion from the crime beat to the city desk. So she played along. At the time that she took the position, nobody had lasted as city editor of the *Herald-Express* for more than two years. Aggie would last seventeen. She was to become one of the

---

* Robert "Red" Manley, although cleared of suspicion of Elizabeth Short's murder, never escaped the shadow of the Dahlia case. He suffered a series of nervous breakdowns and was committed to Patton State Mental Hospital by his wife in 1954. He died in a nursing home in 1986.

longest-reigning and most popular city editors in newspaper history. But she never lost her mean streak. She put a baseball bat on her desk to brandish at overzealous Hollywood press agents, and when it became too quiet in the city room, she would fire off a blank pistol and cry out, "Don't let this paper die on us today!" She was, as the reporter Will Fowler said, in a "class Jim Richardson would never attain."

Still, everyone agreed that there was something fishy afoot when Aggie was kicked upstairs. Who was trying to get the star reporter off the biggest newspaper story of the decade? Who wanted her off their back? Why?

Jimmy Richardson soon had his revenge on Aggie for the exclusive interview with Red. He got the first interview with the Frenches in San Diego. Dorothy French, the twenty-two-year-old cashier at the Aztec movie theater in downtown San Diego, recalled feeling sorry for the black-haired girl who had crashed there in December. She had taken her home to stay with her and her brother at their mother Elvera's house in Pacific Beach, as a "friendly act, when the girl was down and out." "There was something so sorrowful about her—she seemed lost and a stranger to the area, and I felt I wanted to help her. I wasn't sure how. She apparently had no place to stay. I suggested she come home with me and get a good night's sleep, if that would help. She said she was thankful for my generosity."

Dorothy's mother Elvera said that Elizabeth—who liked to be called "Beth" in Hollywood—told the Frenches that she had come to San Diego looking for work, because of the movie strikes that had paralyzed Los Angeles. But she had barely worked a few days in the month she stayed with the Frenches, although she kept claiming she was looking for a job. Most days, she would simply lounge in the living room writing letters, her lacy black underclothes strewn on the Frenches' sofa, the room heavy with her overpowering, musky perfume. Beth talked a lot about her "husband," a Major Matt Gordon, whom she said had been killed in a plane crash over India the previous November. She had given birth to a child by him, she said, but the baby died. She showed the Frenches a newspaper article that she kept in her purse, and which she claimed referred to them as married. But the name of the bride had been scratched out. The newspaper, Elizabeth said, had made a mistake over the bride's name. In mid-December, Beth's former boyfriend, Gordon Fickling, wired her $100 to tide her over.* Such a large amount should have kept her going a few months, but she soon seemed to be broke again. "While she was with us, she apparently needed a great deal of money for something," said Dorothy French. Up to December 21, Elizabeth had dated Red virtually every night; but then from December 22 to January 1 she was out with other men most nights.

The Frenches described Beth as reluctant to talk about her past. She was "polite and secretive." Often she seemed depressed and moody, which Elvera attributed to her failure to find employment. Beth told Elvera she had plans to break into the movies, and that a Hollywood celebrity had promised to help her. Much of the time she appeared on edge and afraid. The Frenches recalled, for example, a strange incident when two men and a woman came knocking on the door. Beth wouldn't answer, but peeked through the curtain. She seemed relieved when the trio finally left. "She was terribly frightened and refused to talk about them," said Dorothy French. "She was evasive when I asked other questions, so I gave up." Beth told the Frenches that a woman had chased her and a friend up Hollywood Boulevard in December. "She seemed constantly in fear of something," said Elvera. "Whenever anybody came to the door she would act frightened." It was during her stay in San Diego that Elizabeth dyed her hair with henna —perhaps in an attempt to disguise her appearance. The reddish henna, as had been reported in the newspapers, was fading when her body was discovered, the hair growing back to its original dark color.

In the end, Beth overstayed her welcome. Elvera got fed up with

---

* Equivalent to over $1,200 today.

tiptoeing around her own house to avoid waking her guest up when she slept late after her nighttime dates. Mrs. French was also worried about the effect of such a plethora of lacy black underwear on her teenage son. She asked Beth to leave. "Our place is very crowded with my son Cory and daughter Dorothy, and I'm a widow," explained Elvera. She showed Tommy Devlin an expensive black hat with a veil. "Beth worked as a hat model. When she left, she gave me this hat that I admired. I think it was her way of thanking me for letting her stay."

Elvera said that Elizabeth left their house alone and on foot on January 8, carrying two suitcases and a hatbox. Around the corner, Red was waiting in his car. He had driven to the Frenches' house in it once before. "He was a big, good-looking fellow with wavy red hair," Dorothy recalled. "He had a wonderful smile. His teeth sparkle, they're so white. When my mother and I saw him, he was immaculately dressed and seemed to be the kind of person who'd always dress like that. He was wonderfully well mannered." A neighbor, Forest Faith, saw Elizabeth as she drove away with Red in his coupe. "Both of them were in good humor, laughing and joking, as they put suitcases in the trunk of the car," she said. Elvera was not much surprised to hear that Beth had suffered mishap on arriving in Los Angeles. "I had a premonition Miss Short was in trouble."

In addition to the Frenches, Tommy Devlin turned up another cracker for Jimmy Richardson in San Diego. He told him that Mrs. French had said the girl had a trunk stored at the American Railway Express office. The company told Tommy that the trunk had been sent to their Los Angeles warehouse for nonpayment of storage, but they would not turn it over to the *Examiner* without permission from the police. So Jimmy Richardson called the LAPD. He got Jack Donahoe, chief of the Homicide Squad, on the phone.

"If I tell you where you can find the Dahlia's trunk will you agree to bring it to the *Examiner* and open it here?"

Jack Donahoe was a big, beefy Irishman who didn't take no shit.

But he was new to Homicide, having just transferred from Robbery, where he had been buried in administration.

"Look, Jim. If I do that every other paper in town will be after my scalp. Don't put me on the spot like that. You've caused me enough goddam trouble the way it is with all those stories you've been breaking."

"You want the trunk, don't you? No deal, no trunk."

Jack groaned. "All right. It's a deal. I'll send a couple of the boys to you. But if you were a friend of mine you'd give me a break."

"If you were a friend of mine you'd give me a break. Let's be friends somehow, Jack."

"All right, but I'm sure gonna catch hell."

The next day, the Dahlia's trunk arrived at the *Examiner* offices.

4

GILDA

The trunk was a gold mine. It contained clothes, photographs, albums, letters from dozens of men. Jimmy also managed to get hold of the Dahlia's two suitcases and hatbox, which she had checked into the Greyhound bus station before going with Red to the Biltmore. Everything was suffused with the same perfume: sweet, sickly, pervaded by a musty note of decay.

They found Elizabeth's autograph book. From this it transpired that she had been the Medford high school beauty, referred to as Medford High's "Deanna Durbin." Of the five Short girls, it seemed, Elizabeth (known as "Bette" at home) had been the prettiest—and the dreamiest. Phoebe Short's husband, Cleo Alvin Short, had vanished in Boston in 1930. When Cleo's car was found abandoned in a vacant parking lot near the Charlestown Bridge, the inference was obvious. Cleo must have taken his life by leaping from the gray bridge railings into the churning depths of the Charles River. It was just another Depression story. The mother brought up her daughters alone.

Phoebe Short often blamed herself for her husband's suicide. Cleo had been running a thriving car repair business in Wolfeboro, New Hampshire. He hadn't wanted to move to Massachusetts, but Phoebe had insisted. The place was peaceful, with libraries, churches, decent schools, and universities. A good place to raise children. So the family left New Hampshire, first for Hyde Park, Boston, and then for the streetcar suburb of Medford. Cleo started a new enterprise making miniature golf courses. At first business thrived. The golf course that Cleo built at Howard Johnson Circle was considered one of the finest around. The family lived in a spacious residence on Magoun Avenue, an affluent, leafy precinct of Medford lined with large, porch-fronted white clapboard houses. Cleo and Phoebe could afford new oak furniture, a brand-new Ford, and singing and violin lessons for their eldest daughter, Ginnie. Then the Depression struck. The business failed. Cleo killed himself. Phoebe and her girls found themselves on a slow downward spiral through ever-smaller rented homes. Finally, they wound up in a third-floor railroad flat on Salem Street.

Salem Street was crisscrossed by trolley tracks running directly from Medford Square. The intersection was next to the old town burial ground, with its magnificent crumbling tombstones of wealthy New England farmers. On the fringes of the cemetery, slaves rested uneasily in unmarked graves. The Shorts' building was a three-decker clapboard apartment block. The backyard was littered with tricycles and washing lines. The Shorts lived on the third floor, in a cramped apartment with a small balcony. Sometimes Phoebe Short or one of her girls could be glimpsed on the balcony, hanging out brightly colored braided rugs to dry.

Life on Salem Street was a monotonous round of school, church, and odd jobs waitressing or babysitting for neighbors. Except for the movies. The girls from Medford High would return from the movie theater and gather on a shady porch on summer evenings, reenacting their favorite scenes. Mary Pacios, a childhood friend who was later to write a memoir of growing up with Beth Short, recalled that, while the other girls were only playing games, for Beth the movie star's life was real. Everybody in Medford remembered Bette's walk: a slow and sensuous sashay of the hips, which had cars jamming their brakes on Salem Street. Perfectly turned out, with matching hat and gloves even for a trip to the local grocery store, Elizabeth Short always seemed to be destined for a different world, something infinitely bigger and more glamorous than the New England suburb in which she had been born. And yet, there was a sadness and sense of loss about her. "She was the manic depressive type, gay one minute and blue the next," recalled her mother, Phoebe. A former boyfriend from Bette's teenage years said, "She wanted to be someone famous. She had stars in her eyes, dreams rather than plans. I think of her as a very beautiful but very private person, with a sadness about her. A void, something missing."

One day Phoebe Short was walking down the street in Medford when she bumped straight into her former husband. Cleo, it transpired, had not committed suicide; the abandoned car was a ruse. Cleo wanted a reconciliation. Phoebe refused. The family was doing perfectly fine without him. Bette, however, dreamed of a life with the father she never knew. In her sophomore year she quit school and wrote Cleo that she would like to come down to live with him in Vallejo, California. She could cook and keep house for him, take care of him. They would be a real family. Cleo agreed. He had served in the merchant navy during the war and was now working in the naval yards doing odd jobs as a handyman. Most of the time, he was drunk. The live-in arrangement with his daughter lasted three weeks. At the end of that time Cleo threw Elizabeth out, "because of her habit of running around and keeping late hours." So she took up the job at the post exchange at Camp Cooke. It was from here that she was dispatched back to Medford after her arrest for underage drinking.

When she alighted from the bus in the fall of 1943, Elizabeth never revealed to Phoebe that she had been sent home to Medford by the Santa Barbara cops. It was just one of many, many things that she did not tell her mother. Life resumed as before. Summers were spent at home in Medford with Phoebe. Winters were spent in Miami Beach, Florida, where Bette would retreat to escape the New England frosts that triggered the bronchial and asthmatic complaints with which she was constantly plagued. But something had happened to Bette since her brief and ill-fated trip to California. She had "gone Hollywood." Medford would, from now on, be too dull and small-town for her.

From December 1943 through March 1945, Elizabeth would stay in Medford just long enough to earn the carfare to head down to Miami Beach. There she boarded at the El Mar Hotel and worked as a waitress, first at the Rosedale Delicatessen, the oldest Jewish sandwich shop in Miami, and then at Mammy's Restaurant on Collins Avenue. It was in December 1944, in one of the swinging nightclubs on a palm-tree-lined boulevard of wartime Miami, that Elizabeth met Major Matthew Michael Gordon, Jr., a decorated United States Army Air Force officer and "Flying Tiger." Gordon was assigned to the Second Air Commando Group, which was then in training for deployment to the Pacific theater of operations. Elizabeth was always attracted to men in uniform. Matt looked the true part of a flying ace, with wholesome, rugged features and a flashing smile. Whether the couple was truly engaged or not is unknown. Unsent letters found in Elizabeth's trunk from April and May 1945, when Gordon was overseas for the end of the war, implied that she thought they were. "Please take good care of yourself for me, darling, because you are private property," she wrote. "Today is VE Day. People are throwing paper from the windows and are ready to run wild. You want to slip away and be married. We'll do whatever you wish, darling. Whatever you want, I want."

Despite President Truman's call for a subdued celebration in light of the "terrible price" the country had paid to rid the world of Hitler, VE Day was characterized by unrestrained jubilation throughout the United States, with crowds flooding the streets from New York to New Orleans. Along with so many thousands of other girls, Beth must have eagerly anticipated the return of her fiancé, the Flying Tiger. But a telegram from Matt's mother three months later dashed her hopes:

Received word War Department Matt killed in crash. Our deepest sympathy is with you. Pray it isn't true. Love.

Major Gordon's plane had crashed over India.

Later, after the brutal murder and the newspapers' transformation of Bette from innocent victim into femme fatale, Mrs. Gordon was to play down the relationship between her deceased son and the vampish Black Dahlia. She expressed disbelief that Matt had ever married, or even intended to marry, Elizabeth Short. The telegram, she said, was a courtesy she had sent to all of Matt's friends.

Was Matt Gordon engaged to Elizabeth Short? The truth will probably never be known. The love letters in Beth's trunk had never been posted. Elvera French had noted that Elizabeth spent much of her time lounging around the house writing letters, spinning tales of her past marriage, her flier husband, her lost child. For Elizabeth Short, the borderline between fantasy and reality was dangerously blurred. The world of her imagination, like the world of the movies, was more real to her than the drab life of suburban poverty she had led on Salem Street. And the many and varied life stories she wove enabled her, with each retelling, to escape the bondage of her reality, to reenact her own life as a movie in which she was cast as the central character, the tragic heroine. But Elizabeth's stories also made it much more difficult for investigators to separate fact from fiction when attempting to solve the riddle of the real-life, brutal drama in which she did, in the end, play her final role.

After Matt's death, Beth went through a string of flings and whirlwind romances. There was Tim Mehringer, a handsome married flier based at the Jacksonville Naval Air Station; Lieutenant Stephen Wolak, an Air Force officer based out in El Paso; another military acquaintance, Paul Rosie. Most significantly, there was Lieutenant Colonel Joseph Gordon Fickling, a former boyfriend with whom Elizabeth took up again after Matt's death. Gordon Fickling was thirty-one years old and came from Charlottesville, North Carolina.

He had served as a B-24 pilot in the U.S. Air Corps during the war. After hostilities ended, he became a pilot on a commercial line flying between North Carolina and Chicago. Elizabeth followed Fickling to Indianapolis in June 1946, and on to Long Beach after a brief stay in Chicago in July. At Long Beach, she signed into the Washington Hotel on Linden Avenue, and afterward at a furnished apartment provided by Fickling. It was at Long Beach that Elizabeth acquired her racy reputation for frequenting a drugstore soda fountain in lacy black clothes. The druggist later told police that she was seen with an Army lieutenant who would get "very jealous" when she turned her attention to a variety of sailors. Likewise, the manager of the Washington Hotel recalled Elizabeth being visited there several times by an Army man, and once by a sailor. The Army man, he said, "seemed jealous of the sailor." Perhaps it was the presence of so many rivals that caused Fickling to break off the relationship. He was later to state that he knew Elizabeth had other dates while she was seeing him, and the thought of her kissing other men made him "crazy."

Whatever the reason, by the end of August 1946, the affair with Fickling was over. "Honey," he wrote in a telegram, "I'm sorry about that wire you sent. Couldn't raise the money on that short notice. Glad you managed OK. I want that picture of you very much." Again, presumably in response to another request for funds, he wrote: "Darling, your request is impossible at this time, other obligations have me against a wall. Try to make other arrangements. I'm concerned and sorry, believe me." Elizabeth and Gordon Fickling continued to correspond. He still cared about her and sent money when he could, wiring her the $100 that she asked for in December, when she was staying with the Frenches in San Diego. But now he was keeping her at bay, concentrating on establishing a new life for himself, in what would prove to be a successful career as a commercial flier. Elizabeth realized that the relationship was over. At first she protested: if everyone waited to have everything all smooth before they decided to marry, none of them would ever be together. Then she seemed to accept the position. "I'll never regret coming west to see you," she wrote. "You didn't take me in your arms and keep me there. However, it was nice as long as it lasted. You had a great deal on your mind, and I was just an extra burden." The final letter Fickling received from Elizabeth was sent from San Diego on January 8, 1947, the day before she left for Los Angeles with Red. In it, she told him not to write her anymore in San Diego, as she was going to Chicago to work as a model for someone called "Jack." It was the last Fickling heard from her.

Before the discovery of Elizabeth's trunk, Jimmy Richardson had lamented the lack of printable pictures in the Dahlia case. Afterward, it became one of the best-illustrated in Los Angeles newspaper history. But the newspapermen soon exhausted the ephemera to be extracted from a brief life lived out of suitcases, borrowed carfare, and cheap motels. In any event, the case was moving on. Phoebe Short had just alighted from a plane in Los Angeles. The inquest into her daughter's death was about to begin.

5

DIAL M FOR MURDER

At 10:30 on the morning of Wednesday, January 22, 1947, the coroners' court in the old Los Angeles Hall of Justice was packed to overflowing. Coroner Ben H. Brown cast a displeased look at the crowd. At fifty-five years old, Brown had reigned over the Los Angeles County Coroner's Office for just two years. In that brief space of time he had come into contact with more movie stars than the average person would in his entire life. Unfortunately, if a movie star was in the presence of Coroner Brown, that star was most likely dead. But no dead movie star in Brown's tenure to date had attracted one sliver of the attention that was being accorded to his latest object of inquiry: Elizabeth Short, the unknown dead girl from Massachusetts.

First on the witness stand was Phoebe Mae Short. Soberly dressed in gray with a black velvet pillbox hat, the mother related how her daughter had left her house in April of the previous year. That, as far as she knew, Elizabeth had worked as a waitress and at the San Diego naval hospital. And of how she came to hear about her daughter's death.

The mother's testimony was deadpan, but the scene at the county morgue the previous day had been anything but deadpan. Mrs. Short, overcome with emotion, had for a long while refused to look at the body that lay draped in a white sheet on the mortuary slab, behind a pane of glass. "I want to remember Elizabeth as she was," she said. With Phoebe was Elizabeth's eldest sister Virginia, now married to a professor at Berkeley. Finally, the mother had forced herself to ask the morgue attendants to remove the sheet from the body. She stared for a moment, then closed her eyes. "It looks like my daughter. But I can't be sure." Ginnie, too, wasn't sure. Finally, Phoebe ventured the fact that her daughter had a large mole on her left shoulder. Did this corpse have such a mole? The answer was the affirmative. "Then that," said Phoebe, "is my daughter."

By the time of the inquest the next day, Phoebe seemed calm. The quiet monotone in which her evidence was given was broken only when the coroner asked if she knew where her daughter had died. "She was murdered here in Los Angeles!" the mother cried, jumping from her seat.

Phoebe Short was followed on the witness stand by Detective Lieutenant Jesse W. Haskins of the LAPD. He had been one of the first police officers at the crime scene on Thirty-ninth and Norton. Haskins said that the body was found on the west side of Norton, in a vacant lot covered with weeds, grass, and rose clippings. There was a fireplug in the center of the block, about equidistant from the intersections with Thirty-ninth and Coliseum. The body was about fifty-four feet north of the plug, toward Coliseum. It had been lying to the north faceup, severed in two, the legs spread. There was a tire track up against the curbing, and what appeared to be the imprint of a bloody heel in the tire mark.* There was one bloodstain on the sidewalk. There was also an empty cement sack lying nearby. It had what looked like a spot of blood on it. The body was clean, and appeared to have been washed. Evidently it had been transported to the scene from another location.

Haskins's evidence was followed by that of Robert Manley, LAPD Homicide Detective Lieutenant Harry Hansen, and the autopsy sur-

---

* According to an early police report filed in February 1947, photographs were taken of the tire tracks. These subsequently disappeared.

geon Frederick Newbarr. Manley repeated the story he had already told the police and Aggie Underwood. Detective Hansen was tight-lipped. Giving nothing away, he stated only that the LAPD was currently following all leads in the case and as yet had nothing to report. Dr. Newbarr ascended the stand to read his autopsy report. However, as he reached the most crucial point—the details of the mutilations—he was cut short by Coroner Brown.

"Doctor, I don't believe it will be necessary for you to read all of this," the coroner said hastily. "It is rather long, and I don't think we need to read all of it here. The essential findings with regard to cause of death have already been expressed; and that is the concussion of the brain and the laceration of the face."

The verdict of the coroner's jury, after the forty-five-minute hearing, was curt and inevitable. Elizabeth Short had died from hemorrhage and shock due to concussion of the brain and lacerations of the face. The injuries had been inflicted on the deceased by some person or persons unknown, at an unknown location. The finding was homicide, with a recommendation that every effort be made to apprehend the person or persons responsible.

Back at the *Examiner* offices, Jimmy Richardson was blowing a fuse. His story was in danger of fizzling out. Immediately after the discovery of the body, detectives had cast a dragnet over the Leimert Park area in search of clues. The house-to-house hunt had turned up three people who reported that they had seen a Chevrolet coupe in the early morning hours, near the spot where the body was found. Another witness, Bob Meyer, who lived a block over, told police he saw what he believed to be an older model, 1936 or 1937, dark Ford sedan stop for about four minutes close by the spot where the body was found, sometime between 6:30 and 7:00 on the morning of January 15. Meyer had not been able to see the driver's face, as it was blocked by tall weeds. None of these sightings had led to any concrete leads.

Jimmy needed more headlines, and he needed them fast. The case had dwindled to a few paragraphs and was about to fade out.

Then, on the morning of January 23, the phone rang, and Jimmy took the call that he would remember for the rest of his life.

"Is this the city editor?" asked a sly, soft voice.

"Yes."

"What is your name, please?"

"Richardson."

"Well, Mr. Richardson, I must congratulate you on what the *Examiner* has done in the Black Dahlia case."

"Thank you." Jimmy was wondering what the hell this was about. There was a slight pause.

"You seem to have run out of material," the voice continued.

"That's right."

There was a soft laugh. "Maybe I can be of some assistance."

Something in the way this was said sent a shiver down Jimmy's spine.

"We need it." Jimmy forced the wisecrack. Again, that sly, soft laugh.

"I'll tell you what I'll do," the voice said. "I'll send you some of the things she had with her when she, shall we say, disappeared?"

Richardson grabbed a sheet of paper and scrawled on it, *Trace this call.*

"What kind of things?" He tossed the piece of paper to his assistant, who was hunched over his typewriter punching at the keys with the first finger of each hand. The assistant read the note and immediately started to jiggle the receiver arm on his telephone to get the attention of Mae Northern, the switchboard girl.

"Oh, say her address book and her birth certificate and a few other things she had in her handbag."

"When will I get them?" Through the cigarette smoke and the chaos of messenger boys passing in and out of the office swing doors, Jimmy could just see Mae in the distance. She had dialed a number and was beginning to talk into her mouthpiece.

"Oh, within the next day or so. See how far you can get with them. And now I must say goodbye. You may be trying to trace this call."

"Wait a minute—" But the line clicked. The phone went dead.

"What was it?" Jimmy's assistant was falling out of his chair, wide-eyed.

Jimmy lit a cigarette. "I think I may have been talking to the killer of the Dahlia."

Two days later, he knew he had.

"I have just had a call from the postal inspector's office," Harry Morgan, the night city editor, told Jimmy. "They have intercepted a parcel addressed to 'The *Los Angeles Examiner* and other newspapers.' Whoever sent it used lettering clipped from newspapers and pasted on to form the words. The inspectors have decided to open it in the presence of representatives from all the papers."

"Goddam him anyway." Jimmy felt the blood thumping in his head. He needed a stiff whiskey. But he had dried out years ago, so he lit a Lucky from the butt of the one that had preceded it instead.

"What are you talking about?" Harry was nonplussed.

Jimmy sighed smoke. "I've been expecting that parcel, Harry. He told me he would send it to me. Why the hell did he let the others in on it?"

"I don't know what you're talking about, Jim."

So Jimmy told him.

"I'll join you, goddam him anyway," Harry said, when he heard the story. "I don't blame you. I've sent a crew to the post office and I'll let you know as soon as I hear."

The parcel was opened at the metropolitan downtown post office in the presence of the Los Angeles postal inspectors, Sergeants Brown and Cummings of LAPD Homicide, and Sergeant Wheeler of the LAPD fingerprint unit. There were also representatives of the *Examiner,* the *Herald-Express,* the *Times,* and the *Daily News.* The parcel had been posted from a downtown mailbox on January 24, the day after the call to Jimmy. It was partially opened. It contained Elizabeth's birth certificate; her Social Security card; a claim check dated January 9, No. R06-97-79, for the two suitcases and hatbox that the *Examiner* had located at the Greyhound bus station; a telegram relating to the trunk that had been held by the Railway Express; various business cards; several photos of Elizabeth with men in uniform; and a brown leather notebook filled with names and phone numbers.

The package, as Harry Morgan had said, was addressed to the "*Los Angeles Examiner* and other Los Angeles papers." Also on the envelope were the words, "Here is [sic] Dahlia's belongings—Letter to follow." The words of the address and message had been cut-and-pasted from newspaper lettering—mainly the *Los Angeles Examiner*, although the *Herald-Express* noted with satisfaction that the word "Dahlia's" had been clipped from the red headline in its sunset edition of the previous Monday. The package was open at one end. The contents gave off a strong odor of gasoline.

There was no doubt in anybody's mind that the sender of the package must have been the killer. The fact that the contents of the parcel had been soaked in gasoline meant that it was impossible to lift any fingerprints from them. One fingerprint was lifted from the exterior of the package, but this was of minimal value, as it was taken from the outside of the envelope, which had already been partially opened. It could have belonged to anybody, including the postal workers. The print quality was poor, with blurs and smudges, but it was still sent to the FBI to seek a possible match with the millions of impressions already filed in the federal agency's massive fingerprint card index. The result came back negative.

The address book was limp and still damp from the gasoline. It was made of brown leather. Several pages had been cut out. The book contained names, addresses, and telephone numbers in no particular order, mostly in Elizabeth Short's handwriting. There were three or four pages in a hand that was not Short's. On the cover, in gold letters, was embossed the year "1937," and a name. It was a name everybody in the post room knew.

—

The promised "Letter to follow" came within a day. It was postmarked January 26 at 6:30 p.m. It was a one-cent United States government postcard, addressed to the *Los Angeles Examiner* alone. The message was handwritten in crude printing.

"Here it is," read the postcard. "Turning in Wed. Jan. 29. 10 a.m. Had my fun at [sic] police." It was signed "Black Dahlia Avenger."

The police noted that the printed postcard had been written with a "new ballpoint pen." This could be a clue because in 1947 ballpoint pens were still something of a rarity. While they had been provided to officers during the war, commercial distribution to the general public only began at Christmas 1945, at the cost of $12.50 each.*

In a public statement, Captain Donahoe of the LAPD said that he believed the postcard was "legitimate." "The fact that the postcard was printed rather than lettered with words cut from newspapers also supports the theory that the killer intends to turn himself in to the police, and no longer needs to take pains to conceal his identity," Donahoe said. The signature "Black Dahlia Avenger" implied that the killer "murdered Elizabeth Short for some avenged wrong, either real or imagined."

All day on Wednesday, January 29, detectives were posted at the doors of the *Examiner* offices. Swarms of newspapermen from all the rival publications hung about expectantly.

They waited.

Finally, Richardson chased the reporters away and called Big Jack Donahoe.

"Get your boys away from here. Nobody is coming in with them standing there all eagle-eyed. If he comes, I promise I'll call you."

"All right, but understand I'm taking him out of there at once," Jack told him. "No deal this time. You can't hide out a murderer without getting yourself in real trouble. You know that, don't you?"

But the murderer never showed.

---

* Equivalent to $137 today.

The next day, January 30, another postcard arrived—this time with a message cut from news clippings like in the package. It read: "Have changed my mind, you would not give me a square deal. Dahlia killing was justified." Shortly after, the police received an anonymous telephone call.

"Don't try to find the Short girl's murderer because you won't," the caller said, and hung up.

The following weeks brought a flood of further letters and postcards addressed to the LAPD and various newspapers. The police believed that the first package containing Elizabeth's belongings was almost certainly sent in by the killer. It was hard to see how anybody else could have gotten their hands on the contents of the girl's purse. On the other hand, the dozens of letters that followed the package might have included some genuine correspondence, or they might have been hoaxes sprung by screwballs and the less scrupulous newspapermen. Nobody could be sure. The view of the FBI's Los Angeles field office was that while the first package was genuine, "No subsequent mail or communications contained any material to indicate writers have any knowledge or connection with instant case." Nevertheless, the police did retrieve and send to the FBI four latent prints that were lifted from a subsequent anonymous letter sent to the LAPD. The five fingerprints—the single, blurred print from the outside of the package and the four from the anonymous letter—were used for a routine cross-check of potential suspects. A positive match would be strong evidence of culpability; but a negative match would not rule out the suspect.

Attention now turned back to the grim relics that had been sent in the package. As with the trunk and suitcase, the newspapermen pawed their way through the contents of the Dahlia's purse. Photographs of Elizabeth with yet more military personnel occupied as many column inches that week as the Communists taking over Poland. Elizabeth Short's address book became a national obsession. Headlines screamed that Captain Donahoe, having seen the names listed in the book, had said, "This book is gonna be dynamite!" But the police refused to name the "big names" mentioned, for fear of "embarrassing" them. The newspapers speculated that the contacts listed in the address book might provide clues as to what had happened to Elizabeth during the mysterious "missing week," a period that still remained unaccounted for. This was the interval between the evening of Thursday, January 9, when Red had dropped her off at the Biltmore Hotel, and the following Wednesday, when her body had been discovered. It was the crucial five days in the course of which things as yet unknown had happened, which were to turn Elizabeth Short, the Hollywood hopeful, into LAPD's Case #30-1268: a butchered carcass tossed onto the grass beside a sidewalk. But there was one well-known name that the police were not able to withhold from the public. It had been plain to see for everybody when the package was opened. It became the next hot lead in the case. Everyone wanted to talk to the man whose name was embossed in gold on the cover of the Dahlia's address book.

6

HOUSE OF
STRANGERS

The minute it was discovered that his name was on the cover of the Dahlia's address book, Mark Hansen was in a jam. For the well-known but publicity-phobic Hollywood businessman, it was bad news. His name might as well have been up in lights over one of his many movie theaters or nightclubs.

At fifty-five years old, Mark Marinus Hansen had come a long way from Aalborg, Denmark, the town of his birth. The "city of smoking chimneys," the Danes called it. Hansen was only nineteen years old when he stepped off the steamer from the Old Country and made his way to the town of Scobey, on the great plains of eastern Montana. Long designated the "Great American Desert," this dauntingly arid land was the last frontier, stretching from the ninety-eighth meridian to the Rocky Mountains. In the first decade of the new century, Hansen had been one of thousands of pioneer homesteaders who flocked to the self-billed "Treasure State." But the boom was so big that it had to go bust. Ten years later when it crashed and burned, Hansen was one of the thousands who "spit on the fire and whistled for the dog." First he went to Williston, North Dakota, where he set up in the motion picture theater business. Then he moved to Minneapolis, Minnesota, and ran theaters there. Finally, he wound up in Tinseltown.

By 1947, Mark Hansen was a wealthy and powerful Hollywood mover and shaker. He owned over a dozen motion picture theaters, from Whittier to Walnut Park. He part-owned the Florentine Gardens, a Hollywood Boulevard nightclub where the famous compere Nils Thor Granlund, or "NTG"—a fellow Norseman—fronted the floor show with a parade of scantily clad females before a partygoing crowd that included the likes of an aging Errol Flynn. At $1.50 for dinner with girlie show included, the Florentine Gardens catered to the "meat 'n' potatoes" crowd. The "caviar set" hung out at plush places such as the Clover Club, Trocadero, or Mocambo. But the Florentine Gardens was still a booming venue, whose only real competition was the rival Earl Carroll's theater, west on Sunset Boulevard. It was the place where the budding actress and dancer Yvonne DeCarlo had first sashayed onto the stage with busty, heavily made-up blond striptease artist Lili St. Cyr. It was also the fateful spot where, in 1942, Norma Jean Mortensen and her first husband, Jim Dougherty, had said, "I do"—before Mortensen abandoned spouse and name to become Marilyn Monroe. Playing to a packed audience, the Florentine shows took place every night in a noisy, barnlike space littered with white tables and jammed with servicemen flush on post–Pearl Harbor pay.

Middle-aged and hawk-nosed, with a marked Scandinavian accent, Mark Hansen worked in a shadowy hinterland between legitimate business and the fringes of the Los Angeles underworld. Hidden within the Florentine Gardens was a secret gambling casino, operated by Jimmy "Little Giant" Utley, archrival of the gangster Mickey Cohen. Utley was one of the toughest hoods in Hollywood. A diminutive Irishman who had begun his racketeering career as a carnival hustler, he was involved in prostitution, bookmaking, drugs, a chain of illegal abortion clinics, and the lucrative bingo parlors at Venice Beach. The rumor was that one of Utley's favorite turn-ons was to dress up as a medical assistant in his abortion clinics and play an active role "assisting" with the "broads" laid out on the table. The word on the street was that Mark Hansen, like Jimmy Utley, was in the abortion racket. Mickey Cohen—kingpin of the Los Angeles underworld—hated Utley for being a snitch and cop-lover who was in league with the LAPD. One day Cohen beat up Utley in the street when he saw him talking to a crooked cop.

Like the Hollywood studio moguls, Hansen and his floor show host NTG operated their own B-version of the casting couch. In addition to his many theaters, Hansen owned two "rooming houses," where would-be Hollywood hopefuls were groomed for semi-nude careers both on and off the dance floor. NTG, Hansen's chief recruiter, searched rodeo shows across the country for jailbait whom he would cajole into coming to L.A. to "dance" for the club.* NTG was a middle-aged Swede with a pale flabby face, bulbous nose, and penchant for shiny suits. Back in the 1920s and '30s, he had defined the New York nightclub scene with big floor shows featuring girls in high heels and G-strings. He financed his New York nightclubs with Irish-American gangster money, specifically from Owen "Owney" Madden, the tough enforcer who was once described as the "preeminent mobster of the Prohibition era." In Hollywood, NTG "discovered" stars such as Yvonne de Carlo, Betty Hutton, Jean Wallace, Marie "the Body" McDonald, and Lili St. Cyr. But more often than not, would-be movie stars "discovered" by NTG would end up as taxi dancers in one of Mark Hansen's dime-a-time joints.

Mark Hansen kept a harem of his favorite girls in his house on Carlos Avenue, just behind the Florentine Gardens. It was an impressive building clad in ornamental stone veneer with a marble porch, shady veranda, and secret corners nestled in the shadow of palms and pepper trees. Hansen had separated from his wife, Ida, who occupied a mansion in the canyon with their daughters. NTG kept a long-suffering spouse, Rose Wenzel, up in New York. The pair lived bachelors' lives. There were parties, hard liquor, hard drugs, and above all, an endless parade of girls. It was on October 1, 1946, when

---

* In 1944, the Florentine Gardens was charged with hiring two underage girls, the fifteen-year-old Stull sisters, Jean and Dean (*Billboard*, July 22, 1944, p. 26).

Elizabeth Short first pitched up at Carlos Avenue. Hansen noticed her immediately. She had a girlfriend with her: a big, heavyset Massachusetts girl with a weakness for liquor, called Marjorie Graham. Elizabeth, Marjorie, and a blond nightclub singer had shacked up together in a seedy rooming house, the Hawthorne Hotel on North Orange Drive, after Gordon Fickling split from Elizabeth. Fellow hotel residents Harold Costa and Donald Leyes, who had dated Elizabeth's girlfriends, recalled that "the kid was broke and hungry." Others said that she was "a fun-loving, always in trouble beauty." At the Hawthorne, according to a hotel clerk, Elizabeth was forever behind on her rent. When she was, a "short, dark man" of about thirty-five or forty years old paid it. The girls had spent a few days downtown at the Figueroa Hotel with Sid Zaid, a shady musician, before turning up on Mark's doorstep on Carlos Avenue.

Several people noticed that to Mark Hansen, Elizabeth Short was different from the other girls who passed through the house on Carlos Avenue. Twenty-five-year-old Ann Toth also lived in a room at Mark's home. Toth was Danish like Hansen, another Hollywood hopeful, and a bit player in the movies. She had a beautiful, pale, pointed face, arched eyebrows, and hair that she wore in curls pinned back with an Alice band. In 1947, although she didn't know it at the time, Ann would reach the pinnacle of her career: an uncredited role playing a woman in the ladies' toilet in Stuart Heisler's movie *Smash-Up*.

"Mark really liked Beth, he had a yen for her," Ann said. Mark, according to Ann, had tried to "make" Elizabeth a couple of times. To fend him off, she had claimed she was a virgin. But being forbidden fruit made Elizabeth all the more tantalizing. The middle-aged businessman seemed to desire her all the more: the fey, aloof Boston ingénue with pale skin, translucent eyes that seemed to change color in the light, and red mouth that slashed her face like a wound. Mrs. Ardis, a Hollywood seamstress who rented one of Mark's apartments, recalled that Hansen invited her around for drinks, to "see the most beautiful creature in Hollywood." The next day Mark came over to Ardis's apartment with Elizabeth and ordered two dresses for the girl, which Ardis fitted and made. They were never delivered. Mark would not tolerate Beth's endless stream of boyfriends. He banned them from the apartment.

After ten days of teasing and frustration, Hansen had had enough. On October 10 he ordered the girls to move on, because, as he later told the police, "this Graham girl, she was inclined to be liquored up and I didn't like it at all; and this Short girl, she had always got some undesirable looking character waiting for her outside and bringing her home." The girls fell in with two young men, Bill Robinson and Marvin Margolis. Bill was living at his aunt's place in the Guardian Arms Apartments on Hollywood Boulevard. Marvin, a premed student at USC, was sharing the apartment with him. Later, the two men claimed that they slept with Marjorie, while Beth slept alone on the sofa. But Ann Toth told police that Bill was in fact dating Marjorie, while Marvin was dating Beth, although Beth always claimed Marvin was her "cousin" when Mark Hansen was around. One chilly morning at dawn, after the girls were supposed to have moved out of Hansen's apartment, Ann Toth spotted them sitting on the marble steps of the front porch. They claimed they had come to collect their mail, but Ann had already given it to them a couple of days before. She assumed it was because they had no place to stay. Once Elizabeth came over to see Ann crying. Bill Robinson had tried to "make" her in the car. When she gave him the cold shoulder, he had punched her in the face and thrown her out of his automobile.

One evening in late October 1946, Mark Hansen returned home to Carlos Avenue to find Marvin Margolis, Beth's "cousin," there. He had a suitcase. Marvin explained that the girls were going back to Boston. Could he leave their baggage at Mark's place for the night? Hansen agreed. When he came back home that evening, the suitcase was still there. And so was Beth Short. Elizabeth tearfully explained that Marjorie had gone back home to Massachusetts. She had nowhere to go. Could she stay? And so, like the sucker he was when it came to the Short girl, Mark let her back into his home.

—

Elizabeth's second stay at Carlos Avenue was dark and stormy. There was, again, the endless stream of boyfriends: soldiers, sailors, fliers, teachers, students, salesmen, advertisers, bank clerks, barmen, brick-layers, mechanics, artists, photographers, estate agents. They came fur-tively, parking their automobiles and waiting on the street corner a block away from Hansen's house, out of sight. "Everybody picked her up a block away, and everybody more often dumped her off a block away," recalled Ann Toth. "She wouldn't dare bring anyone to the house. Well, Mark wouldn't like it anyway. He more or less possessed her from the time she came there." Beth made Mark furious. She made a long-distance call to Texas to her ex-boyfriend, Gordon Fickling, and charged it to his telephone bill. She tried to play the "wife," clearing out Mark's bathroom cupboard and throwing out all the old stuff. After the cupboard-clearing episode, Ann said, Hansen was furious for at least a month.

The final straw came when Beth had a fight with another girl who was staying at Carlos Avenue. According to Ann Toth, Mark had been romancing Beth, claiming he was not seeing other girls. But old habits are hard to break, and one night he came home with his latest pick up. Beth who was sleeping in Ann Toth's room—got angry over the girl. She was a tramp, she said: they never did that sort of thing in Boston. "She had a lot of high ideas, that Betty, believe me, with her Boston family and all that stuff," Ann recalled. "She got up and locked her suitcase, because she thought this girl was going to get into her suitcase, and the girl said, 'I don't want to touch your damn suitcase, I don't want anything in there.' Anyway, words were flying back and forth and there was a beef and a fist fight, and Mark stepped in between them." Mark ordered Elizabeth to move out the next day.

This time, there was no change of heart. Ann helped Elizabeth pack her odd scraps of possessions. The Danish actress secretly arranged for Beth to rent a bed at the Chancellor Apartments, a bald white bunker of a rooming house on North Cherokee. In Room 501, on the top floor of the building, eight girls were jammed into bunk beds like sardines in a can. The fee was $1 each a night.

"She came here for a room last November 13. That's a bad day, isn't it?" recalled Mrs. Juanita Ringo, the caretaker at the Chancellor. "She wasn't sociable like the other girls who lived in apartment 501 with her. More the sophisticated type."

Ann Toth did not dare admit to Mark Hansen that she had helped Beth and found a place for her to stay. Mark, for his part, seemed to be annoyed that Elizabeth was apparently able to manage without his help. Toth would collect Beth's mail when it arrived at Carlos Avenue and bring it over to her at the Chancellor. "I got it before Mark got to it, because he might have wanted to keep it or something," she told the police. "Elizabeth didn't want me to let him get ahold of it." When Ann came over to Carlos Avenue to collect mail, she saw Beth in conversation with Hansen a couple of times. At this point, she thought everything seemed "copacetic" between them. But in truth, Beth hated the Chancellor Apartments. One night, Mark Hansen told the police, he came home to find her having dinner with Ann Toth. She was crying. She had moved in with some bad company, she told him. She was scared. She wanted to move again.

By early December, Beth had run out of money. "When I went up for the rent last December 5, she didn't have it," Juanita Ringo recalled. "I don't think she had a job. That night she got the money somewhere, and left the next morning." The day Elizabeth left the Chancellor, something was troubling her. "The morning she left she was very anxious," said her roommate at the Chancellor, twenty-two-year-old Linda Rohr, who worked at the rouge room at Max Factor. "She said, 'I've got to hurry—he's waiting for me.' We never found out who 'he' was. She was supposed to go to live with her sister in Berkeley." After disappearing for a couple of days with the mysterious male, Elizabeth resurfaced on December 8, alone at the Aztec Theatre in San Diego. There Dorothy French found her.

On January 16, the day after Elizabeth's body was found, Ann Toth called the police. The newspapers had reported that detectives were searching for a friend of the victim called "Ann Todd." They were also, it was reported, looking for a blond nightclub singer who had shacked up with the Dahlia at the Hawthorne Hotel, and who apparently disliked her intensely. Mark Hansen was reluctant to go to the cops, but Ann insisted. When they arrived at the police station, Hansen shied away from the swarm of reporters and flashbulbs, lurking in the background. He was, he claimed, "nobody." He was "Ann's chauffeur." Toth gave an account to homicide detectives of the two occasions when Elizabeth Short had stayed at Carlos Avenue. Hansen verified the statements, but refused to say anything with reporters present. The last he saw of Elizabeth Short, he said, was when she was staying at the Chancellor Apartments, before she left for San Diego.

Now, just over a week later, the discovery of Mark Hansen's name on the cover of the Dahlia's address book put the businessman in the unwelcome spotlight again. Hansen's explanation for the address book was that it was a gift sent to him from Denmark. It had disappeared from the desk at his Carlos Avenue home some time ago. The Short girl must have stolen it. But the press, in particular Aggie Underwood, were now beginning to ask questions about Mark Hansen. About the harem of girls at the house on Carlos Avenue. About Hansen's relationship with the Dahlia.

Then—the day after the surfacing of the address book—Mark Hansen had his greatest stroke of luck. Other things belonging to the dead girl surfaced, which turned the story on its head and caught the attention of every paper in town. There were signs that the killer might have made his first—and to date only—mistake.

THE BIG SLEEP

The shoe was made of black patent leather, high-heeled and open-toed. It was found, along with a shiny black patent-leather purse, in a trash depot on East Twenty-fifth Street.

The purse had been previously spotted in a trash can by Robert Hyman, the manager of a café on South Crenshaw Boulevard. When Hyman saw the purse in the trash can, it contained a pair of high-heeled shoes, but by the time the café manager reported the discovery, the contents of the can had been collected and dumped at the depot. It was only after an extensive police search of the depot that the purse and a single shoe were finally recovered.

As the last person known to have been with the Dahlia, it fell to Robert "Red" Manley to identify the shoe and purse. They were displayed among a selection of similar shoes and bags, dusted with a light coating of ash. Red straightaway picked out the items from the trash can. He knew this was one of Elizabeth's shoes, he said, because he had gotten new shoe-taps fitted for her at her request, when they stayed at the motel in San Diego. This shoe had a double tap, exactly as had been fitted to the Dahlia's shoes. Red also recognized the purse. Not only did it match the one Elizabeth had been carrying, it also still emanated a faint waft of her distinctive perfume.

The purse and shoe were different from the package sent to the

Los Angeles Examiner in one important respect: the killer had not intended that they be found. He had likely tossed them into a convenient trash can shortly after the crime. Did the location of the trash can—at the café on Crenshaw—suggest the location of the murder or the murderer's identity?

The chance discovery of Elizabeth's purse and one of her shoes was a major find, but for every breakthrough in the Dahlia investigation there were a dozen brick walls. After much searching, the cops tracked down the missing blond nightclub singer who had lodged with the Dahlia at the Hawthorne Hotel and vanished the day of the murder. It was said she had expressed a "bitter dislike" of Elizabeth. She was Norma Lee Meyer, a sixteen-year-old runaway from a broken home in Long Beach, who was passing herself off as twenty-one. Norma went by the name of "Lynn Martin." She had frizzy blond hair that haloed her face like a sulky Shirley Temple. She posed for photographers in a trench coat and bobby socks.

Lynn had fled on the day Elizabeth's body was discovered next to the sidewalk and had gone into hiding in a motel on Ventura Boulevard. The cops found her in the company of a forty-two-year-old "salesman" with a rap sheet, known as Edward P. ("The Duke") Wellington. When questioned, Lynn talked about a photographer on Jewett Drive called George Price. Price had brought her to his apartment and taken nude photographs of her. George Price's name was in the Dahlia's address book. Witnesses reported seeing Elizabeth in Price's automobile on Hollywood Boulevard sometime before she left Los Angeles for San Diego. But when the cops questioned Price, he denied knowing Elizabeth. He had no clue, he said, how his name had turned up in the girl's address book.

George Price was not the only peddler in smut whose name was linked to the Dahlia. Arthur Curtis James, Jr., also known as Charles B. Smith, was a middle-aged, self-proclaimed "artist" who told the papers he had painted Beth in the nude. Arthur said he met the Dahlia in a cocktail lounge in Hollywood in August 1944. "I was sitting alone at the bar, making pencil sketches on a bit of paper, when a girl who turned out to be 'Beth,' sitting beside me, showed an interest in my sketches," he told Aggie Underwood's reporter. Arthur's friendship with the Dahlia bloomed over the next three months. He painted several pictures of her—a large oil painting that he turned over to a man in Arcadia, and a sketch he sold to a woman who lived in the Pacific Palisades. But the friendship ended abruptly when Arthur was arrested in Tucson, Arizona. He was with a girl alleged to have been transported there for "immoral purposes." He never, he said, saw the Dahlia again.

The revelations of George Price, Arthur James, and Lynn Martin led to speculation that a clandestine pornography ring was in operation in Hollywood. But how such a ring might connect to the Dahlia killing, if at all, was far from clear. Many years later, some startling evidence was to surface to suggest that Beth Short had indeed been involved in nude photography. But for now, the picture was clouded. And then, to further muddy the waters, there were the "confessing Sams."

The twenty-nine-year-old Army corporal had bloodstained pockets. He carried a clipping of the Dahlia murder.

"I dated that gal on January 9. The next thing, I blacked out. When I came to, I was standing in the Pennsylvania Station in New York." Corporal Joseph Dumais was adamant he had killed the Dahlia. "I get drunk and forget, and I get rough with women."

The Army investigators believed Corporal Dumais at first. But then, nine soldiers came forward to state that they had seen him at Fort Dix between January 10 and 15. It transpired that Dumais had in fact been in New Jersey—more than two thousand miles from the murder scene—over the week of Elizabeth's disappearance and death. Nor did the corporal know the two secret facts about the mutilations that the police had been keeping for questioning.*

Over the weeks, months, and years following the Dahlia murder,

---

* Corporal Dumais continued to claim to be Elizabeth's killer, off and on, for the next ten years.

the crackpots kept coming. Over five hundred in all. Edward Augele was a forty-one-year-old unemployed warehouseman who confessed to the murder to get a free meal and a place to stay for the night. Melvin Robert Bailey was a twenty-two-year-old St. Louis boy who claimed he "cut up" the girl because she refused to move back out East with him. A thirty-three-year-old restaurant porter called Daniel Voorhees, with a rap sheet that included rape, telephoned the cops and confessed because "he couldn't stand it any longer." The problem was that, at the time he claimed to have been having a torrid affair with Beth, she was a teenager living on the East Coast. Voorhees was judged a mental case and booked for insanity.

The "confessing Sams" distracted the police and fed the press, but they also proved to be dangerous. On February 8, 1947, Aggie's newspaper ran the headline "Corporal Dumais Is Black Dahlia Killer." The case, the paper announced, had been solved. Two days later, the newspaper ran another headline: "Werewolf Killer Strikes Again! Kills L.A. Woman, Writes B.D. on Body." In the space of barely three weeks after the killing of Elizabeth Short, another brutal murder had taken place in Los Angeles. This time, the victim was forty-five-year-old Jeanne French, a former aviatrix, bit movie player, and Army nurse. Jeanne's nude body was discovered at about 8:00 a.m. on February 10, 1947, at the intersection of Grand View Avenue and Indianapolis Street in West L.A. She had been stomped, battered, and left to literally bleed to death. Before abandoning the body, the killer had taken a dark red lipstick from her purse. With it he had scrawled on her torso: "FUCK YOU, B.D."

The obvious inference was that the initials *B.D.* stood for "Black Dahlia." Aggie's newspaper was clear in making a link between the two killings with the headline "Werewolf Killer Strikes Again!"

At first, the LAPD agreed with the view that the same man who killed Elizabeth Short also killed Jeanne French. Captain Dona-hoe theorized that whoever killed Short was infuriated by Corporal Dumais's "confession" and the subsequent press attention. He murdered Jeanne French to disprove the claim that the Dahlia killer had been caught. He wrote the initials *B.D.* on Jeanne's body to stamp his signature on the two murders.

But later, the LAPD changed its opinion. The "Dahlia" and the "Lipstick" killings were not connected, the police department stated. The initials on the body were *P.D.* and not *B.D.* It was a rather strange about-turn. Many years later, evidence would surface to question that assertion and suggest that there was indeed a possible connection between the Dahlia and French killings. For now, the Jeanne French murder remained unsolved.* While at least two other nude female bodies were found in Los Angeles soon after the Short and French killings, none of them attracted the attention that the Dahlia case inspired. The lack of press interest prompted UPI news agency executive Bill Payette to complain, "Somebody has to tell these guys you can use these women more than once."

Beyond stimulating copycat murders, the "confessing Sams" were a waste of police time. But the cops had to interview them all because, as the LAPD police psychiatrist Dr. Paul De River said, the Dahlia killer craved publicity. He had publicly displayed Elizabeth Short's body beside the sidewalk like a carcass on a butcher's slab. He had taunted the city editor of a major Los Angeles newspaper. He had sent in a package containing the victim's belongings to the press. Any one of the confessing Sams might be him. So the cops had to check them all.

One confessor, however, was different from the others.

"I knew her as Libby Short in Hollywood. I met her in the bar at the Greyhound depot about 3½ years ago. We visited back and forth in hotels and motels. About four days before Libby died, she was giving me a bad time. She was chasing around with other girlfriends. One was a blonde named Louise, about 20 years old. She was queer too. I flew into a rage and stabbed her. I held her and stabbed her and stabbed her and stabbed her!" The woman had initially telephoned

---

* The Jeanne French killing is discussed further on page 109.

the *Oakland Tribune*. She was later described by the newspapers as "mannish and crop-haired."

"This baby's dangerous," said Lieutenant Walter E. Hawkinson, head of the Oakland Homicide Squad, when the report was radioed over to him.

The "dangerous broad" was thirty-five-year-old Christine Reynolds. She had been shacking up with a female cousin, a Detroit bus inspector, in a motel in Glendale. The pair had argued. Christine hit the cousin with an iron pot and broke her finger, the cousin told Aggie's reporter.

Press and public were fascinated. For some time, there had been rumors flying around that the Dahlia was a "female pervert," and that she had indulged in "unnatural intimacies" with women. One purported sighting of Elizabeth during the missing week was with a woman of "Amazonian proportions" at a gas station. Another was of the Dahlia in the company of a "bossy blonde." There were unsubstantiated sightings of Elizabeth at the Crown Jewel cocktail bar on Eighth and Olive, after she left the Biltmore on the night of Thursday, January 9. The Crown Jewel was a well-known gay bar downtown, and only a couple of blocks from the Biltmore. There were believed to have been some gay women staying at the Chancellor Apartments, Beth's last known address in Los Angeles. The nature of the injuries inflicted on the Dahlia also aroused speculation as to a female killer. The deep vertical gash, inflicted from the pubic bone to the navel, could have been a grotesque reference to female genitalia. But something else Christine Reynolds said grabbed the attention of the cops.

"I cut some of her goddam hair off and shoved it up her fucking pussy."*

This was not exactly, but very, very close, to one of the "secret" facts that had been deliberately withheld from public disclosure.

---

* As transcribed in a confidential police report of the incident. The newspapers reported, in more dignified fashion, that Reynolds had said she had cut off the victim's hair and "treated it in an obscene fashion."

How could Christine, whose recollection of other details of the crime did not correlate with the facts, know this key piece of information? The answer was a black eye to the LAPD. After a police interrogation, Christine broke down. The "secret clue" had been given to her by a girlfriend who had once worked for the Los Angeles police. The woman had told Christine she learned the clue from "a police lieutenant called Rudy."*

Christine Reynolds had been exposed as a phony, as were the other handful of women who stepped forward to "confess" to the murder. But the papers were reluctant to give up on what was described as the "queer" angle in the case. *Examiner* reporter Sid Hughes was especially fired up to catch a killer lesbian. "Sid Hughes wouldn't give up on the lesbian angle. He checked it out pretty thoroughly," said *Daily News* journalist Gerry Ramlow.

The reasons for the postwar reading public's obsession with the Sapphic angle to the Dahlia case were rooted in Tinseltown's deeply ambivalent portrayal of homosexuality. 1940s Hollywood was built on the twin bedrocks of Christianity and Judaism: religions innately antagonistic to same-sex love. The restrictive censorship of the Hays Code,† supported by bodies such as the National League of Decency, forbade all reference to the love that "dare not speak its name." Stars with leanings in the "wrong" direction were forced to conceal their true inclinations by "lavender" marriages, often with a homosexual partner of the opposite sex. Homosexuals, like Communists, Jews, Mexicans, and other nonwhite "foreigners," embodied all that was feared and dreaded in the "Other," defined as anything "un-American." They fueled the hysterical fears of a "fifth-column"

---

* This must have been Lieutenant Rudy Wellpott, the notorious head of Administrative Vice at the LAPD, who was later to be embroiled in the Mickey Cohen and Brenda Allen phone-tapping scandals of 1949. (Discussed on page 148.)

† Hays Code: the Motion Picture Production Code, a set of self-imposed industry rules that set out a restrictive set of "moral guidelines," and which was applied to motion pictures produced by the Hollywood studios from 1930 to 1968. Among other restrictions, the code forbade the depiction of homosexuality in any form.

conspiracy that were to culminate in the witch hunts of the McCarthy years.

But if male homosexuality was condemned, female homosexuality was beyond the pale. Most American women barely knew what a lesbian was. Gay females were, in the public image, loathsome creatures. They were either seen as hard, sophisticated older women who preyed upon younger victims, or sad, misplaced would-be men who dressed in mannish clothing. These images corresponded to the then-current theory that lesbians were men trapped in women's bodies. In fiction and medical literature, they were portrayed as neurotic, tragic, or absurd, inevitably driven to debility or suicide. It would have been impossible for an actress who openly loved women to become a star. Female stars who played in the "twilight zone"—Greta Garbo, Tallulah Bankhead, Barbara Stanwyck, Marlene Dietrich, Joan Crawford, Katharine Hepburn, Judy Garland—were all forced to make a front of social conformity, many ending up living alone, alcoholic wrecks, or in dead marriages. And yet, in many cases—notably those of Hepburn, Garbo, and Dietrich—it was the very aloofness and sexual ambivalence of the "Gillette blades"* that was the basis of their allure. As with so much else, Hollywood played a double standard with this particular manifestation of the "Other." While overtly disapproving of the members of its "sewing circle," the film industry nevertheless exploited them for their ability to titillate the moviegoing masses with voyeuristic glimpses of a deep and complex female sexuality, liberated from the restrictions of convention. So stars such as Marlene Dietrich and Greta Garbo were permitted to appear in androgynous roles, cross-dress, and even—occasionally—kiss another woman on-screen. It was a hypocritical double standard but it sold pictures and it made the "Gillette blades" megastars.

Not to be outdone by Sid Hughes at the *Examiner*, the *Herald-*

---

* "Gillette blades": so called because of the double-edged blade of the Gillette razor, i.e., "cutting both ways."

Express also fully explored the female killer theory. It ran side-by-side photo stories on three infamous homicidal females who had been busted in Los Angeles. Louise Peete, one of only four women executed by the state of California, was a serial killer who had been apprehended when a cop noticed that a flower bed in her blossoming garden looked unnaturally new and bare. It turned out to contain her latest victim. Winnie Ruth Judd had committed two murders in Arizona. She was busted in L.A. when a trunk containing the dismembered remains of her victims began to leak fluids in the baggage claim section of a local train station. Clara Phillips (a.k.a. "Tiger Girl") had murdered a woman whom she suspected was a rival for her husband's affections. She had struck her repeatedly with a hammer, then rolled a fifty-pound boulder on top of the corpse.

Aggie Underwood even hauled out Alice La Vere, a "noted consulting psychologist" and expert-for-hire, to compile a profile of the lesbian Dahlia killer. La Vere opined that the killer was "a sinister Lucrezia Borgia—a butcher woman whose crime dwarfs any in the modern crime annals." According to La Vere, murders left behind them "a trail of fingerprints, bits of skin and hair." The Black Dahlia killer left the most telltale clue of all—the murder pattern of a "degenerate, vicious feminine mind." There were three types of killer, La Vere continued, who might have perpetrated such a crime: a jealous, rejected female; an abnormal, "Well of Loneliness" type whose "twisted mind" combined "the most terrifying criminal tendencies of the warped male and female minds"; and a "psychopathic male" caught between impotency and confused sex tendencies. La Vere urged the police in particular to look for a woman older than the Dahlia. This woman, who either inspired the crime or actually committed it, need not be a female of great strength. Extreme emotion or high mental tension, La Vere noted, can give superhuman strength.

The Hollywood director and screenwriter Ben Hecht also wrote an article for the *Herald-Express* positing a lesbian killer. According to Hecht, the female psychopath in question was a "hyperthyroidic type," with an "over-developed thymus gland." The faulty gram-mar of the killer's letters, such as the statement "Had my fun *at* the police," also (according to Hecht) suggested a female killer. It was a "female malapropism, and an infantile one. . . . Little girls often say, 'Give it *at* me!'" Hecht proceeded to give a description of the female killer straight out of the phantasmagoria of the postwar horror movie, describing her as gaunt, with a "rudimentary bosom." Her face was long and narrow; she had a receding chin; her fingers were long; she had a "European" accent. But then, mysteriously, Hecht finished his article with a cryptic about-turn. The killer, he said, was not a woman, but a man. He knew the killer's name and the reasons for the crime, but was unable to offer "another version." Whether Hecht really knew anything about the killer, or was simply playing some obscure prank, remained a mystery.

The LAPD scoped out the lesbian angle, too. Sergeant Peter Vetcher, an Army officer based in Washington who had had a one-night stand with Elizabeth Short in Los Angeles in the fall of 1946, had told the police that Elizabeth had told him she was "going with a man whom she did not like very much," but that "she did not want to hurt his feelings by stopping going with him." Vetcher also told the cops that, while the pair had made love several times that night, "at no time was she in a passionate mood." The natural conclusion he came to from her sexual indifference to him was that she was likely a lesbian. As further evidence of Sapphic leanings, Vetcher told police that Elizabeth had told him she had at one time frequently visited a wealthy woman who resided in Hollywood or Los Angeles, and that this woman had made "improper advances to her," which she had resisted.

Police reports hinted darkly at the involvement in the murder of a "queer woman surgeon in the Valley." Even more suspect, this queer woman surgeon was Chinese. "Madam Chang," wrote one report, "was a prominent queer" of San Francisco who "spent considerable time partying in Hollywood." She entertained pilots and fliers in the U.S. Air Force en route to the Pacific field of operations during the war. Elizabeth, the reports noted, had been engaged to a Flying Tiger (Matt Gordon), and therefore could have known Madam Chang. The police reports did not disclose further details or information about the sinister "queer female surgeon." Her true story was to be uncovered many years later. It was more incredible than anything a Hearst reporter could dream up, but it had nothing to do with the Black Dahlia.*

Aggie Underwood probably knew full well that the speculations on lesbian involvement in the Dahlia murder were a red herring, but she was happy to let them run. Officially, Aggie had been booted off the Dahlia case. But secretly, she continued to investigate it. Her investigations took several years to come to fruition, but they were to lead finally to the truth.

Moving on from the "queer woman surgeon in the Valley" theory, the LAPD checked out another likely subject. This one was an Oklahoma cowboy with sinister Communist connections. Woody Guthrie, the Okie hillbilly, was at this point a well-known albeit controversial musician living on Mermaid Avenue in Brooklyn with his second wife, Marjorie, and their children. Unknown at the time was that he was suffering from undiagnosed and untreated Huntington's disease.† During a separation from Marjorie in 1948, Guthrie wrote a number of rambling letters to Mary Ruth Crissman, the twenty-eight-year-old sister of a friend of his, who lived in Northern California. There were as many as twelve letters, typed on foolscap legal pad, with handwritten notes in the margins. Woody wrote in forensically technical detail about how he would make passionate love to Mary Ruth. He stuffed into the envelopes pages from New York tabloids with lurid red circles around stories of grisly murders. The packets frightened Mary Ruth. She showed them to her

---

* The true story of "Madam Chang" was uncovered many years later and is discussed on page 210.
† Huntington's disease is a progressive hereditary neurological disorder, common symptoms of which include uncharacteristic aggression, emotional volatility, and social disinhibition.

sister, who telephoned the police. A deputy district attorney visited the Crissman sisters to warn them about Guthrie. They were not to be alone with him under any circumstances. A family friend who worked for the Los Angeles police dropped by with grisly pictures of the disemboweled Elizabeth Short. They wanted to question Guthrie about the murder. "That was the kind of thing this man would be capable of," the officer told Mary Ruth.

In the end, the LAPD eliminated Woody Guthrie as a candidate for Elizabeth's murder. The Dust Bowl troubadour with sinister pro-labor ties was the perfect suspect, save for one problem; he was not in Los Angeles at the time of the murder. Guthrie was indicted by the New York City authorities for sending obscene items in the mail. Through the efforts of his attorney, he got off with a minor sentence.

In addition to chasing unlikely suspects, the LAPD also investigated a number of alleged "sightings" of Elizabeth during the missing week. None of them could be confirmed.

Mrs. Christina Salisbury was a self-proclaimed princess of the Cherokee Indian tribe, who had played several seasons at the Ziegfeld Follies as "Princess Whitewing." She claimed to have seen Beth on the night of January 10 at the Tabu Club on the Sunset Strip. Beth was, according to Princess Whitewing, in the company of two women, a blonde and a brunette.

Mr. and Mrs. Johnson owned the Hirsch Apartments on East Washington Boulevard. They claimed that a girl matching Elizabeth's description checked into the apartments on Sunday, January 12, in the company of a man. They identified him as a man in a photograph found in Beth's trunk. He was of medium height and complexion and refused to sign the register. He told Mr. Johnson to just put down "Barnes and wife." He said the couple were moving out of Hollywood. They did not see the girl again. The man came back Wednesday. Mr. Johnson said, "We thought you might be dead." He got very excited and left. But the clothes Mrs. Johnson described the woman as wearing—beige and pink slacks, a full-length black coat, white blouse, and white bandanna over her head—did not match the outfit Elizabeth was wearing when she left Red. She had been wearing a black collarless suit, fluffy white blouse, and beige coat. A fingerprint check in the room subsequently satisfied the police that it was a case of mistaken identity.

Buddy LaGore, a bartender at the Four Star Grill on Hollywood Boulevard, claimed to have known Elizabeth and to have seen her in the company of two women on the night of January 10. "When she came in that last time she looked as if she'd slept in her clothes for days. The sheer black dress was stained and crumpled. I'd seen her many times before and always she wore the best nylons. But this time she had no stockings on." He added that her hair was "straggly" and some lipstick had been smeared on "hit-or-miss. . . . The powder was caked on her face." The other thing that Buddy noticed was that she "was cowed instead of being gay and excited, the way I'd seen her before."

A policewoman named Myrl McBride stated that on the night of Tuesday, January 14—the night before Elizabeth's body was found in Leimert Park—a girl came up to her on Main Street. The girl was crying. She said to the policewoman, "Someone wants to kill me." She then told of her ex-Marine boyfriend meeting her in a bar and "threatening to kill me if he found me with another man." McBride said she later saw the girl reenter the bar and emerge with two men and another woman. She had told the policewoman she was to meet her parents at the bus station later. But once she was shown the murdered girl's photograph, McBride was said to be less certain about the identification.

None of the "sightings" of Elizabeth in the week between January 9 and 15 were confirmed. The fact that her baggage—which had been checked in at the downtown Greyhound bus station—had never been reclaimed was significant. The cops asked Elizabeth's girlfriend, Ann Toth, if she was the type to borrow someone else's clothes, or spend four or five days in the same white blouse.

"No, she wasn't. She was the type that didn't want anybody to touch their clothes and she didn't want to touch theirs. She washed everything. She was a very meticulous person," said Toth.*

Elizabeth's friends all agreed that she was particularly fastidious about her makeup and dress. She was certainly not the type of girl to have voluntarily spent a week without changing even her underwear. The overwhelming probability was that she had been trapped and tortured in the week before her death, the week in which she had gone missing.† If any of the so-called "sightings" of her during the missing week was accurate, she must have somehow escaped her captor or captors, albeit for a short time. But who had trapped Elizabeth during that week? And where?

Somehow, the police in the Dahlia investigation always seemed to be one step behind the newspapers. The Hearst reporters had big expense accounts. They could pay to shut witnesses up until the papers had finished with them. All the major advances in the early stages of the case—the artist's sketch of Elizabeth, the identification of the victim from Soundphoto copies of her fingerprints, finding Red, the first contact with the girl's mother, locating the Frenches—were down to Jimmy's or Aggie's men, and not Captain Donahoe's. The police were beginning to look like a joke. To the public they were the cliché of Keystone Cops, stumbling around a succession of off-the-wall angles to the case. "Dahlia Case 'Idiot's Delight': More 'Confessions' and 'Letters,'" scoffed a banner headline in Aggie's *Herald-Express*. Captain Donahoe did not do the police department any favors when, in support of the "lesbian angle," he reasoned that Elizabeth must have stayed at a woman's house in order to borrow "a make-up kit."‡ He drew even greater derision when he theorized that

---

* Elizabeth's fastidiousness was also cited by Robert "Red" Manley, who mentioned that, even when sick at the motel in San Diego, she had asked for her suitcases with her clothes and makeup to be brought in to her from the car.

† The *Herald-Express* also pointed out the failure to collect her baggage implied the likelihood that Elizabeth was trapped, and possibly drugged, during the "missing week" (*Herald-Express*, January 23, 1947).

‡ As opposed to the much more plausible explanation that the girl was trapped.

a woman might more likely have cut the body in half, for the reason that she would not be able to carry the entire 123-pound corpse. In a phone call to the FBI in February, Jimmy Richardson warned that there were rumbles of police incompetence in the Dahlia case. The Police Commission had asked the LAPD chief, Clemence Horrall, for a full report. There were questions about whether the local police department was up to handling the case, or whether the FBI should step in to clean up the mess.

Everybody was putting pressure on the LAPD. In particular, the homicide detectives leading the Dahlia investigation—Lieutenant Harry Hansen* and Sergeant Finis Brown—were in the hot seat. Aggie's boys called the homicide cops the "egostupes," a portmanteau term intended to convey a combination of stupidity, arrogance, and ego. But Lieutenant Harry Hansen was not stupid. Admittedly, he had a penchant for pin-striped suits, loud ties, and snazzy watch-bands. Tall, red-haired, and balding, his basset-hound face was long and morose, with Mickey Mouse ears and sleepy eyes. His fedora was glued to his head, earning him the moniker Harry "the Hat." But Harry had served more than twenty years with the Los Angeles Police Department. Originally from Salt Lake City, his parents were Mormons who later moved to Los Angeles. Harry graduated from Manual Arts High School and joined the LAPD in 1926. There, he graduated from patrolman through the Records Bureau, Robbery, Burglary, and, finally, Homicide. With his regular partner Jack McCreadie, he had been responsible for bringing to justice—and the gas chamber—a host of vicious killers. They included such lowlifes as Mrs. Peete of the infamously denuded flower bed, and William Edward Hickman, a child murderer whom Harry had identified from a single fingerprint on the rearview mirror of his Chrysler roadster. Everybody respected Harry "the Hat."

But there was another side to "the Hat," which fewer people saw.

---

* No relation to the Los Angeles businessman Mark Hansen, although both were of Danish descent.

It was recalled by Harry Watson,* a well-known photographer for the *Daily News*. Watson had been summoned one night to the Hall of Justice, to cover a story in which a suspected child molester would be available for photographs. As he entered the conference room in which the prisoner was being held, he saw a man sitting at the table, head in his hands, repeating over and over, "I know my rights, I know my rights." According to Watson, Leutenant Hansen reached out to the man and punched him, knocking him to the floor. He then pushed him back into his seat, where the prisoner sat while the photographers busily snapped pictures of him, the blood dribbling from his chin. Back at the newsroom, the photographers retouched the pictures to erase the blood. On another occasion, Hansen bragged to Watson about how he obtained what he called "Third Street Bridge confessions." If a suspect refused to cooperate with the cops, he would be taken to Third Street Bridge and dangled over the side. If no confession was forthcoming, he would be dropped onto the concrete below.

Lieutenant Harry Hansen's partner on the Dahlia case, Sergeant Finis Brown, was very different from "the Hat." Finis was squat and swarthy, with heavy jowls and rumpled suits. Unlike Harry, he had none of the smooth talker about him. People who knew Finis described him as "real strange," that "you couldn't believe a word he said." If Harry "the Hat" was the one to get heavy with criminals, Finis fraternized with them. According to the veteran Fox television crime reporter Tony Valdez, it was common knowledge that Finis Brown was mixed up with Mark Hansen, that he was the "bagman" who collected the dough from police shakedowns of the hoodlums and racketeers of the Los Angeles underworld. That opinion was shared by the intrepid police correspondent of the *Long Beach Independent* Chuck Cheatham: "'Harry the Hat,' that's what we called

---

* Harry Watson (1922–2001) was a member of a family of child film stars who later became a leading staff photographer on the *Daily News*. In the 1950s he switched to television and became a pioneering cameraman for KTTV. All of the six Watson brothers became news or commercial photographers, and Harry's uncle George went on to manage Acme News Pictures (a forerunner of United Press Photos). .

Lieutenant Harry Hansen. He wasn't on the take, not the Hat. His partner Finis Brown, that's another story." The legendary Los Angeles crime reporter Nieson Himmel was of the same view: "People said that Harry Hansen's partner, Finis Albania Brown, was a bookie. We called him 'F.A.' for 'Fat Arse.'"*

Some years earlier, criminologist and crime reporter Ernest Jerome Hopkins had noted that the LAPD of the era had an absolute disregard for the Constitution, or for law of any sort. Hopkins described how LAPD officers would routinely beat suspects with rubber hoses under interrogation, since a hose left no visible marks. Throughout the 1930s and '40s, the LAPD had a reputation for lawlessness and brutality beyond almost any other police department. The fanatically anti-Labor Los Angeles business establishment, coupled with the city's puritanical new population from mainly Iowa and Kansas, led to a combination of "Red Squad" and "Moral Squad" that clashed viciously with the laissez-faire values of the movie industry community. At the same time, police were caught up with shyster lawyers, stool pigeons, and bail bondsmen in a cycle of graft that saw the proceeds of crime split profitably between lawyers, cops, and criminals. "It was a lousy, crooked department," recalled Max Solomon, who had defended many an L.A. gangster and so could be presumed to know what he was talking about. "You know, in Chicago the gangsters paid off the police but the gangsters did the job. In Los Angeles, the police were the gangsters."

But Sergeant Finis Brown had an asset that nobody else had. His elder brother, Thaddeus Brown, was the powerful commander of the LAPD Patrol Bureau, handling all divisional vice activities of the department. Thad Brown was a cop's cop. The historian of the LAPD

---

* Nieson Himmel (1922–99) was one of the police reporters who defined postwar Los Angeles. Himmel spent a lifetime prowling the city streets for stories and listening to the nightly mayhem of newsroom murder calls. He worked for the *City News* and *Daily News* before joining Aggie Underwood's *Herald-Express*, and was once arrested for trafficking narcotics across the U.S.-Mexican border when on assignment for a story under Aggie's supervision. He ended his career as a police reporter for the *Los Angeles Times*.

Joe Domanick wrote of him that "he loved to drink, loved his men, and they loved him." The elder Brown brother was something of a celebrity. In the early days of the cop radio show *Dragnet*, Joe Friday's self-introduction would invariably include the words, "*The boss is Thad Brown, chief of detectives.*" But like the pudgy, baby-faced police captain Hank Quinlan in Orson Welles's movie *Touch of Evil*, Thad's chummy façade concealed a core of ice. He commanded a network of paid informants in all corners of the city: the management of the Communist Party, a barber in Watts, the head of tongs in Chinatown.* To the average cop in the police department, Thad's word was law. Nobody would dare knock Finis while his big brother was around to protect him.

More than a year after the murder of Elizabeth Short, the police investigation was heading nowhere. Los Angeles citizens were terrorized by a succession of recent unsolved murders in the city, of which the Dahlia and French cases were just two examples. Angelenos complained that their women were unsafe on the streets at night as long as the "werewolf killer" remained at large. The public mood was fast turning from unease to anger. Complaints flooded in to the mayor and civic authorities. Something had to be done. But the months dragged on, and nothing happened.

Then, in late 1948—almost two years after the murder—there was, finally, a breakthrough.

---

* Tong: North American Chinese secret society or clandestine brotherhood.

PART 2
DARK PASSAGE

"Experience has taught me
never to trust a policeman."

THE ASPHALT JUNGLE (1950)

8

THE LETTER

I n the aftermath of the Dahlia killing, Dr. Joseph Paul De River received hundreds of letters from members of the public, offering theories, clues, and solutions.* He read them all.

In the 1940s, the doctor was the sole police psychiatrist employed by the LAPD. He was therefore responsible for screening the nuts, crackpots, and other deluded individuals who stepped forward with a confession or claim relating to the killing. The doctor took them all seriously, because it was his view that the pathology of the Dahlia killer included a deep-seated compulsion to publicize and claim recognition for his act. The doctor was convinced that the confessors "would keep on coming" and that the police would have to talk to them, because "the type of mind that conceived the Elizabeth Short murder will some day have to boast about it."

Dr. De River had already written an article for Aggie Underwood's *Herald-Express*, in which he analyzed the "criminally twisted mind" of the person responsible for the Dahlia murder. According to the doctor, the sadistic killer of Elizabeth Short went about his work with "egotistical satisfaction, elevating his ego and will to power." The doctor was of the view that the killer hated womankind. He was a "sadistic fiend" who delighted in beating and then annihilating

---

* Pronounced *De-RYE-ver.*

his victim. The doctor noted that sadists of this type "have a super-abundance of curiosity and are liable to spend much time with their victims after the spark of life has flickered and died." The killer might even be of the studious type. In the doctor's view, he "delighted in the humiliation of his victim." He was the "experimentor and analyst" in the most "brutal forms of torture."

Dr. De River himself was a unique figure in the Los Angeles Police Department. He had been born in New Orleans in 1892, apparently of French descent. Certainly the surname "De River" carried with it European connotations. It also, as the doctor himself said, evoked the psychiatrist's calling, to "derive" hidden truths obscured beneath the smokescreen of the conscious personality. The doctor's own favorite explanation for his surname came from the fact that he had been born on the Mississippi River, in the course of a boat journey from Cincinnati to New Orleans. His formal training had begun in 1916, in the days when professional psychiatry was in its infancy, with a medical degree from Tulane University.

The doctor himself cut an imposing figure. His nose was impressively hooked. His black eyes stared imperiously at the object of his gaze, above his jet-black mustache. He was seldom to be seen without his pipe in his left hand. He would take a deep puff on it and pause, clearing his throat for dramatic emphasis. As *Life* magazine observed, he very much looked the part of a celebrity Hollywood physician.

The high point in the doctor's career with the Los Angeles Police Department came a decade before the Dahlia, with the case of the three little "Babes of Inglewood." Seven-year-old Madeline and nine-year-old Melba Everett were sisters. They went missing on June 26, 1937, with their eight-year-old-friend Jeannette Stephens. The three little girls were last seen talking to a man at Centinela Park. Two days later, volunteer Boy Scouts found their bodies in a weedy gully in the Baldwin Hills. They had been strangled and sexually assaulted.

Dr. De River visited the crime scene and viewed the bodies in the morgue. He observed that the little girls had been laid facedown, their dresses pulled up, their shoes placed side by side in a row. After considering all the evidence, the doctor described the type of person the police should be seeking: a sadistic pedophile in his twenties who was meticulous in appearance, religious, and remorseful. He might have a past record of annoying children, or loitering where they played. The crime had been planned and the killer had known how to approach the girls without frightening them. They had trusted him.

The doctor's description of the killer fit a school crossing guard by the name of Albert Dyer. Dyer aroused suspicion when, after questioning by the police, he walked back into the interrogation room, took the officer's hand, and thanked him for all the efforts that were being made to solve the crimes. Dyer was therefore brought in for requestioning. This time, he confessed to the murders. He told police that he had lured the little girls into the secluded gully in the Baldwin Hills with a story about rabbits. He had then separated them. He had strangled them one by one and prayed over their dead bodies. Later, when photographs of angry crowds storming Inglewood City Hall and demanding justice for the murdered girls were reexamined, Albert Dyer could be seen in the crowd, yelling with the other irate citizens, "Lynch the S.O.B.!" He was even photographed among the men helping to carry the small bodies of the victims to the morgue. Dyer's wife later admitted that, after the killings, her husband had kept a scrapbook of clippings relating to the case.

Dr. De River's profile of the killer in the Inglewood case was only the second case in history of a criminal profile being used to catch a killer: the first being the landmark profile of the British serial killer Jack the Ripper, which was drawn up by two physicians in the 1880s.* Moreover, the doctor's description of the Inglewood killer had been broadly accurate, although Albert Dyer was thirty-two (not

---

* The London physicians George Phillips and Thomas Bond used autopsy results and crime scene evidence in the fall of 1888 to create a rudimentary but groundbreaking analysis of the personality, behavioral characteristics, and lifestyle of the notorious serial killer known as "Jack the Ripper." This is generally considered the first case of criminal profiling.

in his twenties), and had not previously been arrested for bothering children. Dyer was tried by Judge Thomas P. White, convicted, and sent to the gas chamber.

After the conviction of Albert Dyer, Dr. De River became the new star expert for the Los Angeles Police Department. He was brought onto the payroll of the LAPD as the department's first consultant psychiatrist, charged with interviewing suspects and criminal profiling. He established a one-man Sexual Offense Bureau, and it was through his personal campaigning and the public outcry and indignation over the Dahlia murder that California introduced the first state sexual offender register, in 1947.

Three years after the Inglewood case, the doctor met his first serious challenge. It came in the form of an eleven-year-old girl. On the afternoon of April 4, 1940, Chloe Davis called her father, who managed a Los Angeles grocery store, and told him to come straight home. When Frank Barton Davis arrived at the two-bedroom bungalow on West Fifty-eighth Place, he saw a crowd of neighbors clustered around the house. Chloe stood on the porch, her forehead bleeding. In the kitchen were Barton's three-year-old son Marquis and seven-year-old-daughter Deborah Ann, lying faceup on the blood-soaked linoleum. They had been bludgeoned. In the hallway lay Barton's wife, Lolita. She had been bludgeoned and burned. In the bathroom was his ten-year-old daughter, Daphne. Barton glanced at the blood and pieces of brain spattered on the walls and ceiling. He registered that he had lost his entire family. He ran screaming down the street. His daughter, Chloe, went after him and told him to "brace up."

Chloe, who had superficial injuries, was interviewed by police officers and Dr. De River. Under questioning, she appeared remarkably cold and calm. Chloe claimed that her mother, Lolita, had ordered her to kill her brothers and sisters, and then Lolita herself. She had told Chloe to set her nightdress on fire, and then kill her and the other children. This Chloe had obediently done, pausing for a drink between blows. The evidence in the case was far from clear-cut. On the one hand, Lolita was found with slit wrists, tending to corroborate Chloe's story that the mother intended to commit suicide. Lolita had also been suffering from mental problems at the time of her death, and had apparently asked for chloroform to kill the children when the "demons" came after them. On the other hand, one of the dying children, Daphne, was alleged to have told doctors before she expired that Chloe had attacked her. Neighbors gave witness to the girl's violent temperament, including an incident when she grabbed her mother's hair over a petty quarrel, and banged her head against the wall. Chloe was just a head shorter than her mother, and muscular. She could, it was admitted, easily have committed such an attack.

Chloe's father, Barton, who by now wanted his remaining daughter back, hired top attorneys and a rival psychiatrist to counter Dr. De River's contention, for the LAPD, that Chloe was a "cold" character who lacked "remorse," who had intentionally killed her mother and siblings. There were, the father's expert alleged, "important elements of physical and mental shock to be considered before an adequate appraisal of the girl's reactions can be evaluated." There was also the fact that, under California law at the time, the threshold for criminal responsibility was fourteen years old.

In the event, the coroner's jury ruled that Lolita Davis had murdered her three children and then killed herself. In a blow to De River's career, Superior Judge W. Turney Fox of the juvenile court ruled that the police psychiatrist was not to question suspects under the age of eighteen. Judge Fox's successor in the juvenile court, Superior Judge A. A. Scott, confirmed the ruling, although Judge Scott later defended De River with the statement that "in my opinion, Dr. De River is the best qualified sex psychiatrist in the country."*

---

* The question of juvenile criminal responsibility is a vexed one, to which there has arguably never been found a complete solution. Issues include knowledge of wrongfulness, understanding of criminality and its consequences, the child's psychological development, and lived experience. See, for example, the overview in McDiarmid, Claire, "An Age of Complexity: Children and Criminal Responsibility in Law," *Youth Justice*, August 2013, vol. 13, no. 2, pp. 145–60.

By 1947, however, the Chloe Davis fiasco was in the past and Dr. De River was firmly entrenched in the offices of the LAPD as its resident police psychiatrist. His reputation was that of a somewhat unorthodox and controversial practitioner, but all agreed that he did seem to have an uncanny ability to read the mind of the sexual criminal. Set against the Chloe Davis failure were successful prosecutions in over twenty cases where the doctor had acted as expert witness. He had, he was proud to say, never lost a case for the city of Los Angeles in court. Certainly the doctor was conservative in his views on criminal responsibility and the registration of sexual offenders. But he was by no means extreme for the time. In the 1940s, the terms "degeneracy" and "perversion" included homosexuality and oral and anal sex.* When the sexual offender register was introduced in California, punishments proposed for "sex psychopaths" included castration, tattooing on the forehead, and trimming the ears of sexual offenders to a sharp peak so that even children could identify them. America, in the late 1940s, was in the midst of a "sex crime panic." The sexual license of the war years had been shut down, and the political discourse of civil liberties and procedural justice was, as yet, two decades away.

One of the most ardent supporters of Dr. De River was Aggie Underwood. Their friendship had started back in 1937, when Aggie was a police reporter on the beat, covering the Inglewood case. At one point during the trial of Albert Dyer, Judge White remained in his chambers to allow Aggie to grab a snack in the coffee shop around the corner from the courtroom. When Aggie returned, the judge mounted his bench to receive the jury's guilty verdict. Judge White, Aggie Underwood, Dr. De River, and district attorney investigator Eugene Williams—who brought De River into the process of interviewing the Inglewood suspects—remained lifelong friends

---

* Sodomy laws, or laws proscribing certain types of sexual activity as "unnatural"—notably homosexuality—were not declared illegal on a federal basis in the U.S. until the 2003 Supreme Court ruling of *Lawrence v. Texas*. Even today, fourteen U.S. states have not as yet revised their sodomy laws in line with the federal court's ruling.

after the case.* De River wrote columns for Aggie's newspaper. During the investigation of the Dahlia murder, the police psychiatrist met the city editor secretly at her home. Publicly, the *Herald-Express* continued to keep Randolph Hearst and the reading public happy with stories of confessing Sams and Sapphic sadism. Privately, Aggie and Dr. De River pored over the serious evidence in the case. They discussed the theories. They evaluated the suspects. They drew psychological profiles of the killer. "Aggie met surreptitiously with Dr. Paul De River," recalled Aggie's daughter-in-law, Rilla. "They'd meet at Aggie's house late at night and pore over the books De River had written, discussing theories and drawing psychological profiles of people. Some were quite prominent, and others were low-level hoods and hangers-on."

On October 28, 1948, a letter arrived on Dr. De River's desk that particularly caught his attention. It had been typed on paper stamped Miami Beach, FLA. The return address was a post office box in Miami. The letter was from a person signing himself under the name of "Jack Sand." It referred to a magazine report of the Dahlia murder, and stated that the writer had been associating with a person who fitted the "pattern" of the "infamous one." The letter went on to say that the writer had met the suspected Dahlia killer the previous March in San Francisco, and had associated closely with him for two months. Whether he was capable of such an act, however, the writer could not be sure. The writer of the letter went on to state that he had "never knowling [sic] associated with a murderer," but that the man he had met in San Francisco had a motive for the killing, and by his own admission was "present at the time," and "knew the characters involved." He went on to offer his help in tracking the suspect down, stating that there were many more circumstances that led to his suspicions.

---

* Judge Thomas P. White (1888–1968) was a distinguished member of the Los Angeles appellate court. Among his rulings as an appeals court judge was the successful appeal of the Latino defendants in the notorious "Sleepy Lagoon" case.

Something about the letter from "Jack Sand" fired a neuron deep in Dr. De River's brain. The magazine article to which the writer referred was in fact one that had been planted by the doctor, in a deliberate attempt to lure the Dahlia killer. It was the cover story of the October 1948 edition of a pulp crime magazine called *True Detective*. The story was entitled, in the plural, "The Black Dahlia Murders." The cover of the edition was blood-red, featuring the white faces and avenging stares of half a dozen female "victims." The author of the article cited Dr. De River's published profile of the killer, noting his view that the murderer had manifested "a sadistic component of a sado-masochistic complex." It also cited the doctor's opinion that the killer might "be of a studious, scientific bent," and would, by his very nature, "be impelled to boast of the crime that shocked the nation."

Three weeks after receiving the letter from "Jack Sand," the doctor sent a response. He was intrigued, he wrote, to know more about the fellow that Mr. Sand had met in San Francisco in March 1947, who knew so much about the Dahlia murder. The doctor himself was writing a textbook dealing with behavioral problems, and was interested to find out about the backgrounds of such individuals, in particular their childhood, which was often "the basis of complexes. . . . I am interested," the doctor wrote, "in any person that fits into any pattern that is like the Elizabeth Short case."

On November 27, the doctor received a response from "Jack Sand." Jack described his relationship with "Jeff," the man he had met in San Francisco. Jack and Jeff had spent six weeks together. Jack had once watched Jeff have sexual relations with two women they picked up at a bar. Jeff told Jack that he knew Elizabeth Short, and that he frequented the bars that she did. The police had questioned several people he knew in relation to the case. Jeff had therefore fled from Los Angeles, to escape questioning himself. Jeff had encouraged Jack to try to break into screenwriting for Hollywood. Once, Jeff made a pencil sketch of Jack. Jack enclosed the sketch with his letter. It was signed, "Jeff '48." The sketch showed an interesting pattern of shading, or "crosshatching." It evoked the intricate, crisscross lacerations on the Dahlia's pubic bone and right hip. The doctor was convinced that "Jack" was not the writer's real name.

Further letters from Jack Sand to Dr. De River followed. Jack admitted to a strong interest in sexual sadism. On December 11, he wrote that Jeff was a very "loyal lad." If he had any information that Jack was the real culprit, he doubted that anybody would hear of it. Jack wrote that Jeff had been attracted to him by the "abundance of lovely girls" he had seen with him, and had thought that, by making his "acquittance" [sic], he would be able to meet some of them. Jack wrote that Jeff was very "dissapointed" [sic] when he found out these girls did not in fact visit his hotel room.* The sensitive and tender side of Jeff's nature, wrote Jack, was very "predomonate" [sic], also a touch of cunning and slyness. Finally, Jack proffered a hypothetical explanation of the genesis and motive for the Dahlia killing. Was it not possible, he wrote, that an associate of Elizabeth, after an affair "not considered proper by the average person," had been "mocked or threatened exposure by her to his friends?" He therefore might, out of revenge, inflict "pain of some nature on her and experience a new sensation by accident. . . . Thus leading to the complete annihilation of her and other victims."

The letters from Jack Sand contained errors of spelling, grammar, and syntax ("aquittance," "dissapointed," "predomonate"). There were also errors on the envelopes in which the letters were sent: one, for example, was addressed "Especial delivar." There had, as the doctor was aware, been a number of grammatical errors in the purported Dahlia killer letters: "Here *is* Dahlia's possessions"; and "Had my fun *at* the police." Elizabeth had also, in her final letter to Gordon Fickling, referred to going to work as a model for someone called "Jack."† A further curious point was that Jack, in his letters, referred to the murder victim always as "Elizabeth"—never "Elizabeth Short"

---

* The girls did not visit Jack's hotel room because, as was later discovered, he was a pimp.
† See the letter from Gordon Fickling referred to on page 44.

or "the Dahlia case." It was a term of intimacy that the doctor found striking. Most significantly, Jack's act of coming forward to the police manifested, in the doctor's opinion, the very desire for publicity, the need "to boast of the crime that shocked the nation," which he was convinced that the Dahlia killer harbored.

Dr. De River and Aggie Underwood were sure they were on to something. The doctor in particular wanted to find out more about "Jack Sand," to establish exactly who he and his friend "Jeff" were, and the nature of their relationship to the Dahlia. To do this, he would need to obtain the clearance of the LAPD top brass. So the doctor went to see the LAPD chief, Clemence Horrall.

9

THE SUSPECT

Police Chief Clemence B. Horrall was a rarity in the Los Angeles Police Department in that he held a college degree. He was also probably the only officer who kept a farm of pigs, chickens, horses, and cows at his home in the Valley. His wife milked the cows every morning.

Horrall had been appointed the forty-first police chief of the LAPD in 1941 by Los Angeles Mayor Fletcher Bowron, as a weapon in the mayor's war against corruption. For the police department had, by Mayor Bowron's election, been rocked by scandal after scandal. The police chief before Horrall, Arthur C. Hohmann, had been forced to resign after a corruption bust involving the head of the LAPD Robbery Squad. And only three years before that, there had been an even worse public relations disaster.

On January 14, 1938, private investigator Harry Raymond got into his car and turned on the ignition. The car was blasted to smithereens by a black powder bomb hidden under the hood. Miraculously, Raymond survived. At the time of the bombing, Harry Raymond was employed by the crusading Los Angeles restaurant owner Clifford Clinton.* His beat was to investigate police-protected brothels and

---

* Clifford E. Clinton (1900–1969), founder of the Los Angeles restaurant chain Clifton's Cafeterias, was a leading philanthropist and campaigner against corruption who, among other charitable acts, founded "penny restaurants" to feed the needy before the government introduced relief agencies.

gambling parlors in the city. But when Raymond was rushed to the hospital filled with shrapnel, he dropped a bombshell bigger than the original bomb that had blasted him. The individual responsible for the car bomb attack, he claimed, was none other than the then-head of the LAPD Police Intelligence Squad, Captain Earle Kynette. Captain Kynette and other LAPD officers were involved in the police-protected rackets of the city. Harry Raymond and Clifford Clinton, by their poking around, were getting too close to exposing what was going on. The threat they posed had to be, in police parlance, "neutralized." Kynette, naturally, denied the allegations. He was, he claimed, at home nursing an eye complaint with boric acid the night of the attack. Unfortunately for Kynette, the fact that he and other members of the LAPD had rented a $50-a-month house opposite Harry Raymond's home in order to spy on him, together with the detonating wire found in Kynette's garage, told another story.

Despite establishment attempts to dampen the flames, the evidence against Earle Kynette was just too damning. After indictment by the 1938 Los Angeles grand jury, Kynette was tried, convicted of attempted murder, and sent to San Quentin. The then–LAPD chief, James "Two Gun" Davis, was forced to resign. The incumbent mayor, Frank Shaw—who managed Los Angeles like his private piggy bank—was ousted. In Shaw's place as mayor came the sober ex-judge and staunch ally of Clifford Clinton, the self-avowed white knight against corruption Fletcher Bowron. At the time of Mayor Shaw's recall, police corruption was so widespread that it was said that, when the mayor stepped down, dozens of Los Angeles police officers "retired" to Mexico.

The new mayor vowed to change all that. Fletcher Bowron eschewed the dapper panama hats, shiny suits, and Oliver Hardy–esque mustache favored by his predecessor, Frank Shaw. Flashiness—all too reminiscent of the gangster—was replaced by gray suits and spectacles. The new mayor was nostalgic for the dusty old Los Angeles of his childhood, when wagons trundled along dirt tracks and the word "freeway" had yet to invade the American dictionary or way of life. In Bowron's shake-up, over two hundred police officers were demoted or fired. Two new chiefs tried and failed to manage the unruly police department before Clemence Horrall was finally appointed to the post.

On Mayor Bowron's orders, Chief Horrall and his assistant, Joe Reed, devised a strategy for controlling the gangsters in town: a new, elite special detail. The detail—known as the Gangster Squad—was charged specifically with the task of clearing the hoods out of the city. It was headed by a tough little officer from the Seventy-seventh Street Station, on the edge of Watts: Lieutenant William Burns. The prime targets of the Gangster Squad were the local gangsters— Mickey Cohen, Bugsy Siegel, the Mafia's local capo Jack Dragna, Jimmy "Little Giant" Utley, and the like. But they also spied on corrupt cops. That, and any other "special assignment" given to them by the chief.

It was just such a "special assignment" that Chief Horrall had in mind when he called Willie Burns into his office late in December 1948. Present at the secret meeting were Dr. De River, Assistant Chief Joe Reed, and Captain Francis Kearney of Homicide. Captain Kearney had replaced Big Jack Donahoe —who had been transferred back to Robbery—as head of the Homicide detail a year back.

By the time Chief Horrall called the meeting with Willie Burns, a lot had happened since Jack Sand's original letter to Dr. De River. Throughout the winter of '48, the doctor had continued his correspondence with Jack, discussing psychological profiles of the Dahlia killer. In the meantime, Chief Horrall and Assistant Chief Reed had sent an undercover officer of the LAPD—Officer Jones*—to Miami, to tail Jack.

Officer Jones was, at first, unaware of the purpose of his mission. He reported that Jack spent hours staking out a restaurant called Wolfie's on Collins Avenue, where his wife worked as a waitress. As

---

* Officer Jones's mission was kept highly secret and his first name was never revealed.

Dr. De River had suspected, "Jack Sand" was a pseudonym. Jack's real name was, in fact, Leslie Duane Dillon. He was twenty-seven years old, tall and lanky, sloop-shouldered, with glasses, and he was given to dyeing his hair in different colors.

Leslie Dillon had grown up in Cushing, Oklahoma, a small town riddled with pipelines and infused with the odor of gasoline from the massive refineries of the Creek County oil fields. His father, Ray, was a metal worker. By the time he was eight years old, Dillon's parents had separated. His mother, Mamie, was living as a single parent in his grandmother's home in Cushing, working as a cook in a local restaurant. During the war, Dillon served barely a year in the Navy before he was dishonorably discharged for stealing watches. In January '46 he was arrested and charged with pimping in San Francisco. Shortly thereafter he married, had a baby daughter, and firmly settled into what would become a lifetime of drifting. Throughout the late '40s he meandered from state to state with his wife and daughter, crisscrossing the country from coast to coast with stays in San Francisco, Los Angeles, Florida, and Oklahoma City. His aliases were many: "Jack Sand," "Jack Diamond," "Jack Dillon Maxim." His changes of occupation reflected the chameleon-like changes of his name and hair color: bellhop, rumrunner, bootlegger, beer bottler, pimp, gambler, taxi driver, dance instructor. He never stayed at any one place, or did any one thing, for long.

After a few weeks of being tailed by Officer Jones in Miami, Leslie Dillon got wind of something afoot. This was not surprising, as he was called in and raked over the coals by the Miami postal inspector about his P.O. box. Suspicious that he was being watched, Dillon even turned himself over to the local office of the FBI. He told them he believed he might be wanted for some offense—possibly murder—in Los Angeles. Did they want him?* The Feds told him they did not

---

* This incident makes it clear that Leslie Dillon, contrary to his later assertions, was well aware from an early stage that he was being watched as a potential suspect in the Dahlia murder.

know what he was talking about and let him go. The FBI also picked up Officer Jones. They let him go, too, when he explained he was on assignment from the Los Angeles Police Department. Aware that he was being watched, Dillon went into hiding in his room for two days. An Italian taxi driver friend, Larry Fanucci, brought him food.

Finally, Dillon left his room in Miami. Officer Jones took the opportunity to search his lodgings. The place was a mess. Violently torn clothes were strewn around. It appeared that Dillon was a voracious reader, not just of detective stories, but of everything. Jones found two newspaper clippings in the room. One showed a picture of a man lying dead, killed by a prison guard at the Cook County jail. The guard was being congratulated by the warden for having killed the man. The other newspaper clipping showed the headline "Shoots Out Girl's Tooth."* There were also unsigned samples of "creative writing." They included an account of what appeared to be the rape and shooting of a woman.† In addition, Jones found the copy of *True Detective* magazine that Dillon had referred to in his original letter to Dr. De River, under the alias of "Jack Sand." The article featured a picture of the telegram that Red Manley had sent to Elizabeth in San Diego. Next to Red's signature, Dillon had inscribed the curious squiggle that he added under the *a* of "Sand" when signing his name as "Jack Sand." The annotations to the magazine article had been made with a ballpoint pen—the kind of pen with which the printed postcard sent to the *Examiner* about "turning in" had been written. Finally, the penny dropped, and Officer Jones realized the purpose of his assignment: to track a suspect in the Dahlia murder. He immediately sent a report back to Chief Horrall stating, "This is the man."

Leslie Dillon's strange behavior and the material collected by Officer Jones in Miami convinced Dr. De River that he needed to at least meet with and talk to him. However, Dillon—who had initially

---

* "Shoots Out Girl's tooth": this clipping is discussed further on page 104.
† The unsigned writing samples are discussed later on page 237.

offered to help in the investigation and advise on the psychology of the Dahlia killer—now seemed to show a remarkable reluctance to head out to the West Coast to meet the doctor in person. So, the doctor reasoned, an alternative meeting location would need to be found. The mechanics of how such a meeting with Leslie Dillon could be arranged was the subject of the secret meeting between Chief Horrall, Assistant Chief Reed, Homicide Chief Francis Kearney, Dr. De River, and Gangster Squad Chief Willie Burns. Chief Horrall's brief for Burns was as demanding as it was unusual. As head of the Gangster Squad, he was to team up with Francis Kearney, head of the Homicide detail. The chiefs of the two details were to give all requisite support to Dr. De River in his efforts to secure a clandestine meeting with Leslie Dillon, wherever that would eventually take place. In practice, this meant chauffeuring De River and Dillon around, once the meeting place had been agreed. It also meant setting up telephone taps to record future conversations between the doctor and Dillon.

There was much that was highly unusual about Burns's "special assignment." It was, to begin with, the first and only time that a key aspect of a homicide investigation had been assigned to members of the Gangster Squad. More unusual still, while the secret assignment was known to the head of the Homicide detail, Captain Kearney, it was not revealed to the two homicide officers in charge of the Dahlia case: Lieutenant Harry "the Hat" Hansen and Sergeant Finis Brown. They were completely unaware of the secret operation. Finis, in particular, was kept out of the way. All through December 1948, the sergeant was assigned to the detail of guarding the Berlin picture exhibition* held in the county museum of Exposition Park.

What prompted the Homicide and Gangster details, in planning the Leslie Dillon mission, to go over the heads of the lead police

---

* Berlin picture exhibition: an exhibition of paintings, mainly from the Kaiser Friedrich Museum in Berlin, captured by the American Third Army during World War II and exhibited in the U.S. in 1948.

officers assigned to the Dahlia case? The official explanation was that to involve Harry "the Hat" Hansen and Finis Brown would have immediately alerted the press to the clandestine operation. And it was true that Jimmy Richardson's men were watching Finis's and Harry's every move. But Harry and Finis were not only kept out of the Leslie Dillon assignment. They were not even told about it. Why? The answer lay, possibly, in the allegations of incompetence that had dogged the Dahlia case from the beginning. But there might well have been another reason. The calling in of the Gangster detail at this juncture implied the possible involvement of organized crime and the presence of police corruption. And the fact that the assigned officers were not told about the mission hinted that the department's top brass did not fully trust them. Specifically, that they did not trust one officer in particular: Finis Brown, commonly known as "Fat Arse," the cop who was rumored to have links with organized vice through his connection with Mark Hansen and the Florentine Gardens.

While Finis Brown was admiring masterpieces of the Dutch and Flemish schools at Exposition Park, Willie Burns quietly assembled his team to accompany and support Dr. De River in his clandestine mission to connect with Leslie Dillon. Burns himself would deal with the bugging of conversations, with the help of Homicide's Captain Kearney. But Willie still needed an undercover cop to act as chauffeur for Dr. De River. Such a man would need to have the muscle to protect the doctor in an emergency. But he would also need to have a brain, to lie low and play the dumb chauffeur and not blow their cover. It took some time and thought before Willie came up with a name. Why had he not thought of it before? He had just the man.

BEHIND LOCKED DOORS

ergeant John J. O'Mara (or "JJ") had been assigned to the Seventy-seventh Street Station when Willie Burns picked him to join the Gangster Squad. A big, blue-eyed Irishman, O'Mara was one of the squad's musclemen. At his local Catholic church of St. Anselm, the priest had selected him especially to pass around the collection basket. The Irishman's ice-blue stare ensured that even the most reluctant members of the congregation coughed up their widow's mite. Like the other members of the Gangster Squad, O'Mara kept a tommy gun concealed in a violin case under the bed. When he was selected by Willie Burns to serve on the squad, he had already been causing ripples at the Seventy-seventh Street Station for busting a burglary ring that included the teenage son of a police commander. Some of his colleagues were of the view that he should have let the case "disappear." He hadn't. O'Mara's specialty was to escort local hoodlums up to a secluded spot in the Hollywood Hills. He would, as he put it, "have a little heart-to-heart talk with 'em, emphasize the fact that this wasn't New York, this wasn't Chicago, this wasn't Cleveland. And we leaned on 'em a little, you know what I mean? Up in the Hollywood Hills, off Coldwater Canyon, anywhere up there. And it's dark at night." In the darkness, O'Mara would put a gun to the hoodlum's ear and utter his dreaded catchphrase: "You want to sneeze?".

Willie Burns knew that JJ—cool, tough, and dependable—was just the man to chauffeur Dr. De River on his mission to connect with Leslie Dillon. On December 28, 1949, O'Mara therefore received his instructions from the chief of the Gangster Squad. He was to drive the doctor wherever he wanted to go, and protect him in all situations that might arise during the assignment.

Now that the operation had been set up, Dr. De River contacted Leslie Dillon and told him he would like to meet him to discuss the Dahlia case further. He would also like to see if Dillon's friend "Jeff," whom Dillon had hinted had committed the murder, might be persuaded to come to Los Angeles and receive psychiatric treatment. Dillon agreed to meet, but indicated that he did not want to come to Los Angeles. De River told him he was making a trip to New Orleans and then on to New York, and that he was going to be in Phoenix and Las Vegas. The doctor gave Dillon a number of options to meet. He hoped for Las Vegas, as it would likely be easier to get police cooperation to extradite Dillon from there if necessary. Dillon agreed to a meeting in Vegas. Police department funds were spent to buy Dillon a plane ticket. JJ O'Mara, Willie Burns, and the doctor checked into a Vegas hotel to await Dillon's arrival. A couple of days later, unknown to Dillon, Captain Kearney of Homicide joined Burns in Las Vegas. When Dillon arrived in the hotel lobby, he seemed excessively nervous. He had changed his hair color from the peroxide blond he sported in Florida to red-brown.*

It proved impossible to obtain suitable rooms for the party in Vegas. O'Mara was therefore instructed to drive the doctor and his suspect to a health resort and hotel in Banning, near Palm Springs. On the cold December desert trip from Vegas to Palm Springs,

---

* Clemence Horrall, in a letter to the FBI dated January 10, 1949, was to state that Dillon's hair was "red-brown, which appears to be dyed." Dillon's hair had been previously dyed blond.

O'Mara drove while the doctor conversed with Dillon in the backseat of the rusty old Ford jalopy. JJ was too busy focusing on the road to pay much attention, but he recalled later that there was a conversation about embalming and the proper way to bleed a corpse. Dillon told De River that he had once worked for three weeks in a mortuary, Hahn's Funeral Home in Oklahoma City. He and the doctor discussed the procedure of making a cut in the leg of a corpse in order to bleed it, and the method of inserting a tube to drain the blood. Dillon also talked endlessly about "women, women, women." He spoke in a "very soft, well-modulated voice."

The wind was keen as a knife and snow glinted on the peaks of the San Jacinto Mountains when the old Ford arrived at Palm Springs. Briargate Lodge was a long, low, rambling white 1930s building buried in the forest north of Banning. The lodge was perched on the edge of the San Gorgonio Pass, one of the many rifts in the California desert created by the shifting of the great tectonic plates of the San Andreas Fault. It had been built originally as a sanatorium, but by the end of the war had become a hotel. The main building featured along its length a shady porticoed veranda, where creaking basket-weave easy chairs hailed back to its early days as a place of rest, recuperation, and quiet death. Around the principal building clustered individual guest cottages. Dillon, O'Mara, and the doctor were housed in one cottage. Captain Kearney and Willie Burns arrived a day later and were housed in another. They installed the bugging equipment to record the conversations between the doctor and Dillon. Dillon was not supposed to know that Burns and Kearney were anything other than hotel guests.

O'Mara had a room adjoining Dr. De River's, and Leslie Dillon was placed in a room on the other side of the doctor. Later, JJ recalled that Dillon spent a great deal of time prowling around the lodge buildings at nightfall and in the early morning, before everybody else was up. Dillon called O'Mara "JJ," as did the doctor, but a couple of times he called him "Jeff." Much of the talk that O'Mara remembered centered on Dillon's friend "Jeff," who turned out to be an individual called Jeff Connors, and how he was a likely suspect for the Dahlia murder. During the long conversations between the doctor and Dillon in the doctor's room, O'Mara would listen in through the wall from his adjoining room. He remembered that Dillon and the doctor discussed Jeff's portrait of Dillon. Dillon made a sketch of Jeff, in profile.

Leslie Dillon and the doctor also discussed in detail how Jeff had accomplished the Dahlia murder. According to the doctor, Dillon proffered an explanation as to why the Dahlia's body was cut in half. The killer, Dillon said, would have wanted to see how far his penis went into the body of the woman. The doctor asked Dillon about how the body would be cut.

"Well," said Dillon, "if Jeff cut the body one way he would cut it up high, if, for another purpose, he wanted, he would cut it low."

"Well, why would he want to cut the body low?"

"Well, Jeff is a funny fellow. He would like to see the effect of his sexual organs, the far end of an act after the body had been cut."

Dr. De River asked Dillon where the cutting of the body was effected. Dillon said maybe a bed, the floor, or a bath. The doctor asked him how Jeff had drained the blood from the body.

"Oh, he probably hung that up on something in a shower, or something like that."

"Where would Jeff have committed this crime?"

"Oh, in a hotel."

"Well, I don't know of any hotel where he could get the body out without having to lug it downstairs."

"Oh, there are ground-floor hotels."

"You mean motels?"

"Yes," replied Dillon, "motels, something like that."

The conversation went back and forth until eventually De River said, "Do you mind taking off your shirt, Mr. Dillon?"

"No." Dillon stripped off his shirt and showed a very powerful build.

The doctor was surprised. "You are not the type I thought you were at all—or maybe you are." Then, after a pause, "We are just among men here. Have you any objection to dropping your trousers?"

Dillon hesitated. Then he dropped his trousers. According to the doctor, this revealed that he had a "juvenile penis," about "typical of an eight-year-old boy." For the doctor, this was the "first explanation" for the vertical incision that had been made in the Dahlia's body above the pubic region to the navel. For, from the "psychological point of view," it intimated to him that while "Jeff"—the man with the string of female conquests—could be a rapist, it was the "under-developed chap, however powerful he may be"—and Dillon had revealed himself, when stripped, to be a powerful man—who was typical of the "sadist type, the frustrated fellow." The juvenile penis also potentially explained the hypothetical motive for the murder that Dillon had proffered previously, in his written correspondence with the doctor: that Elizabeth's killer, after an affair "not considered proper by the average person," had been "mocked or threatened exposure by her to his friends." He had therefore, out of revenge, inflicted "pain of some nature on her," to the point of experiencing "a new sensation by accident. . . . Thus leading to the complete annihilation of her and other victims."

Could Elizabeth have "mocked" Dillon, or "threatened exposure" of him to his "friends," thus enraging him and provoking the "complete annihilation of her"? Most chilling, if this were the case, who were the "other victims"? In this context, one of the newspaper clippings that had been discovered by Officer Jones of the Gangster Squad at Leslie Dillon's lodgings in Florida was revealing. It was headlined "Shoots Out Girl's Tooth."[*] It related how John B. Elias, age eighteen, had shot out a tooth of Amalia Chipley, age fifteen, with a spring BB pistol, as she ate her lunch in the schoolyard of Everett Junior High School in San Francisco. Elias shot Chipley because the group of girl students had, apparently, been "insulting" him.

One circumstance above all convinced the doctor that Leslie

---

[*] For the discovery of the news clipping by Officer Jones in Florida, see page 97.

Dillon was either guilty of the Dahlia murder or at the very least heavily implicated in it. From the very beginning of the investigation, two key facts relating to the mutilations that had been inflicted on Elizabeth Short's body had been deliberately withheld by the police from public disclosure. Only a handful of officers, and the doctor himself, were aware of them. They were facts that only the killer would know. The facts were these: What did the killer do with the pubic hair and the rose tattoo that he cut from the victim's body? According to Dr. De River, Leslie Dillon knew the answers to these two questions. The pubic hair had been inserted into the rectum. The rose tattoo had been inserted in the vagina. In addition, according to both the doctor and the LAPD, Dillon knew further details about the crime that even the police did not know. Those details were to come to light much, much later.

Throughout the stay at Banning, Dillon was deeply suspicious of O'Mara. "He was pretty sharp," JJ recalled. "He was a pretty wise man, and hard to fool around. You had to change the subject around. At one point he asked me, if I ever thought of taking a police examination. I told him I did, but I was too short. He looked me over pretty carefully." Dillon talked about his interest in law enforcement, including a past application for the post of deputy sheriff in Los Angeles. While he became quite cocksure when the doctor, his "friend," was around, he always seemed to become very nervous when De River went away. On several occasions, he returned to his room as if to check whether somebody was going through his belongings.

JJ also recalled a particular conversation between Dillon and the doctor that took place in the doctor's room on New Year's Eve of 1948. O'Mara was watching and listening through a crack in the door. The pair had been discussing a sketch of the Madonna, whom Dillon likened to Elizabeth Short. Dillon liked the hair of the figure in the sketch, and also mentioned that he liked girls with "big mouths." At this point, Dillon was looking at the doctor intently. He had such an expression of "rage and hate" contorting his face that JJ immediately went on alert as to the doctor's safety. According to O'Mara, Dillon was "an individual that I have never seen the likes of before, and will probably never see again. His facial expression would change, and his temperaments would change, very quickly." He was not a stupid person. In fact, he was "super cunning. . . . He would shoot a few statements and watch your reactions," recalled O'Mara. "He was very, very clever, in my opinion. You had to more or less spar with him, box with him."

One night when there was a shortage of rooms, the question came up whether Dillon might share a room with O'Mara. Dillon said, "I'll sleep with JJ." "He got quite a laugh out of that," JJ remembered. "I wouldn't sleep with that fellow, not even in the same room, unless I was wide awake. He's not stupid, in any sense of the word." For JJ, there was "something about the man that raises a man's animal instincts, makes the hair on the back of your neck bristle up."

While he did not drink much, Dillon did do drugs. He told O'Mara he would take bennies, or benzedrine,* "for pep," and "cut the paper and drink whiskey with the fellows." He referred to them getting a "great kick and bang out of it." He also told JJ about how he would get phenobarbital,† grind it up into powder, "put it on ice-cream or food," and give it to women, as "it knocks them out." Dillon told JJ about a large quantity of phenobarbital that he had obtained from some nurses staying at a hotel in which he had been working.

After four or five days in Palm Springs, O'Mara was ordered to drive Leslie Dillon and the doctor west to Los Angeles, in a bid to track down Dillon's friend Jeff Connors. After the party checked out of Briargate Lodge, the police searched Dillon's room. They found a pair of women's loafer-style black suede shoes, with platform heels. The hotel manager swore that they had not been in the room before the party arrived. The shoes—nine and a half inches in length—

---

* Bennies/benzedrine: an amphetamine-based drug originally marketed in the form of inhalers by Smith, Kline & French and quickly adopted for recreational use in the mid-twentieth century.
† Phenobarbital: a drug used for the treatment of epilepsy and seizures with the side effects of inducing sedation and hypnosis.

were much bigger than the petite size 6 worn by Elizabeth Short. Although women's shoes, they were equivalent to a man's shoe size of the time.*

Leslie Dillon appeared to be very reluctant to travel to Los Angeles. JJ noticed that, as they approached the outskirts of the city, he began "fidgeting and watching the street markers." They stopped at the La Bonita Motel on Garvey Avenue in El Monte. It was a red-roofed, dirty white Spanish-Colonial-style bungalow building, flanked by amputated date palms and twisted jacaranda trees petrified in the cold. Once again, Willie Burns and Captain Kearney, this time with the help of Gangster Squad Officer Con Keller, bugged the rooms. O'Mara and the doctor, meanwhile, had another task. They had a little surprise for Leslie Dillon.

---

* One of the shoes Elizabeth had worn—open-toed and high-heeled—had in any event been found dumped in a trash can on Crenshaw Boulevard and identified by Robert "Red" Manley in January 1947. (See page 62.) The possibility of the Dahlia killer having some form of transvestite fetishism was hinted at by the fact that, according to Aggie Underwood's early reports in the *Herald-Express*, the big toenail on each of Elizabeth's feet had been painted red. (See page 11.)

DEADLINE
AT DAWN

T he brakes of the old Ford creaked in the cold. Along the sidewalks, frost choked the gum trees and cypresses, while the
palm trees trembled in a sky that glinted like the tommy gun
under the car's front seat. Los Angeles winters were never like this.
Except in January 1949.

The Ford headed down from El Monte to Long Beach, where
Leslie Dillon had told the doctor he had stayed at a trailer park on
the Pacific Coast Highway, back in 1946. Called the A1 Trailer Park,
it was a scattering of white trailers parked along dirt paths lined with
young palms. Telegraph poles and slack clotheslines crisscrossed the
chicken-wire fencing that separated the lots. When the Ford parked
at the entrance to the trailer park, Dillon opened the door and rushed
into the small office beneath the park's signboard. JJ and the doctor
waited for a moment, but Dillon failed to reappear. So they got out of
the car and went to the office, where they found Dillon engrossed in
conversation with the man at the front desk.

"I noticed him pointing down to the ledger," JJ later recalled. "It
turned out to be a book, a record of people in attendance at this
trailer court." Dillon, JJ saw, was busy erasing entries in the ledger.
He was nodding his head toward JJ and the doctor as he talked to
the man at the front desk. "It was a hurried-up deal," O'Mara said.

"He more or less rushed in there, wanted to get something changed, before we made our way in there."

The owner of the trailer park was an elderly man called Jiggs Moore. The doctor asked him what he was doing. "Well, I made a little change here, correction in the book for Mr. Dillon here about the time he was in this place, the days he was in here, and the date of his departure."

The doctor made a mental note to get police officers back to the trailer park to question Jiggs Moore further. For now, they made their way back to the car. Dillon stopped by the camp's pay phone and jotted down the number.

The Ford sped away from the park and up toward Hollywood, headed for the doctor's office on Hollywood and Vine. Dillon volunteered to O'Mara that the best way to get there would be via La Brea. JJ ignored Dillon's suggestion and headed up Western Avenue, turned on Manchester, and proceeded up Crenshaw Boulevard toward Leimert Park. Dillon protested that this route was "erroneous" and "way out of the way." When they got to Thirty-ninth Street, JJ tried to turn up an alleyway. "You can't get that way," Dillon told him. They tried another alleyway. "That alley won't get you through," said Dillon. So they proceeded to Coliseum and Norton. "At the time," said O'Mara, "it struck me as awful funny that he knew what alleyway didn't go through." It was clear that Dillon was thoroughly familiar with the area.

They went to Norton and pulled over and parked. Dillon became very agitated.

"Do you recall now," the doctor said, "this was where the body was found?"

"What body do you mean? You mean the woman who was stomped and kicked?"*

"You know what body I mean."

---

* Apparently a reference to the murder of Jeanne French, or the "Red Lipstick Murder," which occurred in Los Angeles in February 1947. (See page 66 and footnote.)

To O'Mara's surprise, Dillon made no reply. He did not—as JJ would have expected—exclaim indignantly, "Are you accusing me of this murder?" or words to that effect. He seemed to be feeling ill. He became "woozy," and "began to weave." The doctor asked him what woman he meant.

"Oh some woman. English. English. English."

"Are you sure of that?"

"Well, what is the difference? English. French."*

They drove back to the motel in El Monte. Dillon wanted to stop en route and get a drink. They stopped at a service station and he got a Coke from the Coke machine, but did not touch it. As the doctor questioned him on the way back, Dillon crouched in the corner of the backseat, sticking his hand out through the wind wing, crowding close to the door, as if he were about to try to clamber out of the automobile.

Back at the motel in El Monte, JJ and the doctor were exhausted by the stress and fatigue of the day. Dillon, however, now seemed "full of vitality" and kept "bouncing back" after all the questions. "I had the impression he was taking narcotics, or something," recalled O'Mara.

On January 3, the doctor and Dillon drove with O'Mara from Los Angeles to San Francisco, continuing the search for Dillon's friend Jeff Connors. The doctor, by now, was convinced that "Jeff" was a projection of Dillon's imagination, a psychic doppelgänger or "double," upon which Dillon had displaced the responsibility for a murder that he had in fact himself committed.†

While JJ and the doctor slept from exhaustion in their hotel beds in San Francisco, Dillon was up and buzzing, flitting between the hotel bellboys, with whom he exchanged whispered confidences.

---

* Again, this appears to be a reference to the Jeanne French murder, with a feigned confusion between the names "English" and "French."

† There was some justification for this belief to the extent that Dillon did frequently use his friends' names as aliases, and had in fact used the alias of "Jeff Connors." (See page 117.) Note also O'Mara's recollection that Dillon sometimes addressed him as "Jeff."

When JJ and De River awoke, they tailed Dillon, who led the detective and the doctor on a merry dance down the frozen streets of San Francisco, from hotel lobby to hotel lobby. Dillon seemed to know every Brylcreemed front-desk clerk, every brass-buttoned and pillbox-hatted bellboy in town. But they never found Jeff Connors. Finally, they returned to Los Angeles.

Back in Los Angeles, the party checked into the downtown Strand Hotel on South Union Avenue, a red-brick building slashed by jagged iron fire escapes. They booked into a suite under the name "O'Shea." Here, Dillon finally began to tire of the cat-and-mouse game with the doctor. On January 10, he sailed a postcard out of the hotel window. It read, on one side, "If found, please mail," and on the other:

I am being held in Room 219–21, Strand Hotel, phone FE 3101 in connection with the Black Dahlia murder by Dr. J Paul De River as far as I can tell. I would like legal counsel.
[signed] Mr. Leslie Dillon.

The postcard was addressed to the Los Angeles attorney Jerry Giesler, at his downtown office in the ornate Chester Williams building at 215 West Fifth Street on Broadway. Giesler was lawyer to the stars and the highest paid attorney of the age. His celebrity clients included the actor Errol Flynn, whom he had represented on charges of statutory rape; Robert Mitchum, whom he defended for marijuana possession; gangsters Bugsy Siegel and Mickey Cohen; and, in later years, the actresses Lana Turner and Marilyn Monroe. Also on the postcard was written the name of Dillon's wife, Georgia Stevenson, c/o the Golf Park Hotel or Wolfie's Restaurant, Miami Beach, Florida; and a telephone number for Dillon's wife's aunt in Los Angeles.

It was snowing in Los Angeles for the first time in seventeen years when Leslie Dillon's postcard was found trodden in the leaf- and mud-choked gutter at the intersection of Seventh and Union. By an incredible coincidence—perhaps too incredible—the postcard was "discovered" by one of Aggie's men, the *Herald-Express* reporter William Chance. Aggie, from her close friendship with De River, knew what was going on at the Strand Hotel. And, of course, one of her men just happened to be on the spot when the great news event occurred.

When the *Herald-Express* telephoned Willie Burns and revealed that a postcard written by one Leslie Dillon had been found floating in a gutter downtown, the cat was finally out of the bag. Burns had little choice but to order the arrest of the LAPD's new prime suspect. Dillon was taken into custody in the downtown drugstore that nestled in the shadow of the Angel's Flight Railway at Third and Hill. At 2:45 p.m., he was booked at the Highland Park Police Station. This was the moment when Harry Hansen and Finis Brown were first told about what had been going on.

Harry "the Hat" was having a day off when Captain Kearney called him at home on the afternoon of Monday, January 10.

"How soon can you get downtown?"

"Why, what's up?"

"Well, something pretty hot, how soon can you get down?"

"Well, just as soon as I can get cleaned up, change clothes and drive down."

"Come on then."

Harry hightailed it downtown to Highland Park. The captain told him that there was a man in custody by the name of Leslie Dillon, and that he was a pretty good suspect in the case. Finis Brown was called, too. Now he also found out for the first time what his fellow officers had been up to, while he had been inspecting the masterpieces at Exposition Park. Dillon was taken to Chief Horrall's office for questioning, then on to the police academy for further interrogation into the night. In the meantime, his suitcases were searched. In them were found some seven hundred phenobarbital pills; seven safety razor blades; and a dog leash with a heavy, massive strap. The lock end of the dog leash was new and unscratched, but the last third of it showed evidence of being very thoroughly scrubbed and scraped. The strap appeared to have been run through the noose, and a heavy weight suspended from it so that there was an angle to the end of the noose. The leash was sent to the LAPD crime lab for testing.

As the arteries of the city clogged and ground to a halt in snow-drifts, a bevy of reporters sped to the offices of Chief Horrall at City Hall for a press conference. Horrall's announcement was a sensation. The LAPD had, the chief said, apprehended the "best suspect yet" in the Dahlia investigation. The man was Leslie Dillon, alias Jack Sand, twenty-seven, a former hotel clerk and bellhop with an admitted interest in sadism and psychopathy. Dillon, Horrall said, had voluntarily told the LAPD police psychiatrist Dr. Paul De River about "secret details" relating to the crime. The police had kept back a series of "key questions" that only the killer could answer. "Dillon had all the answers," said the chief. "More, he knew things even we didn't know about the murder." Under interrogation at a downtown hotel, Horrall went on, Dillon "without prompting revealed details of the crime which police have never been able to explain. These details include significant explanations of the mutilation of Miss Short's body, and her movements before she died." Horrall added that "Dillon's presence in Los Angeles at the time of the slaying has been definitely established."*

This was a pip indeed. The chief's revelations were a bombshell in a case that had become mired in a tide of fantastical Sapphic conspiracies and other confabulations. The newspapermen rushed to track down all the information they could find on the "hottest suspect yet." Jimmy Richardson's men reported that, when Dillon was not living sporadically in Los Angeles in the late forties, he had worked as a pimp and bellhop in San Francisco. There he had lived on Sacramento Street with his wife, Georgia, and his baby girl. Dillon had met Georgia in Oklahoma, his own home state, and married her there. He had, it was reported, worked as a mortician's assistant

---

* It is important to note that at the January 10 press conference the LAPD asserted categorically that it had been established that Dillon was definitely in Los Angeles on January 15, 1947, the date of the murder. This assertion was subsequently reneged by the police department.

in Oklahoma, and had personal knowledge of embalming methods. When in Los Angeles in the summer of '46, Dillon had lived in a trailer at the A1 Trailer Park on the Pacific Coast Highway. Later, he stayed with his wife's aunt, Nellie Mae Hinshaw, on South Crenshaw Boulevard, where he parked his trailer in the forecourt. Mrs. Hinshaw told Jimmy's men that she could not remember whether he was staying with her at the time of the murder. "But the police," the *Examiner* went on to state, "can prove Dillon was here." In Los Angeles, the newspaper reported, Dillon and his wife had also stayed with his mother-in-law, Mrs. Laura Stevenson, on South Normandie. The *Examiner* quoted Mrs. Stevenson as saying, "They came down from San Francisco just a few days after Christmas 1946 and moved in with me at my place on South Normandie Avenue. They stayed for two months, later moving to Oklahoma and then Florida."

It transpired that Leslie Dillon had three regular addresses in or around Los Angeles, even when he was officially based in San Francisco: the A1 Trailer Park near Long Beach; his mother-in-law's house on South Normandie; and the house belonging to his wife's aunt on Crenshaw Boulevard. The Crenshaw Boulevard address was less than four miles—or eleven minutes' drive—from Leimert Park. An astonishing coincidence that was overlooked by all was the fact that the aunt's house was also only two blocks away from the café on Crenshaw where Elizabeth Short's purse and shoes had been discovered dumped in a trash can by the café manager Robert Hyman, back in January 1947.*

Leslie Dillon's mother-in-law, Laura Stevenson, told the newspapers that Dillon and her daughter had separated more than a year ago. Wife and child were living in Miami. When confronted with the news of her husband's arrest, Dillon's estranged wife Georgia was reported by the *Los Angeles Examiner* as being "half hysterical" yet "strangely reticent." "I have no comment to make—now," she repeated, over and over. "She accented the *now*," reported the

---

* For the discovery of the purse and shoes, see page 62.

newspaper, "as if to hint that when she felt the time ripe, she might have plenty to tell."* The landlady of the Normandie Avenue address where Dillon's mother-in-law lived was quoted by the *Examiner* as saying that Dillon had owned a black Ford coupe during the two months he had resided there, from January to February 1947. In the summer of 1947, after the murder, he had headed out to Oklahoma City, where he was arrested for bootlegging. The *Examiner*'s report continued:

> Six feet tall, slender, dressed in what would be called "natty" clothes—a camel's hair top coat, neat small-checked slacks and sports shirt, the man smiled at cameramen whilst he posed. For the few minutes of picture taking the police unlocked the manacles that bound his wrists. Then they clicked them shut again, and under a five man guard, took him away and wouldn't tell where.
>
> "We're going to let nobody talk to him—except ourselves—until we've got a closed case," a police spokesman said.
>
> So "hot" a suspect did the police consider Dillon that he was under guard by five men.

Dr. De River was quoted in the press as saying that Dillon knew "more about the Dahlia murder than the police did, and more about abnormal sex psycopathia than most psychiatrists do." The doctor added: "From what he told me, I gathered that in the past two years Dillon has lost 40 pounds. These are the two years since the Dahlia was murdered. Dillon also told me that because of a 'certain event' in his life two years ago, he had been trying to achieve a complete change of personality. But he wouldn't say what the certain event

---

* Georgia Dillon's official statement to the police, including, crucially, any evidence she may have given as to Leslie Dillon's whereabouts on the night of January 14/15, 1947, has never been released.

was." While Dillon denied that he ever knew Elizabeth Short, Deputy Police Chief William Bradley told the newspapers, "We have two witnesses who say Dillon knew the Dahlia, went out with her."* The shadowy world of hotel bellhops, pimping, and bootlegging in which Leslie Dillon operated was the same territory covered by the underworld operations of girls and gambling run by associates of Elizabeth Short such as Mark Hansen and his pals Jimmy Utley and NTG. Was there a nexus between them? If so, where?

Dillon was questioned at the police academy into the early hours of the morning on Tuesday, January 11, and then into the night again. Drafted in to help with the interrogation were veteran Deputy District Attorney John Barnes, along with Deputies Fred Henderson and Adolph Alexander. John Barnes was quoted in the press on Tuesday as fully supporting the LAPD. "From what the police have learned," he told the *Examiner*, "I am convinced that Dillon must be held and guarded carefully whilst the whole story he tells is checked out to the ultimate." In the meantime, Dillon's mother, Mamie, had, through an attorney, obtained a writ of habeas corpus on Dillon that was returnable at 1:30 p.m. on Wednesday, the next day. In effect, the police had to charge Dillon by the time the writ expired or release him. In the meantime, Dillon's fingerprints were sent off to the FBI to be compared with the five latent prints collected from the various items of anonymous correspondence sent to the police. The FBI failed to produce a match, but that wasn't a surprise. The only print to come from the package purportedly sent by the killer was from the outside of the envelope, and blurred; the other four came from a later letter that, as the FBI had noted, gave no indication of knowledge of or a connection with the killer.†

De River's case up to now had been that "only the killer himself, or a man directly connected with the crime, could know the things

---

* The identities of these "two witnesses" were never revealed. The evidence of the various people who connected Leslie Dillon with Elizabeth Short is discussed further on pages 131–135.

† For a discussion of the five latent fingerprints relating to the case that were sent to the FBI, see page 52.

that Dillon knew." Leslie Dillon's response was to refer back to his "friend" Jeff. It was Jeff, he repeated, who had given him the "secret details" of the Dahlia killing. "A friend of mine, named Jeff Connors, is the man I suspect of having killed Beth Short. He told me the inside facts of the murder which I told you." The doctor's settled belief that "Jeff" was an alter ego who existed only in Dillon's imagination received support when a photograph of Leslie Dillon was shown to the manager of a San Francisco hotel at which Dillon had worked. The manager identified the photograph of Dillon as "Jeff Connors." This implied that Dillon had, in fact, used the name "Jeff Connors" as an alias.* "The existence of Jeff Connors is seriously doubted by the investigators," reported the *Examiner*. "The belief is that he is a mythical alter ego of the blonde, blue-eyed man in custody."

By the morning of Wednesday, January 12, only a few hours remained before the writ of habeas corpus expired and Leslie Dillon would have to be charged or released. And yet there was still no sound from the LAPD. The minutes crawled past on the great clock at Los Angeles' Union Station. In the monolithic *Examiner* headquarters on Eleventh and Broadway, the cast-iron printing presses were ready to roll into action. The lead plates were cast, the giant paper rolls mounted, the ink tanks filled. Jimmy Richardson reached for his white pills. Aggie Underwood had her rewrite men on standby at their telephones. Everybody waited for the call from City Hall. The call that would pull the trigger on the biggest news story of the decade. Hypothetical headlines ricocheted off the office walls of every city editor's office in town: "Dahlia Killer Apprehended— Sadistic Sex Fiend Reveals Hidden Details of Butcher Murder."

Finally, at 11:30 a.m.—just two hours before the deadline for expiration of the writ of habeas corpus—the call came through from the reporters at City Hall. When it did, nobody could believe it. There must, Aggie thought, have been some mistake.

---

* Leslie Dillon did in fact use the names of other friends and acquaintances among the many aliases by which he passed (page 96).

BREAKING POINT

L eslie Dillon was to be released.

The official explanation for the stunning about-turn was simple: Jeff Connors had been located. He was not a psychological projection of Dillon's subconscious, as Dr. De River had thought. He was a real human being of flesh and bone, residing in the old gold rush town of Gilroy, nestled in the foothills of the Sierra Nevada. Jeff's alias, it transpired, was Arthur (or "Artie") Lane. He was a forty-something cafeteria busboy, cosmetics peddler, pulp magazine writer, and failed actor turned utilities man for the movies.

On the night of Thursday, January 13, Jeff Connors was booked and held for questioning. In the meantime, Leslie Dillon walked out of the old red-brick building of the Highland Park Jail a free man. It was left to Deputy Chief William Bradley to explain to the press the LAPD's extraordinary volte-face.

"We have insufficient evidence to warrant holding Leslie Dillon. Until this morning, we thought his story was phony and that the 'Jeff Connors' he told us about was a figment of his imagination. But then Jeff Connors was arrested in Gilroy—and now what can we do but believe Dillon."* Bradley paused, then added: "And I guess that now, we'll have to sugar Dillon up a bit."

While Chief Horrall had previously stated that the LAPD had incontrovertible evidence of Dillon's presence in Los Angeles at the time of Short's murder, the story now changed. Dillon, the deputy chief said, had been in San Francisco at the time of the murder. Nothing was now said about the "secret facts" relating to the crime, which Horrall had previously stated Dillon knew.

Aggie, Jimmy, and just about everybody else in the press corps were stunned. Only two days after the Los Angeles Police Department had declared "the best ever suspect" in the Dahlia case, the police were sheepishly releasing the twenty-seven-year-old bellhop from jail. Not only that, they were apologizing to him. Now it was Detectives Harry "the Hat" Hansen and Finis "Fat Arse" Brown who played the bellhops, carrying Dillon's suitcases to a waiting automobile. It was Dr. De River who played the chauffeur, driving Dillon back to his wife's aunt's house on Crenshaw Boulevard.

But Leslie Duane Dillon was showing no sign of willingness to be "sugared up."

"I have been in custody for a week. I was handcuffed as early as January 3—a week before my arrest was announced. I have been guarded in hotel rooms by detectives ever since," Dillon told the newspapermen. "I'm going to have to talk to my attorney before I decide whether or not I'm going to sue anybody for what's been done to me."

Dillon told the *Los Angeles Examiner* a "strange story of unorthodox police behavior," including being held for several days in secret police custody. He said he could hardly believe that, as a result of a "helpful letter" to the LAPD police psychiatrist, "these things hap-

---

* It is unclear how the mere fact of Jeff Connors's separate existence was sufficient to demolish the case against Leslie Dillon, particularly given the evidence that Dillon had in fact gone by Connors's name in the past.

pened to me." He had been whisked by airplane across the United States. He had been promised a job as the doctor's secretary. He had been flattered as "the most intelligent man" the doctor "had met in a long time," and as someone who knew "more about sex psychopathia than most psychiatrists." And then he was suddenly handcuffed, kept in custody for over a week, and flatly told that he had killed the Black Dahlia, Elizabeth Short.*

"They had me just about convinced," claimed Dillon, "that I was crazy or something. That maybe I DID kill the Dahlia—and then just forgot about it." He had never, Dillon said, intimated that he knew who the Black Dahlia killer was, or implicated his friend Jeff Connors as the murderer.† "They slapped handcuffs on me. Dr. De River wanted to know whether I'd have truth serum or a lie detector, which? I said either, but first for God's sake let me call my wife and a lawyer. They wouldn't." (Dillon, in fact, initially agreed to take lie detector and scopolamine tests, but subsequently refused both.)

Dillon told the press that he had been stripped nude and photographed.‡

"They handcuffed me to a radiator. Then they questioned me. They really turned on the heat. They said they had traced me two years, could blast all my stories. I was only telling them the truth. Dr. De River sent the detectives outside, then worked on me alone. He

---

* While the questioning of Leslie Dillon was certainly "unorthodox," it should be remembered that, prior to the Supreme Court decision in *Miranda v Arizona* in 1966, there was no codified procedure in the United States for detaining suspects or informing them of their rights. As recorded by the criminologist and news reporter Ernest Jerome Hopkins in his 1931 book *Our Lawless Police*, much routine police procedure of the time was unconstitutional and would today be considered illegal. Harry "the Hat" had himself boasted to the *Daily News* photographer Harry Watson about his favored technique of dangling suspects from a bridge over concrete to extract a confession (see page 77).

† This was contradicted by Leslie Dillon's initial letter to De River as "Jack Sand" (see page 89), where he wrote that his friend Jeff had a motive for the crime and hinted that there were other things which led to his suspicions. The "motive" that Dillon later proffered was rage at the girl "mocking" the killer. (See page 104.) See also Dillon's interview with the *Examiner* on January 12: "A friend of mine, named Jeff Connors, is the man I suspect of having killed Beth Short. He told me the inside facts of the murder which I told you."

‡ De River's version of this was that he had suggested Dillon drop his pants, as they were "among men." (See page 104.)

said, 'What you tell me is in confidence. We'll treat you like a sick boy, not a criminal.' He wanted me to confess I killed the Dahlia. I couldn't." In Los Angeles, Dillon continued, three two-man detective teams had joined them. They had held him incommunicado at the hotel on Seventh and Olive. In desperation, he had managed to scribble the postcard to Jerry Giesler and drop it into the street. It was found. Inquiries were made. And then, for the first time since Dillon had been transported cross-country and elsewhere under police guard, the police had announced he was being held. They had booked him on suspicion of murder, and called him "the best suspect they ever had." They had continued their incommunicado tactics. Newsmen were not allowed to question him. No lawyer could get to him. Then, when Jeff Connors was finally discovered to be a real person—blowing the doctor's doppelgänger theory out of the water—they had dropped the case and run for cover.

Dillon went on to state that he had retained the Los Angeles attorney Morris Lavine to examine all aspects concerning his arrest. A former newspaperman, Lavine had won notoriety defending local gangsters such as Mickey Cohen and the Mafioso Johnny Roselli. In 1930 he had been jailed for hatching a scheme to extort $75,000 from a trio of organized crime figures in exchange for keeping their names out of a newspaper story. Ten months later, he was out of the can after fighting his own appeal. A question that was obvious but which nobody asked was how Leslie Dillon—an unemployed bellhop—was able to engage the services of such an expensive attorney as Morris Lavine.*

While Leslie Dillon regaled the press with his histrionic account of his alleged mistreatment at the hands of the Gangster Squad and the doctor, his former "friend" Jeff Connors—a.k.a. Arthur or "Artie" Lane†—was being questioned at City Hall by Deputy Chief Bill

---

* In 1956, Morris Lavine would take over the local Criminal Bar Association, replacing the previous, equally notorious incumbent, Jerry Giesler.
† According to Sergeant Finis Brown, Jeff Connors's real name was Artie Loy.

Bradley and Captain Kearney of Homicide. Harry "the Hat" Hansen and Finis Brown were also there. Connors admitted that he had known Leslie Dillon casually in San Francisco. But he denied that he ever discussed the Dahlia case with him. At first Connors told the press that he knew Elizabeth Short by sight. He had been with her and his wife in a bar the night before the murder. He had, he said, reported the matter to the Hollywood police division the day the body was discovered. No action had been taken by the LAPD. Connors told the press that he had cleared out of Los Angeles after the murder, because a lot of his friends were being questioned about the killing and he wanted to get away.*

Later, however, Jeff's story changed. Now he claimed he never knew the Dahlia. Jeff's ex-wife, a platinum blonde sometime model going by the name of Grace Allen, posed for the newspapers with a winning smile. "Jeff was a screwball," Grace said. "Always imagining things. He never acted in pictures as far as I know, but he told people he did. He was on a studio labor gang, I think." She said she had not seen her ex-husband for a year and a half. They had gotten a divorce in Tijuana. Jeff, Grace said, was given to "Walter Mitty–style" dreaming. "So far as I know, he never knew the Black Dahlia. I think when he said he saw her in a bar he was just dreaming up the whole thing."

Allen told the newspapermen that, to the best of her recollection, Jeff Connors was with her the night before the Dahlia's body was discovered. He was working as a laborer at Columbia Studios from 2:00 to 11:00 p.m.

Grace Allen's statements appeared to give Jeff a watertight alibi. But the pretty blonde omitted certain details. She did not reveal that she was friendly with Mark Hansen, or that she had stayed in his home on Carlos Avenue when she separated from Jeff. Nor that, on that occasion, some helpful police officers had collected her belong-

---

* This correlates with what Leslie Dillon claimed Connors told him in his correspondence with De River. (See page 90.)

ings from the couple's home on Camerford Avenue. Nor did Grace mention the fact that, after Leslie Dillon was released from custody, he had called on her at her home. He had tried to threaten her into not speaking to the press or police. She had not let him in.

Jeff Connors's original admission that he knew Elizabeth Short, his assertion that he and his wife had been with her in a bar the night before the murder, his connection to Leslie Dillon, and his wife's connection to Mark Hansen, tightened the nexus of associations linking the Dahlia, Leslie Dillon, and the shady Danish nightclub owner. Way back in 1947, in the immediate aftermath of the murder, Officer Myrl McBride had reported that, the night before Elizabeth's body was found in the vacant lot, a girl had come up to her on Main Street and begged desperately for help.* Her boyfriend, an ex-Marine, had been threatening to kill her. Later, the same girl had exited a bar with two men and a woman. Dillon was an ex-Marine. Connors, Dillon's friend, had claimed he and his wife were in a bar with the Dahlia the night before the murder. Dillon had threatened Connors's wife and told her to keep silent. Connors had told the press that he ran away from Los Angeles after the killing, to escape police questioning.†

In the tangled web of accusation and counter-accusation, confusion and confabulation, it was difficult to see how a clear picture of the relationship between Jack, Jeff, Grace Allen, and Mark Hansen could be obtained without a confrontation between Dillon and Connors. Such a confrontation was proposed. It never took place. On January 14, 1949—the two-year anniversary of the Dahlia's murder—Jeff Connors walked out into the winter sunlight and across the vaulted courtyard of City Hall, disappearing forever into the crowds milling on Spring Street.

---

* For Officer McBride's account, see page 74.

† Compare also the account of the Frenches and their neighbors, that two men and a woman had visited Elizabeth at their home in San Diego one night in December 1946, and frightened her (page 35).

———

Now came the first signs that Dr. De River's star was in a steep decline.

INVESTIGATE BLACK DAHLIA FIASCO

So ran the headline in the Los Angeles *Daily News* of January 20. The article, written by a journalist named Sara Boynoff, contained an interview with Dr. De River. In the interview, the doctor pointed out that it was Leslie Dillon who had initially contacted him, claiming that he could "put the finger on the A-No. 1 suspect" in the murder of Elizabeth Short. "I have only acted in good faith—doing my duty," said the doctor. He added, hinting darkly, "In good time, I'll give you a very good story. Right now I can't make any statement. I would be more than pleased if police authorities urged me to tell everything I know." When Boynoff asked the doctor about his medical training, De River said, "I've had exceptional training, if I do say so myself." He spoke of his medical degree from Tulane University, and his past employment with the Veterans Administration as a specialist in brain and reconstructive surgery.

But Sara Boynoff did her own digging. Soon, she had unearthed the previously unpublicized judicial order that arose from the Chloe Davis case, banning the doctor from questioning juvenile suspects. She approached Judge Scott and Judge Fox, who had issued the order. However, Judge Scott would only state that "in my opinion, Dr. De River is the best qualified sex psychiatrist in the country."

The next day's issue of the *Daily News* went full steam ahead.

DR. DE RIVER BACKGROUND REVEALED

Sara Boynoff's new headline, splashed across the cover, made what was described as a "shocking" and "sinister" revelation. The doctor's birth name, apparently, was not "Joseph Paul De River" but

"Joseph Israel." He had changed it in the San Francisco Superior Court in 1923.* Boynoff also said that City Councilman Ernest E. Debs had made a resolution calling for a public hearing into De River's background and professional qualifications. "I want to know about this man whom we have hired," Debs was quoted as saying, "and what his skills and qualifications are. This is not the first time he has been under fire. I wonder if we passed blindly in hiring this man."

Dr. De River's hearing before the City Council, investigating his professional qualifications and fitness to act as a police psychiatrist, took place on March 8, 1949, in the marble-pillared vault of the council chamber at Room 340 of City Hall. Councilman Don Allen presided over the proceedings. Councilman Debs asked most of the questions.

First on the witness stand was Assistant Chief Joe Reed. He was forthright in his support of the doctor. "Speaking for the Chief of Police, as he has already authorized me to, and speaking for myself, as the Assistant Chief of Police, I would say that the work that Doctor De River is rendering to the Los Angeles Police Department is exceptional. We feel that his work is a very beneficial part and without his services the Los Angeles Police Department would be handicapped in the prosecution of sex cases."

When the doctor himself took the stand, councilman Debs accused him of lacking the requisite professional psychiatric qualifications. De River's response was that, while there was no dispute that he had the requisite medical training, his lack of formal psychiatric qualifications was simply due to the fact that such training was "established long after I went into psychiatry. The young men are

---

* It is curious that the fact that the doctor had changed his (originally Jewish) name was highlighted as sinister, when this was common practice among not only Jewish immigrants, but immigrants of many other nationalities to the United States in the early twentieth century. It was also strange that Sara Boynoff chose to highlight this particular issue, as she was herself the first-generation daughter of Russian-Jewish immigrants to California.

taking it, but the older men, a great many of them, are not taking it. It is not necessary for us to take it."

The doctor's case was seconded by letters of support from friends and colleagues, including a letter from a William A. Miller, addressed to Councilman Allen. Miller wrote that he had no doubt whatsoever that the "vicious, personal attack" on the doctor had implications that went far beyond his part in the current investigation of the Dahlia case. He would like, he wrote, to known just who was behind the "smear campaign." He had a hunch that, if the facts were brought to light, it would "amaze a lot of people." Why the *Daily News* had gone to so much trouble to point out that the doctor's real name was Israel, could only be guessed at; but, wrote Miller, "I don't believe it would take a genius to figure out the angle there."

Strangely, the City Council proceedings were deafeningly silent about the Dahlia case. The hearing focused exclusively on the professional qualifications of the doctor to hold his position. The so-called "Dahlia Fiasco"—the handling of which had supposedly triggered the *Daily News* investigation of the doctor in the first place—was never referred to at any point. Nor was the name of Leslie Dillon.

By a seeming miracle, Dr. De River escaped the City Council hearing with his job. The respite was not to last long. Nor had Leslie Dillon gone away. A month previously, he had filed a $100,000 claim* for false arrest against the city of Los Angeles. According to the writ, Dr. De River and members of the LAPD "unjustifiably arrested Leslie Dillon, transported him from place to place, handcuffed him, and held him incommunicado without justification or charges having been lodged against him." Dillon, the writ continued, was "nationally degraded by said incompetent agents of the city in that without any basis or legal excuse, he was represented in the press as a 'hot' suspect in the Black Dahlia murder case."† This time, Dillon's claim

---

* Worth over $1 million in today's currency.
† Leslie Dillon eventually dropped his case against the city of Los Angeles when he was threatened with prosecution for robbing a safe during a period working as bellhop for a hotel in Santa Monica.

was filed by L.A. attorney Arthur Brigham Rose: a lawyer even more hard-boiled than Morris Lavine. "Arthur Brigham Rose," wrote Aggie Underwood, "is one of L.A.'s most spectacular trial lawyers, often throwing courtrooms into an uproar. Judges have become weary of holding him in contempt, a proceeding which he argues with authority." On one occasion, Aggie recalled, a policeman, tired of Rose's bullying questions, told him he was too much of a coward to act up in such a way out of court. Rose reached over to the cop, pulled him out of the witness box, and "slugged him." Once again, Dillon—the unemployed bellhop—had somehow found himself elite and expensive legal representation.

In the meantime, while "Jeff" and "Jack" walked free and Dr. De River battled to save his career, the Gangster Squad did not stop its investigation into Leslie Dillon. Officially, the case against Dillon had been dropped with his sudden and unexpected release in January 1949; but in secret, the Gangster Squad persevered.

They had more to learn.

THE LODGER

T he ongoing, clandestine investigation into Leslie Dillon throughout 1949 was carried out by some of the toughest members of the Gangster Squad.

Archie Case was a six-foot 250-pounder. His specialty was the rabbit punch. Case had earned his reputation in the predominantly black neighborhood called Mud Town. He was known on the street as the "Mayor of Watts." James Ahern was Archie's longtime partner. He was as squat, stolid, and tough as his teammate. Loren Waggoner—a rookie who had been a cop for less than four years—had proved his mettle in Central Uniform and Felony divisions before joining the Gangster detail. He partnered Ahern when Case was rushed off to the hospital for an appendectomy in January. When Case returned, Waggoner continued on the Dillon investigation. Finally, Con Keller was another six-footer, a redhead from Iowa farm stock who had come out of the war with a brace on his leg. He was good at bugging and picking locks.

First stop was the A1 Trailer Park on the Pacific Coast Highway, where Dillon had stayed in the summer of 1946. Officers Ahern and Waggoner interviewed Jiggs Moore, the elderly owner of the park. Jiggs told them that Dillon had stayed at the trailer park several times in the course of 1946. He drove different automobiles. "Dillon

told Moore that if he wanted a new car, he (Dillon) had an over*
in Hollywood, that he could get him a car over there, a new one,"
Ahern recalled. "But this man had no income that we could find
out about." Dillon, Moore said, had stayed at the park with his wife,
Georgia. But there had been another girl with him there in October. "The way Jiggs remembered her," said Waggoner, "was through
her hair and the way she dressed, and he remembered that she had
very large bosoms."† Jiggs also mentioned that, after the murder in
January 1947, the police visited the trailer park and several people
made the comment that the girl who had been killed looked "an
awful lot like" the girl who had been at the park the previous year.
Jiggs had not, however, thought to report this to the police. Jiggs was
shown a photograph of Elizabeth Short. "That's the girl," he said.
He would not be moved to say anything else. Jiggs also confirmed to
Waggoner that Leslie Dillon had come to the park in January 1949
and erased certain entries from the registration cards.‡ The records
that remained indicated that Dillon had lived at the trailer park from
June 8 through August 31, 1946, a period that overlapped with Elizabeth Short's stay at Long Beach with Gordon Fickling.§ But Ahern
believed that Dillon returned to the camp later that year.

Ahern and Waggoner also interviewed an old man at the trailer
park called Mr. Carriere. "Carriere remembered Leslie Dillon being
in the trailer court, he lived right across the aisle from him. We asked
if he remembered any woman being with him, and he said he did,
and he described a dark-headed woman," said Ahern. Dillon's wife,
Georgia, was a natural blonde. Ahern and Waggoner showed Mr.
Carriere a picture of Elizabeth Short. "Well, that looks just exactly

---

* An over: i.e., a contact.

† It was generally accepted that Elizabeth Short was small-breasted. However, according to
Ann Toth, like many other women of the time she wore "falsies" to augment her breast size,
which would have given the appearance of larger breasts.

‡ This was the incident witnessed by Dr. De River and JJ O'Mara, described on pages 108–
109.

§ Overlap with Beth's stay at Long Beach: see page 43.

like that woman who was here with Dillon," said Carriere. The old man told Waggoner that Dillon had said to him that he would like to have the girl he was with "come and work for him" up in San Francisco. Waggoner asked what he meant by that. "Well, Dillon was a pimp in San Francisco," Carriere said. Like Jiggs Moore the old man Carriere was adamant that the girl at the park with Dillon was Elizabeth Short, and that he was not mixing her up with anybody else.

Another witness, aspiring Hollywood author and model Ardis Green, also connected Leslie Dillon with Beth Short. Ardis said she had seen Beth at the Ace Cains Nightclub in the company of a tall, blond, slender man about six-one or six-three.* She was shown a picture of Dillon in civilian clothes, from the time he worked in Florida. "I can almost positively say that this is the man that was with Beth Short the night that I was introduced to her, but I can't say positively until I could see him smile or see him in person," Ardis said. She recalled the date of the encounter with Beth and the man exactly, as it was her birthday: August 27, 1946. It was the day Beth split with Gordon Fickling† and moved into the Hawthorne Hotel with Marjorie Graham.

Leslie Dillon's mother, Mamie, had mentioned, in interviews with the police, that Dillon—in addition to staying at his mother-in-law's house on Normandie Avenue, the A1 Trailer Park, and Nellie Hinshaw's house on Crenshaw Boulevard—had spent time at a downtown motel in Los Angeles called the Aster Motel, on South Flower Street. The Gangster Squad detectives decided to check it out.

The Aster Motel consisted of a low-lying strip of ten concrete cabins near the intersection of Flower and Twenty-ninth Streets, in a part of downtown set back from Broadway and Main. It was a closed place, shut to the world: a place of secrets, where men in dark suits

---

* Dillon was six feet tall with a slim build. His hair was naturally brown but he is known to have dyed it blond.

† Gordon Fickling, although tall at six-one-and-a-half, had very dark, wavy hair, and bore no physical resemblance to Leslie Dillon.

paid cash to closet themselves in cabins with nameless associates and women in red lipstick and high-heeled shoes. Officer Ahern, when asked if the Aster Motel had an "unsavory reputation," replied, "Very much so." While it was not an actual house of prostitution, Ahern said, "prostitutes stayed there."*

The owner of the Aster Motel in 1947 was a man named Henry Hoffman. The Gangster Squad tracked him down. Hoffman was a syphilitic ex-con who had spent time in Leavenworth Penitentiary for mail fraud. He told Waggoner that on a morning that Waggoner calculated was January 15, 1947, he found cabin 3 of the motel covered in blood and fecal matter.† The blood and feces were spattered over the floor, the bathroom, and up the sides of the bathroom walls. The place was in so bad a state that Hoffman had to clean it up himself. Hoffman's wife, Clora, had tried to come into the cabin, but there was such a mess that he told her to keep out because he was afraid she might be sick. The sheets on the bed were so saturated with blood that they had to be soaked in a pail of water before being sent to the laundry. The blankets also were soaked with blood and had to be sent out to be cleaned.

The Gangster Squad officers spoke to Clora, who had by now divorced Hoffman and remarried to become Mrs. Sartain. She was running a restaurant downtown on Grand Avenue. Clora also remembered the "mess" in cabin 3 in January 1947. There were human footprints in the blood and fecal matter smeared over the floor. The footprints and shoe prints looked, by their size, like men's prints. She also remembered the bloody sheets and blankets on the bed in cabin 3.

Clora told the Gangster Squad cops that, on the same morning as the discovery of the "mess" in cabin 3 of the motel, a pile of clothes

---

* The Aster Motel's connections with organized crime in the 1940s and '50s were underlined in 1954 when the gangster E. D. Spencer, on the run after a café shooting, was arrested there with his wife, Nan.

† Leslie Dillon, during interviews with Dr. De River in Banning the previous December, had stated that the murder had taken place in a motel. (See page 103.)

was found neatly tied in a bundle on the bed in cabin 9. The clothes were wrapped in brown paper with a cord around them, as if they were to be mailed in the post.* The bundle, Clora told Waggoner, contained a small-sized woman's skirt, blouse, and a pair of men's shorts. They had blood spattered on them. She had been planning to wash the blouse and skirt and give them to her daughter, Pamela, but her husband told her to burn all the clothing in the incinerator. Waggoner asked Clora what she thought had gone on in cabin 3. "Well," she replied, "I thought some sex fiend had been in that room."

Clora told the Gangster Squad officers that the regular police had come around to the motel shortly after the "mess" was discovered. They were looking for an Army sergeant who had been associated with the Dahlia.† Why, Waggoner asked, had Clora not told them about the "mess" at the time? Well, Clora replied, she and her husband had been having trouble with the police, and she didn't want to have anything to do with them. (In fact, Henry Hoffman had been arrested on Saturday, January 11, for a domestic disturbance with his wife and had spent the night in jail.) Mr. Hoffman also told Waggoner that he had not reported the matter because he had enough trouble with the cops, he did not want any more.

The Gangster Squad then interviewed the maid at the Aster Motel, Lila Durant. Lila recalled the incident with the bloody cabin and clothes in January 1947. She remembered that Clora told her she had burned the clothes in the incinerator, because she was afraid. "Lila Durant," said Ahern, "described the clothes, to my way of thinking, fairly close to what Elizabeth Short was purported to have been wearing at the time she disappeared. She said it was a white blouse with ruffles on the front of it, and she said it was a black skirt,

---

* Compare the parcel sent to the *Los Angeles Examiner*, containing the contents of Elizabeth Short's purse. Did the killer originally also intend to send in the bloody clothing, later changing his mind?

† This was likely one of Elizabeth's many boyfriends, possibly Carl Balsiger, who had stayed with her in a motel shortly before she left Los Angeles for San Diego in December 1946. (See page 244.)

and the blouse had a sprinkling of blood on it, and there were a pair of men's shorts—she thought they were size 32—and they had blood all over the crotch, like they had been used to wipe the floor.* She stated that she thought the skirt was about a size 13 or 14,† if I recall it." Lila also recalled a spot of blood that had soaked through the saturated sheets and blankets onto the mattress of the bed, "about the size of a large clock." Lila had not cleaned the cabin herself that day. It had been cleaned out by Mr. Hoffman, although this was not his usual habit. "There was an unusual circumstance there," Ahern said. "I was suspicious on my part of Hoffman, because of the fact that, although he didn't have the habit of cleaning the place up, he was very determined that he be the one to clean this place up." The motel had only opened up for business in December 1946, so until then there had been no laundry bill. But shortly after the murder, Ahern recalled, there had been an excessively large bill charged for laundry.‡

Around this time, Clora Hoffman's brother, Burt Moorman, and his wife, Betty-Jo, had been staying at the motel. "He's a very precise witness, this fellow Moorman," recalled Ahern. "You can't shake him on anything. He is very determined on what he saw." It was Burt who first revealed the discovery of the bloody room. He and Betty-Jo had arrived at the motel around January 7, 1947. They had left around January 18. They had stayed in a trailer for most of the time, and for one night in cabin 1. Effectively, this put the Moormans at the motel

---

* The U.S. male pant size 32 corresponds to a slim/medium build.

† The Sears 1955 catalogue for the "Misses" range gives for size 14: thirty-five-and-a-half-inch bust, twenty-seven-inch waist, thirty-eight-inch hips. This would correspond roughly to a modern U.S. size 6 or UK size 10, that is, a medium build. While Elizabeth Short's precise measurements are not known, the LAPD dead body report gave her as five-foot-three and weighing 118 pounds, putting her into the normal category for body mass index. Officer Ahern in his evidence recalled the clothes being discovered at the motel fitting the type and size of those worn by Elizabeth Short at her disappearance.

‡ The only documented case when the motel had an excessive bill for laundry was January 17, 1947. The items were identified as two blankets/bedspreads, and a rug. The pick-up date could have been January 13 or 15. However, no alternative explanation was given for an unusually large pick-up on January 13 (document entitled "Summary of Elizabeth [Beth] Short Murder Investigation," DA grand jury documents).

over the whole of the crucial "missing week," that is, the period from Elizabeth Short's disappearance (Thursday, January 9) to the discovery of her body in the vacant lot (Wednesday, January 15).

Burt Moorman recalled that Mr. and Mrs. Hoffman fought a lot. He remembered the bloody room, and that the two Army blankets on the bed were so saturated with blood that "it looked like somebody had taken a gallon of red paint and poured it over those blankets." He also remembered Mrs. Hoffman taking some bloody towels out into the backyard, and some bloody clothes, which she showed his wife Betty-Jo and then put in the incinerator. Ahern asked Moorman how much blood there was on the bed. "I worked in a mortuary," Burt replied. "We used to drain bodies of blood. We used to drain off half of it and then put in the other fluid. I thought that the blood on this mattress would be what a human body would probably contain. It was that much. The smell there at that time was enough to drive you out, even though the cabin had been cleaned up."

Burt Moorman's wife, Betty-Jo, confirmed her husband's account. She drew a diagram showing where the blood in the bathroom was located, next to the shower door. Betty-Jo could not remember exactly in which cabin the "mess" was discovered. But she did recall seeing "large men's footprints and shoe tracks" in the feces. She had seen her husband's sister Clora Hoffman carry bloody items to the incinerator.

In late April 1947, the Hoffmans sold the Aster Motel to new owners. The motel registers for April showed that Leslie Dillon had stayed there during that month. The Gangster Squad asked Clora Hoffman if they could see the motel registration cards from January 1947, to check if Dillon had stayed there earlier in the year, at the time of the murder. Clora told them to come back the next day and she would give them the cards. But when the cops returned to see her, she told them she was sorry, but she had burned them about a month before. They had been living in a small apartment with the children; the cards were getting in the way; so she had destroyed them. When Waggoner asked Henry Hoffman if Leslie Dillon had been at the motel, he initially said that he had been there in March or April 1947. Waggoner asked him if he could remember Dillon ever being there anytime before that. Hoffman said no, he couldn't remember exactly, but he might have been there. If he had, he just didn't remember it.

Once again, Leslie Dillon seemed to have the benefit of a convenient record erasure. But the officers of the Gangster Squad were not about to give up. They were convinced there was something more in this deal with Leslie Dillon up on Flower Street. They tracked down an old associate of Dillon's called Tommy Harlow, a longtime petty thief and crooked real estate dealer originally from Dallas. Harlow told Officers Waggoner and Ahern that he first met Leslie Dillon through Dillon's half-brother Henry, who operated a restaurant on La Cienega Boulevard. Henry, Harlow said, persuaded him to take Dillon on as a real estate salesman, to teach him about real estate. The date of this meeting was early December 1946. On this day Harlow and Dillon went to the A1 Trailer Park on the Pacific Coast Highway, and Dillon introduced Harlow to his friend Jiggs Moore, who owned the trailer park.

From December '46 through January '47, Harlow said, Dillon worked on and off for him. He would show up at Harlow's office on West Olympic. Sometimes Harlow would take him out with him, and sometimes not. Dillon was occasionally away from Los Angeles for three or four days; when he was away, he was in San Francisco. In March, Harlow put Dillon to work refurbishing an old house. Dillon worked for Harlow for about three weeks, and during that time Harlow would pick him up at the home of his wife's aunt, Nellie Hinshaw, on South Crenshaw. Dillon had his pale blue trailer parked outside the house. It was a two-room affair, with a stove and refrigerator for cooking. One day Harlow looked into the trailer and saw Dillon's wife and little girl. Dillon drove his brother Henry's old black Buick, and also an old 1936 two-door black sedan during this period.* Harlow did not know to whom the black sedan belonged, but he thought it was Dillon's. A woman at Harlow's real estate office, Mrs. Pearl McCromber, recognized a picture of Leslie Dillon and told the officers that, to the best of her knowledge, he had worked for Tommy Harlow on Olympic Boulevard during the month of December 1946 and the early part of January 1947. He would come, she said, on a bus from San Francisco, although she could not be specific about dates.†

According to Tommy Harlow, Leslie Dillon asked him to buy a house that he, Dillon, would run as a house of prostitution. Dillon said, "My buddy and I will operate the house and get the girls. All you have to do is get the house." The "buddy" referred to was an unidentified Italian man.‡ Harlow didn't go for it. According to Tommy, Dillon was "all the time running around with different women." As long as Harlow knew him, "he was always talking about women, operating houses of prostitution, hot jewelry,§ and other talk of similar topics."

In further interviews with the Gangster Squad cops, Harlow told them that the Aster Motel had been built in late 1946 for a "friend of his called Hansen."¶ The motel was completed and put on the

---

* Old 1936 two-door black sedan: compare the eyewitness reports of a 1936 or 1937 dark Ford sedan seen at the body dump site (page 47).

† The LAPD later attempted to discredit Tommy Harlow's evidence by claiming that he had gotten his dates wrong, and that Leslie Dillon only started working for Harlow from March 1947. Dillon did, in fact, do some work for Harlow in March and April of that year. However, Harlow's clear recollection was that Dillon had also worked for him earlier, *when the motel was being built*, and this could only have been in December/January. Mrs. Pearl McCromber's account supported Harlow's but her full statement has never been released.

‡ Unidentified Italian: compare Officer Jones's report that Dillon hung out with an Italian taxi driver called Larry Fanucci in Florida (page 97).

§ Hot jewelry: Dillon was in fact wanted by the Santa Monica police for robbing the safe of the Carmel Hotel, where he worked in March 1947. There were unsuccessful attempts to extradite him from Oklahoma in mid-1949 to stand trial for the robbery. The threat of prosecution for the robbery was one of the reasons Dillon eventually dropped his claim for false arrest against the city of Los Angeles.

¶ No official connection between the ownership of the Aster Motel and Mark Hansen has been proved. The original owner, on the face of the motel registration documents, was Clora Hoffman. Mark Hansen did tell district attorney investigators that he owned two "rooming houses" for girls. The addresses of these were never publicly identified. (See page 56.)

market that December. He, Harlow, was appointed as agent to sell it. He visited the motel two or three times in December 1946, and once or twice in January 1947. Leslie Dillon was with him. Dillon, Harlow said, complained of not having a place to stay. Harlow therefore told him to go ahead and sleep at one of the units at the motel: it was not completely finished, and no one would bother him if he stayed there.* Henry Hoffman also, having initially denied that Leslie Dillon ever lived at the motel before March or April 1947, came up to Officer Ahern one night at his ex-wife's café on Grand Avenue and confirmed Harlow's account that Leslie Dillon was the man who had visited the motel with him during the period it was on the market in December and January.

Tommy Harlow also remembered that, at one point, there was a dark-haired girl staying at the motel.† Henry Hoffman was fooling around with the girl, and his wife, Clora, had a big argument with him about it. When Harlow saw the girl, she was lying in bed with just a sheet covering her up. She looked to Harlow like she had been sick, or was "just coming off of a drunk."‡ Waggoner asked Harlow if the girl could have been Elizabeth Short. "Well, you go talk to Mr. Hoffman first," Harlow said. "And after you talk to Mr. Hoffman and have him describe that girl, you come back to me and talk."

The trouble was, Henry Hoffman did not want to talk about the dark-haired girl at the motel. Every time anyone from the Gangster Squad tried to broach the subject, he veered away. Loren Waggoner fared best with him. Somehow, the old con and the young cop seemed to hit it off. In July 1949, after months of effort, the rookie detective managed, finally, to win the confidence of the cagey old man. "I had

---

* This means that Dillon must have stayed at the motel in late 1946/early 1947, not just in March/April 1947, because by then the motel was completed.

† Elizabeth had hennaed her hair at the Frenches' house but by the time of her death the dye was growing out, showing the original dark strands and giving the appearance of dark brown (page 11).

‡ The possibility that Elizabeth Short was held captive at the motel in a drugged condition was mooted, but not investigated. The contents of Short's stomach were sent off for analysis for the presence of narcotics, but were somehow lost. No official analysis was ever produced.

two pictures of Elizabeth Short in my pocket, and we were sitting in the car talking," Waggoner recalled. "I pulled these pictures out, and he was sitting in the back seat. I had them in my hand, I was hitting them on the seat, and he said, 'Let me see that picture.' I showed him the picture. He asked me, 'Why didn't you ever show me this picture before? This is the girl that was there at that motel.'" Suddenly, during that meeting in the car with Waggoner and his partner, Garth Ward, Hoffman began to "remember things that he would not tell investigating officers before." He told the officers that, on a night in January—he believed it was around January 9, 1947—a dark-haired girl came to the Aster Motel. He believed she stayed in cabin 9. After two days, the girl had no more money to pay for her room. His wife said she had to go. He thought she did go, but it was possible she stayed there longer, without his knowledge. Altogether, he had seen the dark-haired girl about six times in the cabin. She had told him she was a waitress somewhere up on Broadway. When he saw the girl, she was lying on the bed with no clothes on, just covered by a sheet. He had sat on the bed with her and run his fingers through her hair. He had tried to talk her into having sex with him, but she had refused.

During the interview with Waggoner and Ward in the car, Hoffman also suddenly "remembered" the parcel of bloody clothing that his wife had described. It was later found in cabin 9, he said, where the girl had stayed. He had not told the cops about the black-haired girl before because he was afraid they would try to pin the murder on him. Hoffman looked at the picture of Elizabeth Short for a long time. Finally, he said, "Now that I recognize this picture, I believe that the Black Dahlia was killed at the Aster Motel." Waggoner asked him why. "Because of the bloody clothing and the bloody sheets."

James Hurst was a suspicious old man who lived across from the motel on Flower Street. Like most of the people in the area, he did not like cops. But, for some reason, he took a liking to Archie Case. Mr. Hurst also recalled the black-haired girl staying at the motel. According to Officer Case, "Hurst said that this black-haired girl, who was living at the motel at the time that the girl was killed, came over and approached him as he was going into his house, and said she would like a quarter to go over to Long Beach." Hurst told the girl he was a poor man. He didn't generally give anybody anything. But this girl had a "desperate look on her face," she looked "like she had been crying for about a week." So Hurst said, "Why don't you get it from your friends at the motel?" She said, "They won't give me anything." And so he gave the girl fifty cents. Hurst's identification of the girl was "like most of the others—black-haired, and he thought she very closely resembled the pictures of Elizabeth Short that were shown." Hurst told Archie he had seen the girl leave her cabin and go into the cabin where the Hoffmans stayed. He also recalled that around Sunday, January 12, he had seen a man who seemed to be ill somewhere around the cabins toward the center of the court,* and that someone had forced this man back into the cabin. He heard someone mention they should call a doctor. A short time afterward, a man arrived who seemed to be a doctor, but after talking to the others, he refused to enter the cabin. Later, the sick man left in a taxi. Hurst was shown a picture of Leslie Dillon. He thought Dillon looked like the man who had been sick.

The cleaning maid, Lila Durant, also spoke of the black-haired girl. She told Ahern that Mrs. Hoffman had said to her, "You know what that black-haired so-and-so that lived back there in no. 10† had the nerve to do this afternoon?" Lila said, "No." "She came up here and had the nerve to ask me for two bits to go to Long Beach." Clora, however, subsequently denied that she had said any such thing to Lila. Mrs. Hoffman, in fact, never made a positive identification of Elizabeth Short from photographs as the black-haired girl who lived at the motel. The most she would say was, "It looks like her." Clora's brother Burt Moorman also told the police about the black-haired

---

* Cabin 3 was toward the center of the strip of cabins, which ran from 1 to 10.
† The general view was that the black-haired girl lived at cabin 9, not 10. This was probably a slip by Lila.

girl who stayed at the motel, although he was confused as to which room she had been in. He corroborated that she was in bed under just a sheet, and he also recalled seeing a man at the door of one of the cabins, who he believed could have been Leslie Dillon.

The appearance and behavior of the black-haired girl at the Aster Motel corresponded with what the Gangster Squad knew of Elizabeth Short. Elizabeth, Archie Case noted, "had a habit of begging." When Case was making inquiries about her at Long Beach, he was told that she would repeatedly beg people for a dime, a quarter, anything she could possibly get.* And then there had been the original "sighting" by Officer Myrl McBride way back in '47, the night before the discovery of Short's body in the vacant lot, of a girl begging for help. The girl had exited a bar on Main Street with two men and a woman.† Leslie Dillon was known to frequent the seedy dives of Main Street; Tommy Harlow had once seen him at the intersection of Fifth and Main with a girl for whom he was pimping. Could the girl that Officer McBride saw that night on Main have been Elizabeth, briefly escaped with the half dollar that Hurst had given her?‡ Had she somehow been persuaded to return to that motel, which on that night was to become her death chamber?§ Everybody at the motel agreed that whoever the "black-haired girl" who stayed there in January '47 had been, she disappeared without trace after the murder. And not one of the people at the motel could give the Gangster Squad officers any clue as to where she might be found.

---

* She had also begged Gordon Fickling for money. (See page 43.)

† The threatening presence of "two men and a woman" returns repeatedly in accounts of Elizabeth's last days. In addition to Officer McBride's account, Dorothy French also recounted how a nocturnal visit by such a trio frightened Beth shortly before she left San Diego. If—as Jeff Connors first stated to police—Elizabeth was with him and his wife in a bar the night before the murder, it is possible that Leslie Dillon was the second man, the "ex-Marine" boyfriend of whom she was so afraid.

‡ The bars and clubs of Main Street in downtown Los Angeles were only two and a half miles from the Aster Motel, so just a short trolley car ride away. This area of town was also very close to the Biltmore Hotel.

§ Officer McBride's statement, which would have given a description of the "two men and a woman" seen with the girl who begged for help on the night of January 14, 1947, has never been released by the LAPD.

—

When Henry Hoffman finally opened up to Waggoner in the car in July 1949, he began to remember quite a bit about what had happened at the Aster Motel. Hoffman told the young policeman about a "fellow from Batavia"* who had stayed at the motel for four or five days, about the same time the black-haired girl was there. Before he came, there had been a call notifying Hoffman of his arrival from the "Dutch Embassy or Danish consulate"—he could not recall which. The man from Batavia had a large amount of baggage with him. He arrived around Saturday, January 11, the day Hoffman was arrested for assaulting his wife, and stayed in cabin 8.† According to Hoffman, he was about forty-five or fifty years old. He had hair that was graying around the temples.‡ He spoke with some sort of a foreign accent—Swedish or Norwegian, or something like that.§ He told Hoffman he was going to stay in Los Angeles for a few days, and then fly up to New York to buy road machinery. One day he asked Hoffman to take him to Earl Carroll's nightclub in Hollywood¶ to get tickets for the show. Hoffman drove him there and waited for well over an hour. Finally the man returned and paid Hoffman five dollars for waiting. Hoffman introduced the man to Tommy Harlow, and the pair discussed the real estate business.

"I'm the main witness in this case, I hope those gangsters over in Hollywood don't try and kill me," Hoffman told Waggoner.

Waggoner was surprised. "What do you mean making a statement like that?"

"Well, this Mark Hansen, he's the main suspect in this."

---

* Batavia: the old name for Jakarta, the former capital of the Dutch East Indies, now capital of Indonesia. Batavia was much in the news in the late 1940s due to the Japanese occupation and the Indonesian struggle for independence. Clearly, in this case, the identity was a fake, probably a cover for a foreign accent.

† The cabin next to the one occupied by the black-haired girl, i.e., cabin 9.

‡ This corresponds to a description of Mark Hansen, although Hansen was slightly older at fifty-four years old.

§ Mark Hansen, as Officer Waggoner noted, had a distinctive Scandinavian accent.

¶ Earl Carroll's nightclub on Sunset Boulevard was the main rival of Mark Hansen's Florentine Gardens Nightclub on Hollywood Boulevard.

Waggoner had never mentioned the name "Mark Hansen" to Hoffman before. He asked Hoffman where he got it from.

"Well, that fellow that was mixed up in that Black Dahlia killing. I just put two and two together, and figured it was him."

Later, Hoffman was shown a picture of Mark Hansen. He thought he could be the "man from Batavia," but could not say for sure unless he saw Hansen in person. Hoffman told Waggoner that he was more than willing to cooperate in the case, if he was not accused of the murder. But if he was to get up and testify against Mark Hansen, he wanted the police to guarantee his protection.

"Why?" asked Waggoner.

"Because I'm afraid of Mark Hansen. Hansen is one of the gangsters of Hollywood, and if I get up and testify against him, he is liable to have me shot or something."

Burt and Betty-Jo Moorman also recalled the "man from Batavia" who stayed at the motel. Burt described the man as forty-five or fifty years old, with blue eyes, dark gray hair, and a large nose. He was five-foot-nine, weighed about 160 pounds, and was casually dressed in expensive clothes. The description fit Mark Hansen. Burt told the Gangster Squad that the man from Batavia had asked him and his wife to drive him to a downtown location,* where he collected a large suitcase. Afterward, the man invited them to his cabin for a drink, and they went out for dinner together at a Mexican restaurant on Slauson Avenue.

On June 18, 1949, the Gangster Squad took Burt Moorman out to the Florentine Gardens. There, in the parking lot, he was able to observe Mark Hansen from a distance of twenty feet, for five minutes. Burt thought that Hansen looked like the man from Batavia, but wanted to corroborate with his wife first. On June 21, Betty-Jo was taken to observe Mark Hansen in a restaurant on Hollywood Boulevard, for about an hour. She thought he looked like the same man. Hansen, Betty-Jo said, had the same stooped shoulders and

---

* This "downtown location" has never been revealed.

hesitant walk of the "man from Batavia." Like the man from Batavia, he had "watery, glistening eyes." He also "wolfed down" his food with his left hand, as the man from Batavia had done.

Clora Hoffman also recalled the "man from Batavia." He must have stayed at the motel at the time the bloody clothing was found, she said, because the Moormans were there at the same time, and they left on January 18. Clora Hoffman thought that photographs of Mark Hansen looked like the "man from Batavia," but like her ex-husband, she wanted to see Hansen in person to be sure. Waggoner told Clora that Mr. Hoffman now remembered the dark-haired girl who stayed in cabin 9, and had recognized the picture of Elizabeth Short. "It is about time," Clora replied, "that he started to remember some of the things that happened at the motel."

By the summer of 1949, the Gangster Squad had made impressive headway at the Aster Motel. From an initial tip given by Leslie Dillon's mother, they had managed to establish that a room in the motel—cabin 3—had been discovered splattered with blood and feces on the morning of January 15, 1947. That, at the time of the Dahlia's murder, a dark-haired girl fitting her description had been staying there. That the girl appeared to have been trapped, possibly drugged some of the time, afraid, and desperate to escape. That she seemed to be incapacitated, lying naked on a bed. That she had been the subject of disputes between the owner of the hotel, Henry Hoffman, and his wife, who wanted her out of there. That a pile of bloody clothing fitting the description of the clothes last worn by Elizabeth Short had been found there on the morning after the murder. That the motel had an unusually large laundry bill during that week. And that a man corresponding to the description of Mark Hansen had stayed at the motel, posing as the "man from Batavia." They had also found out that Leslie Dillon had definitely stayed at the motel in the spring of 1947, and apparently knew of it and used it as a place to crash in Los Angeles before then. Two witnesses—Henry Hoffman and Dillon's former employer Tommy Harlow—categorically stated that Leslie Dillon was at the motel when the black-haired girl was there. Two further witnesses—Burt Moorman and Mr. Hurst—said a man corresponding to his description was seen at the time. If the police had drawn a plan of the occupancy of the motel cabins in the week of the Dahlia's disappearance, as had been described to them by the witnesses, it would have looked something like this:

Occupation of ASTER MOTEL, Flower Street, Los Angeles
Circa. January 9–15, 1947

Flower Street Entrance

CABINS									
1	2	3	4	5	6	7	8	9	10
Burt and Betty-Jo Moorman*		"The Mess"					"Man from Batavia"	Dark-haired girl/parcel of bloody clothes	Henry and Clora Hoffman

*When not staying in their trailer in the yard.

And yet, despite the compelling evidence the officers of the Gangster Squad were uncovering, they never seemed to make headway with their investigation. The path was always blocked. On June 10, 1949, Officer Waggoner was told abruptly that he was to be transferred from the Gangster detail to the University Division. It was the day that he was due to take a statement from Henry Hoffman. Willie Burns told Waggoner that the statement was to be taken by Officer Ahern instead.

"Don't you want me to interview him?"

"No, you come in and work nights."

"Don't you want me to work this case anymore?"

"No."

Waggoner was surprised. He could think of no good reason why he was being taken off the case. "I just couldn't figure it out," he later said. "The case could have been solved if we had been allowed to carry on our investigation. I was suddenly taken off the case and I never did learn the reason why."

For a few weeks, the young cop continued to work the Dahlia investigation from University, with his partner Garth Ward. It was during this time that he secured the crucial interview in the car with Henry Hoffman, in which the old man finally opened up. But the allocation of resources to the case at University was so poor that Waggoner and Ward both asked to be taken off it. The nocturnal lifestyles of the people at the Aster Motel meant that interviews had to be carried out mainly at night. And yet, somehow, no night patrol cars were ever available. Clearly, the young officers' investigation was being blocked. Why or by whom, they did not know. And so, toward the end of July '49, Officers Waggoner and Ward, at their own request, were transferred. The two officers submitted a final joint report to the officer in charge at University. Then, they moved on to other things. Once more, the Dahlia investigation stagnated.

But then, in the summer of 1949, an extraordinary series of unforeseen events occurred. The LAPD became embroiled in the biggest corruption scandal of its history: a scandal that was to change the police department, and the course of the Dahlia case, forever.

KISS TOMORROW GOODBYE

C lemence Horrall was gone. It was the summer of 1949, and the downtown trolley cars clanked along the intersection of Temple and Broadway as usual. But in City Hall the chief's office was bare, with just the desk and the empty cot in which old Horrall used to nap while his assistant Joe Reed ran the show. In the former chief's position there was now a new man.

General William Worton was a decorated Marine officer. He had been appointed interim chief of the police department by the mayor, Fletcher Bowron, pending appointment of a permanent replacement for Horrall. Worton had accepted the post reluctantly, having literally retired from his previous position earlier the same day. The general knew a great deal about administration. He knew next to nothing about the internal politics of the Los Angeles Police Department. But he had taken the position out of duty, a sense that his mission was to save one of the largest police departments in the country. A department that was, at that moment, in the throes of the biggest crisis in its history.

And it had all begun with—of all people—the local gangster, Mickey Cohen.

—

By the spring of 1949, Mickey Cohen was hacked off big time with the LAPD. For years now, the diminutive gangster had been the totemic fall guy for Mayor Bowron, in his weekly Friday radio broadcasts. Every time the mayor made one of his many public proclamations that the City of Angels must be swept clean of mobsters, it was little Mickey who was cited as the kingpin of them all, the prime target of the mayor's efforts. And yet, as far as the Mick was concerned, he was the fatted calf from which they all fed. He was being squeezed from all sides, especially by the LAPD Vice Squad, which extorted huge amounts from him in protection money. The last straw came in January 1949, when a group of LAPD officers arrested one of Mickey's key sidekicks, Harold "Happy" Meltzer, for possession of an unlicensed gun. Meltzer told his boss that the gun was a plant. Mickey was furious. This time, he swore, he was going to teach the LAPD a lesson.

The first shot in Mickey's war against the cops was fired by Meltzer's attorney, Sam Rummel.* Rummel claimed that the planted gun was part of an eighteen-month campaign by the LAPD's Vice Squad to shake down Mickey Cohen. Why, Rummel asked pointedly, did the cops never actually arrest Cohen himself? Because, of course, "They did not want to kill the goose they hoped was going to lay the golden egg." In return for an end to the constant harassment, claimed Rummel, Sergeant Elmer V. Jackson of administrative Vice, and his boss Lieutenant Rudy Wellpott,† had tried to squeeze some $20,000

---

* Sam Rummel, a.k.a. the "mouthpiece," acquired notoriety as the fast-talking attorney for mobsters including Mickey Cohen. His downfall came during the Guaranty Finance scandal of 1950, when it was discovered that members of the Los Angeles Vice Squad and sheriff's department had been in cahoots with Cohen on a massive book-making operation, with Rummel as their lawyer. On December 11, 1950, Rummel was summoned to a secret meeting with members of the Los Angeles Sheriff's Department to discuss the scandal. That same night he was shot dead at his luxurious Laurel Canyon Boulevard home. The perpetrators of the killing were never found.

† The same "lieutenant called Rudy" who was accused by the fake confessor Christine Reynolds of having divulged secret details of the Dahlia mutilations to her girlfriend. (See page 68.)

off Cohen. Recklessly pushing the limits, Rummel brazenly claimed that Jackson had told Mickey the money was to fund Fletcher Bowron's reelection campaign: Mayor Bowron, who even then was crusading against the infiltration of "Eastern gangsters" into the City of Angels. Mickey, Rummel said, frequently picked up checks for LAPD vice cops at restaurants like Slapsy Maxie's and Musso's Bar & Grill.

But the allegation that the gun was a plant was just the opening round in Mickey's war against the LAPD. Two years previously, Sergeant Elmer Jackson had already come under fire when he was caught in a car in the company of Brenda Allen, Hollywood's leading vice queen. But now, Rummel said, Mickey Cohen had conclusive proof that Brenda Allen was not only Elmer Jackson's girlfriend, she was also paying him protection money. Brenda, who had a vast number of the Hollywood establishment on her client list, was rumored to be raking in $9,000 a day. A third of it was earmarked for bribes, physician and attorney fees, and bail bondsmen. Rummel said that Mickey had in his possession audio recordings of Brenda and Elmer engaged in hanky-panky. He was prepared to play them in court. To prove it, Mickey showed up at Meltzer's hearing with an ominous "sound-recording machine" and an "electronics expert," who was none other than Jimmy Vaus, a wire-tapper who was two-timing the LAPD by secretly working for Cohen.

Meanwhile, another member of Hollywood Vice, Sergeant Charles Stoker, had already testified secretly before the Los Angeles grand jury criminal complaints committee. Stoker had told the committee about overhearing the conversations between Brenda Allen and Elmer Jackson. Worse, Stoker said, the police establishment had gotten wind of the Allen/Jackson relationship fourteen months earlier and had started an investigation, which had mysteriously stalled.

The scandal occasioned by the revelation of payoffs between cops and madams in the Meltzer trial meant that a grand jury investigation into the LAPD Vice Squad's activities was inevitable. Chief Clemence Horrall and his assistant, Joe Reed, were duly summoned before the jury. The old chief was accused of taking one too many naps while his police department ran rife with corruption. He cut a sorry figure as he tried to explain away his lack of vigilance as the result of an overwhelming number of ceremonial duties. But the star of the show was, naturally, Brenda herself. Heavily made up, in dark glasses and immaculate dress, the redheaded siren told the jurors in a soft voice, with the hint of a Southern twang, about her payoffs—in money and kind—to Sergeant Jackson. The grand jury also heard about members of the Vice Squad beating up nightclub owners who refused to sell out to syndicates enjoying police protection, and allowing million-dollar bingo parlors to operate freely while charity lotteries were raided.

The fallout from the grand jury investigation of the Brenda Allen scandal was prodigious. On June 28, 1949, Chief Clemence Horrall resigned. The old chief was tired, and while few believed he personally knew anything about the antics his Vice Squad had been up to behind his back, his negligence was no longer acceptable. One month later, the grand jury indicted Lieutenant Wellpott and Sergeant Jackson for perjury and accepting bribes. The grand jury wanted everybody involved in the scandal, including Brenda Allen herself, to take lie detector tests. In the end, none of the cops who had been indicted were convicted, and Elmer Jackson notably went on to serve many years in the police department. Jimmy Vaus, the wire-tapper who had been two-timing Mickey Cohen and the LAPD, never did play his incriminating tapes. Just as he was about to do so before the grand jury, he announced that the six spools of wire recordings had been mysteriously stolen from the trunk of his car. Then he said they were buried in his backyard. Finally, he claimed he had lied about what was on the recordings and went to jail for perjury.[*]

One of Chief Worton's first acts as the new head of the LAPD

---

[*] Jimmy Vaus was later to be "converted" by evangelist Billy Graham and devoted the rest of his life to preaching the path of the light. However, it appeared that he was never moved by the spirit to tell the true story of what happened to the missing recordings.

was to do what he did best: administration, in the form of a reshuffle of the police department. The former deputy chief, Bill Bradley, was moved from the position of chief of detectives to a new Bureau of Corrections. And the powerful, now-vacant job of chief of detectives went to the one man the Gangster Squad would have least wanted it to go to: the former head of the Patrol Division, with strong connections to the rival Homicide Division, Thaddeus Brown. But perhaps it didn't matter what the Gangster Squad thought, because the squad itself no longer existed in its previous form. The former chief of the detail, Willie Burns, was transferred to day watch in the Venice Division. The other Gangster Squad officers were dispersed. Some—including Archie Case and JJ O'Mara—merely changed departments rather than their job descriptions. Archie and JJ now found themselves working for a new internal espionage division, set up by Worton. It was called the Intelligence Division.

The departmental reshuffle by Chief Worton reorganized and renamed the Gangster Squad, demoted its chief Willie Burns, and put Thad Brown in a position of power. This fundamentally changed the dynamics of a battle that—since the secret mission to investigate Leslie Dillon—had already been playing out between the Gangster Squad and the Homicide Division on the Dahlia case. Now it was the Homicide Division that was in the dominant position. As far as the Dahlia investigation was concerned, it was the first nail in the coffin.

15

PANIC IN THE STREETS

Before the Brenda Allen scandal and the subsequent near-collapse and reorganization of the LAPD, the Gangster Squad had been making impressive progress with the people at the Aster Motel. Officer Waggoner had extracted extraordinary revelations from the former motel owner, Henry Hoffman. Officers Case and Ahern had even persuaded Burt and Betty-Jo Moorman to permit them to tap their trailer so they could listen in on conversations between the Moormans and Mr. Hoffman's ex-wife, Clora. Everybody, including the Moormans, felt that the Hoffmans had not been straightforward about the events that had taken place at the Aster in January 1947. Bugging the Moormans' trailer might lead to revelations from Clora, in conversation with her brother Burt and his wife.

But then, at the end of June 1949, Horrall went, Worton came, and Thad Brown was promoted to chief of detectives. The consequences for the investigation of the Dahlia case were sharp and swift. Within a week, Case and Ahern were given a new order. The Gangster Squad was to stop all work on the Aster investigation forthwith. The officers were to re-interrogate the witnesses at the motel, in the company of Finis Brown. And then they were to turn the case over to Homicide. Nobody in the gangster detail was able to explain why the plan to bug the Moormans' trailer was summarily abandoned, or why the case was abruptly handed over to Homicide. The most Ahern could offer as an explanation for the transfer was that it was due to "a change in administration. A change in the command of the police department."

Aggie Underwood was, at this point, officially off the Dahlia story. She had, after all, been kicked upstairs way back in 1947 to stop her from interfering with matters that did not concern her. But through her close friendship with Dr. Paul De River, Aggie had gotten wind of something afoot. Nor was she the only one. Rumors abounded that the death chamber of the Dahlia had been located; that there were strange connections between it and a prominent local nightclub owner known to have friends in the LAPD; and that someone, somewhere, was trying to cover things up. Suspicion reached such a fever pitch that the 1949 grand jury, fresh from its investigation into police corruption in the Brenda Allen scandal, announced its intention to look into the LAPD's handling of the Dahlia case, too. "There's a bad situation over there in the police department, and we feel we are being deceived," said a grand jury spokesman.

Somehow, Aggie had gotten her hands on Loren Waggoner's last report. It was the report he had filed with Garth Ward, recording the revelations that Henry Hoffman had made in the car; the final report the rookie cop had submitted before, disillusioned, he and Ward had asked to be transferred off the case. Aggie read it and then, just as with Robert "Red" Manley, whose innocence she had fearlessly pronounced, she now pointed the finger at the man of whose guilt she was certain. It was a daring, perhaps unprecedented move for a Los Angeles journalist of the time. For, while the press loved sensational murders, the cozy relations between cops and the newspapermen meant that the papers tended to steer well clear of stories involving any hint of police graft or corruption.

On September 13, 1949, the *Herald-Express* ran the following article, under the banner headline, "Black Dahlia Murder Room Located":*

SLAIN IN HOUSE ON BUSY STREET

Death Chamber Where Beauty Was Mutilated Finally Has Been Found, Investigators Reveal

The "Black Dahlia" death chamber finally has been located, according to expert investigators. The Herald-Express is able to disclose today as the County Grand Jury prepared to probe the butcher murder mystery, still officially unsolved after more than two and one-half years.

Blood-stained clothes of the same size worn by the "Black Dahlia," Elizabeth Short, 22 year old dark-haired beauty, and blood-covered sheets are known to have been seen in the suspected death room, investigators declared.

Near Death Lot

The quarters in which the victim is believed to have been slain and her body mutilated and bisected are situated in a structure on a busy street less than 15 minutes' drive from the weed-covered lot in which the body was found Jan 15, 1947.

The lot, near Norton Avenue near Coliseum Drive, is located almost on a bee-line with the place where investigators contend Miss Short's gay life was ended in fiendish death.

The Grand jury will subpoena a number of witnesses who have information about the death chamber, a jury spokesman said today.

---

* An unsigned, undated, typed draft of this newspaper article is carefully preserved in the papers of Aggie Underwood, now held by the California State University of Northridge. This suggests that, while the article does not have a byline, Aggie either wrote it herself or was closely involved in its writing.

Nationwide Hunt

The murder of the "Black Dahlia" who was so nick-named because of her penchant for wearing sheer black clothes, touched off a nationwide manhunt in which hundreds of persons were questioned, and scores were arrested, only to be released when investigators cleared them.

Many notoriety-seeking fanatics and chronic alcoholics in Los Angeles and other cities throughout the country even "confessed" the murder, but they were freed when their stories proved false or incoherent.

The follow-up article in the *Herald-Express* the next day, September 14, was even more explicit.

LINK L.A. MOTEL ROOM WITH DAHLIA MURDER

Identify Photo of Victim
Owner Feared Trouble, Failed to Tell Police

A heretofore undisclosed police report* which placed the "Black Dahlia" Elizabeth Short, 22, in a South Flower Street motel room in which blood-saturated clothing and sheets were found by the motel owner was located by the Herald-Express today.

The report states that H. H. Hoffman, the motel owner, identified the dark-haired beauty as the girl who occupied the room three days before her bisected body was discovered in a vacant lot in southwest Los Angeles on Jan. 15, 1947.

Hoffman said his wife found blood-covered shorts, blouse and skirt in the room which he said the Short girl had occupied, according to the report on file with the police department.

---

* The "undisclosed police report" referred to the final report of Officers Waggoner and Ward, filed at the end of July 1949, and referred to on page 145.

Sheets discovered in the room were so saturated with blood that Hoffman said he had to "soak them in a bucket of water" before he sent them to the laundry to be cleaned.

Girl Identified

The report, filed approximately six weeks ago, stated that officers had shown Hoffman a picture of the murder victim and that he had replied:

"That is the girl who was here."

Hoffman said he did not report the information to the police at the time of the murder because he "didn't want any trouble with the police," according to the police record.

Hoffman said that the Short girl "must have been killed in the motel because of the bloody clothing and sheets," the report continues.

Suspect Named

In a later interview, recorded in the same report, Hoffman named a man he said "came to the motel and stayed about four or five days" in the room next to the one he said the Short girl occupied.

The man, police said, was a known acquaintance of the Black Dahlia.

The man who was "named" in the police report, but not in the newspaper article itself, as the man who had stayed in the cabin next to the Dahlia, was of course, Mark Hansen.*

Curiously, while Aggie's explosive story of the leaked police report was picked up by many other local newspapers, no sign of it appeared in the *Herald-Express*'s archrival, the *Los Angeles Examiner*. But the

---

* Henry Hoffman said that the black-haired girl stayed in cabin 9 (where the parcel of bloody clothes was found), and that the "man from Batavia," whom he identified as Mark Hansen, stayed next door in cabin 8. (See page 141.)

next day, September 15, a brief article did appear buried in the inside pages of Jimmy Richardson's newspaper:

POLICE DENY DAHLIA "CLEWS"

Police were busy yesterday denying a new rash of rumors that "new clews" in the 32-months old slaying of Elizabeth Short, the "Black Dahlia," had been found.

"All of these supposed clews are matters checked by police and found to be without substance months ago," said Chief of Detectives Thad Brown.

The most recent report held that a witness had identified a photo of Miss Short as that of a girl who stayed overnight in a motel on South Flower Street a few days before her body was found in a vacant lot in the 3800 block of South Norton Avenue.

"We found this witness to be entirely unreliable," Brown commented.

There were several curious facts about the report buried in the *Examiner*. First, while the newspaper published Detective Chief Thad Brown's knockdown of the Aster Motel story, it had never actually published an article about the "rumors" surrounding the motel in the first place. Second, not just one, but several witnesses had identified Elizabeth Short as the dark-haired girl who stayed at the motel in January '47.* Third, the *Examiner* article made it clear that in practice, the Aster Motel investigations had not been "transferred" from the Gangster Squad to the Homicide Division when Thad Brown took over. They had, in fact, been terminated.

---

* Motel owner Henry Hoffman and neighbor Mr. Hurst both positively identified a photograph of Elizabeth Short as the dark-haired girl who had stayed at the motel. Clora Hoffman, Burt Moorman, Lila Durant, and Tommy Harlow all referred to a dark-haired girl staying at the motel in early January 1947, although because their statements have never been released it is not clear if they identified her as Elizabeth Short.

—

Despite the very strenuous efforts of the LAPD to keep a lid on the scandals, over the long, hot summer of 1949 they seemed to be interminable. Close on the heels of the Brenda Allen debacle and Chief Horrall's resignation, it was now the turn of the Brown brothers to find themselves in the headlines. The cause of the unwelcome publicity this time was a plump, blond, heavily rouged taxi dancer from Oakland called Lola Titus. After an argument with her mother over the "kind of life I had been leading," Lola had left home and taken a bus down to Los Angeles to find the nightclub owner, Mark Hansen. "I made up my mind that he was either going to love me, marry me, or take care of me, or I was going to kill him," she later told investigating officers. Arriving at Hansen's bungalow on Carlos Avenue on July 15, Lola invited the nightclub owner to check out her taxi dancing progress. The pair withdrew to the bedroom. Afterward, while Hansen was shaving in the bathroom, Lola shot him through the back with a twenty-five-caliber automatic pistol. Just before she shot him, she accused him of being a "goddam cop lover." Lola, who was alleged to have been a friend of Elizabeth Short, also accused Hansen of being involved in the Black Dahlia murder. While Mark Hansen staggered to the telephone to call for help, Lola got up, dressed, and left the house. Hansen was taken by ambulance to Hollywood-Leland Hospital, where his first words were, "Get me Brown." As Finis Brown was off on leave, it was his big brother Thad who rushed to Hansen's bedside.

Lola was arraigned for assault with intention to commit murder and locked in the prisoners' detention room on the seventh floor of the Hall of Justice. When a police sergeant came to take her to the courtroom, he found the curvaceous blonde spread-eagled and nude on the floor. The sergeant withdrew and shouted to her to get dressed. Lola emerged briefly in a blue satin dress for the photographers, then promptly withdrew again into the detention room. When the sergeant came to fetch her, she was nude once more. The only explanation that the young blonde could offer the court for her dis-robing was, "It's hot in there."

In court, Lola's attorney claimed that Mark Hansen "made a prac-tice of taking young Hollywood girls and promising them careers in the movies, theatres and night clubs. But Miss Titus fell in love with him, he promised to marry her, and didn't." According to her attor-ney, the taxi dancer had spent a year "knocking around Hollywood" trying to get a break. She had met Mark Hansen over Thanksgiving in 1948 and moved into his home for about a week. Hansen's testi-mony was that they were merely business acquaintances. "I never touched her," he claimed. But Lola told the judge that they had been intimate on numerous occasions: "I could recall every one of them if you had the time." At that point, Judge Byrne's gavel came down, and he ordered the jury out of the courtroom so he could admonish Lola to answer only the questions that were asked.

At the end of her trial, Lola was convicted and sent to the Patton State Hospital for the insane. Her short, sad life was to end in that red-brick, neo-Gothic pile only a decade later, at the age of thirty. But Lola's brief, meteoric, satin-bedecked track through the headlines of Tinseltown was more than just pathetic. It served—yet again—to buttress the rumors of a link between Mark Hansen and the Dahlia murder. Even more significantly, the fact that Hansen had called out, "Get me Brown," on being shot, imprinted on the public conscious-ness the idea of a close connection between the businessman from Aalborg and the Brown brothers. Months later, the episode was to come back to haunt Sergeant Finis Brown.

By the fall of 1949, Aggie Underwood and Paul De River were buoyed by the promise of a full re-investigation of the Dahlia case. The newspapers and public were baying for it. "A grand jury inves-tigation of the police handling of the 'Black Dahlia' murder, with a Hollywood millionaire as the central figure in the probe, is shaping up," reported the *Long Beach Independent* in September. "The jury intends to look into sinister reports that a racket tie-up involving the police has stalled the investigation of the slaying, unsolved for more than 2½ years." Aggie's *Herald-Express* was more explicit. Under the banner headline "Link Rich Hollywood Figure to Stalling of Dahlia Probe—Racket Tie-Up Is Charged," the paper reported:

> Sinister reports that a racket tie-up involving Los Angeles police has stalled the lagging investigation of the "Black Dahlia" murder mystery, unsolved for more than two and one-half years, will be probed by the county Grand Jury, the Herald-Express learned today.
>
> The jury will examine reports that powerful interests affecting the embattled and faction-fighting police department have sought to suppress or minimize crucial evidence in the butcher slaying, a jury spokesman admitted.
>
> Besides one or more suspects in the actual slaying of the "Black Dahlia"—Elizabeth Short, 22, whose mutilated body was found January 15, 1947 in a weed-covered lot on Norton avenue near Coliseum drive—the evidence involves a wealthy Hollywood figure, according to the report.
>
> For several months the Herald-Express, which brought the current police vice investigation to Grand Jury attention, has been checking the reports of irregularities in the "Black Dahlia" case.
>
> Results of this checking were presented to members of the Grand Jury, whose official interest was disclosed in a story printed exclusively by the Herald-Express Tuesday.
>
> "The reasons for the on-again, off-again investigation have become as big a mystery as the 'Black Dahlia' murder mystery itself," a Grand Jury spokesman said today.
>
> "In the face of the reports, we want to give interested parties opportunities to explain or justify their actions—or lack of actions."
>
> Efforts of duty-devoted policemen to determine what

part, if any, the wealthy Hollywood figure played in the life and ghastly death of Miss Short have been thwarted, they charge, by high-ranking police personnel.

In the mystery within the mystery, these policemen, convinced that they were on the brink of solving the case, were suddenly called off the investigation and assigned to other duties.

These officers met a mysterious stone wall of opposition among some of their superiors when diligent cross-checking disclosed the name of the wealthy figure who is known to be on close personal terms with one of the more powerful members of the police department.

"I don't know why anybody should be excited by what happened to the 'Black Dahlia,'" one high-ranking police executive is quoted as having declared. "She's just another butchered ____.*"

Another high ranking executive fell asleep during questioning of a prime suspect, later released, in the case.

The article—printed in the *Herald-Express* on September 8—revealed the full extent of Aggie's pioneering investigative journalism. It made clear that under her stewardship the newspaper had, "for several months," been "checking the reports of irregularities in the 'Black Dahlia' case." Moreover, that the paper had itself presented the "results of this checking" to the grand jury. As an aside, the report revealed an astonishing indifference to the case on the part of "higher executives" at the LAPD. Elizabeth Short was "just another butchered ____." Nobody should be excited by her murder. One top police officer had even fallen asleep during the questioning of a prime suspect who was later released (presumably Leslie Dillon).

With public anger at an all-time high, the time was ripe for a showdown, a confrontation in which the citizens of Los Angeles

---

* Presumably an expletive, redacted in the original article.

would at last call to account their police department, through investigation by their chosen representatives on the grand jury. After two and a half years of smoke and mirrors, the press and public would finally get to the bottom of what was going on in the Dahlia case. Or so they thought.

PART 3

RAW DEAL

"It's like any other business,
only here the blood shows."

—*CHAMPION* (1949)

KEY WITNESS

While Aggie Underwood carried out her newspaper exposé of the irregularities in the Dahlia investigation, Dr. Paul De River drew attention to them in a different way. He alerted the Los Angeles grand jury privately to what was going on. As his mouthpiece, he used an old friend.

Fred Witman was a seasoned private investigator who had been in the detective business for ten years. In 1949, he ran a licensed PI business downtown, near the intersection of Spring and Fourth Streets. It was a ten-minute walk from the Biltmore Hotel, in a part of town where the trolley cars clanged as they transported women in cheap shoes and brash makeup to the incandescent streetlights and taxi-dancing halls of Main Street. As a gumshoe, Witman specialized in defense cases. He had also handled technical investigations for the mechanical pencil corporation Eversharp. He had known De River for thirteen years.

At the beginning of July 1949—around the time that Thad Brown took over as chief of detectives—the doctor made an urgent telephone call to Fred. He showed Witman the file on the Dahlia case. He told the private investigator he had also shown the file to an appellate court judge.* The doctor knew that, with Thad Brown in a position

---

* This was most likely the distinguished Judge Thomas P. White, presiding judge on the Albert Dyer case, appellate judge on the "Sleepy Lagoon" case, and a lifelong friend of Dr. De River and Aggie Underwood. (See page 86.)

of unprecedented power, the Dahlia file would be suppressed. It had to be sent to the grand jury without delay, even though such an action would—as the doctor well knew—kill his career in the Los Angeles Police Department. On September 9, 1949, Fred Witman sent the doctor's file to the grand jury criminal complaints committee. "The cause of the obstruction to this inquiry is far more mysterious than the crimes themselves," wrote Witman in his covering letter to the committee. He was, he stated, "appalled at the splendid leads that had been neglected" in the case. Leslie Dillon, he believed, ought to be judged by a "jury of his peers," and "not by a police department torn by internal embarrassments."

On the morning of September 23, 1949, Fred Witman arrived at the Hall of Justice for a secret meeting with Deputy DA Arthur Veitch and Leo Stanley, chief of the DA's Bureau of Investigation.* He was sworn in and his testimony to the prosecutors was given under oath.

"My interest in the Dahlia case," Witman told Veitch and Stanley, "began rather casually, I should guess about three months after the killing, at which time I phoned my friend Dr. De River and made two suggestions: one, that there was considerable reason in my mind to suspect the killer was an embalmer or had experience in an undertaking establishment.† The other suggestion was this: that there was no need to try to find the killer because of the nature of the crime and my knowledge of such persons. I felt that there was a strong probability that the killer would reveal himself. Dr. De River concurred."

Witman told Veitch and Stanley about the early correspondence between Leslie Dillon and Dr. De River, and the shadowing of Dillon in Miami by Officer Jones from the Gangster Squad. He recounted the strange history of the relationship between "Jack," alias Jack Sand/Leslie Dillon and "Jeff," alias Jeff Connors, and Connors's

---

* The transcript of the sworn evidence given by Witman to Veitch and Stanley of the Los Angeles DA's office remained secret, and was not released until the 2000s.

† Leslie Dillon had allegedly worked for some weeks in a mortuary. (See page 113.)

subsequent arrest and sudden release, without any promised "confrontation" occurring. He repeated De River's conviction that Dillon's behavior manifested the need to be identified with his crime by getting somehow mixed up with the investigation, by putting himself on center stage. "He has to check in. He's very much like a pyromaniac. He sets a fire and helps the Fire Department put out the fire. You have the case, too, of Albert Dyer, who led the authorities in the search for the body of the child he had killed. Dillon has to put himself forward in this in my judgment."

Witman went on to tell the prosecutors that a bellhop friend of Dillon's called Woody had informed the police that, a few days before the murder, Dillon had left his employment at a San Francisco hotel. Shortly after January 15, he had returned to San Francisco, cleared his apartment, and returned to Los Angeles. Just after this statement was taken, however, a member of the Los Angeles Police Department visited Woody in San Francisco. He convinced the bellhop that his recollections were faulty: Dillon had not been in Los Angeles, but San Francisco at the time of the murder. The first policeman was "young and inexperienced," and his statement was therefore "discounted." Witman also told Veitch and Stanley about the leaking of Officer Waggoner's report by Aggie Underwood in the *Herald-Express* earlier that month, only to be blown down by Thad Brown in the *Examiner* shortly afterward.

Next, Witman showed the prosecutors a photograph of the dog leash that had been found in Dillon's suitcase, along with the razors and phenobarbital pills.* The leash, Witman said, had been examined by the police department, who claimed that there was no blood on it. However, Witman asserted, the leash had subsequently been subjected to fluoroscopic examination, and definitely revealed a blood spot.

Witman also showed Veitch and Stanley a sketch that Dillon had made, apparently showing the layout of a building. "I have studied

* See page 112.

this sketch at some length before I ever went to the motel on South Flower Street," he told the prosecutors. "When I went down there and saw the place, I said, 'My God, that explains the whole thing!'" Witman pointed to a part of the sketch. "He came in here. There are the sounds of the screams and whatnot. He walks out and goes over here, dumps the body and going back to his word, 'completely annihilates it, blots it out.' This drawing here has undoubtedly great phallic significance. These dots all around, the character of the dots are Dillon through and through, and appear in other communications." When Dr. De River confronted Dillon with the sketch, Dillon "acknowledged it as his own, and was unable to explain it." Thus, according to Fred Witman, Leslie Dillon had actually drawn a detailed sketch of a building plan that, in Witman's and De River's view, exactly corresponded to the layout of the Aster Motel.*

Witman went on to tell Veitch and Stanley that the LAPD had sent its chemists out to the Aster Motel, to test the cabins for blood. The chemists had reported positive samples of human blood. And yet, "Four days after the report came in, I am advised that the Police Department refused to put reliance on it because certain substances were found also to be there, and the substance that the police department claimed to have been mixed in with the blood to make the findings unreliable, were the substances that Dillon said that Jeff Connors would have used to clean the blood off the body."† Witman also proffered an explanation for the lacerations to the sides of the victim's mouth, extending it to "hideous proportions." Dillon, he said, had told Dr. De River in correspondence that Jeff Connors preferred girls with "big mouths." Furthermore, Dillon—as both the doctor and the LAPD had previously stated—knew the secret facts about

---

* A copy of the sketch was admitted into evidence by Fred Witman and examined by Veitch and Stanley at the secret hearing. It appears to have subsequently disappeared.

† The findings of the LAPD's forensic testing of the rooms at the Aster Motel are discussed in more detail on page 261 onwards.

the mutilations that had been deliberately held from the public, facts that only the killer would know.*

But Witman's biggest revelation to the prosecutors was to come. From his file, the PI produced a previously unpublicized close-up of a photograph from the crime scene.

"I told you that Dillon initials nearly everything that he touches. You will see the letter 'D' carved in this pubic [region] after the pubic hair had been shaved off and slashing been done on the body."

Prosecutor Veitch took a close look at the photograph. "There is also apparently an 'E' or an 'F' there."

Stanley examined the photograph. "Definite 'E.'"

"Looks like 'E D,'" said Veitch.

"I don't know," said Witman, "but the 'D' is there, and here a picture of the same again, showing that 'D.'" He showed the investigators another close-up photograph.

The photographs showing the purported carvings of the initials "D" and "E/F" on Elizabeth Short's body had never been released by the LAPD. But they were admitted by Fred Witman into evidence at the secret hearing, as photographs #295-771, 1-15-47 G.L.†

Fred Witman's explosive evidence before the DA investigators made a grand jury inquiry into the Dahlia case inevitable. Within a few weeks, even the acting police chief, William Worton, was supporting the lobby for an inquiry into the case. The retired Marine general, who seemed finally to have gotten wind of something afoot, called a press conference to report on his first three months in office in October. "I frankly believe that the Dahlia investigation was not properly handled," the chief said. "However, I wish to assure you that this case is now being properly studied and should shortly be ready for

---

* See page 113.

† This was a generic serial number on all the Dahlia crime scene photographs: it gave number of photograph, date, and the initials of the photographer.

investigation by the grand jury." There had, the chief admitted with masterful understatement, been some "bungling" in the investigation, the result of "petty chiseling within the department."

It was an unprecedented situation. A police chief was personally handing over, for the grand jury's independent investigation, one of his department's own cases. A stronger vote of no-confidence would be hard to imagine. In fact, the new chief was all too ready to admit, "I can't trust a soul in the whole department."*

What Chief Worton did not reveal at the press conference was that the decision to refer the Dahlia case to the grand jury had been the result of a secret meeting between himself and the DA's office, a meeting called after Fred Witman gave his evidence to Veitch and Stanley. At that meeting, it was decided that the DA would effectively re-investigate the case on behalf of the grand jury, concentrating on a short list of prime suspects drawn from an examination of the police files. At the top of the suspect list were Leslie Dillon and Mark Hansen. The stage was therefore finally set for the Dahlia investigation to be taken over by nineteen good men, on behalf of the citizens of the City of Angels.

For as long as anyone could remember, the Los Angeles County grand jury had sat in Room 548 on the fifth floor of the old downtown Hall of Justice. It was here that, back in 1937, indictments had been handed down on Earl Kynette and his LAPD cronies for the bombing of Harry Raymond in the Clifford Clinton affair. And it was also here that, earlier in the summer of '49, similar indictments had been handed down against Chief Clemence Horrall, his assistant Joe Reed, and Sergeant Elmer V. Jackson, for their roles in the Brenda Allen scandal.

---

* The chief's referral of the Dahlia case to independent investigation by the grand jury could only mean that he did not have confidence in his own officers to investigate it. It is possible that Worton saw evidence of an implacable standoff between the Gangster and Homicide details on the case, and was reluctant to enter the fray.

The official purpose of the Los Angeles grand jury, chosen annually from the ranks of the good citizens of the City of Angels, was to investigate the conduct of public authorities. To this end, every year each of sixty-five superior court judges would select two prospective jurors. The original list of one hundred and thirty would then be winnowed down to thirty names. The thirty names would be placed in a wheel. Nineteen names would be withdrawn from the wheel. Each juror received two dollars a day, plus fifteen cents a mile one way from his home. The presiding judge of the Superior Court selected the grand jury foreman.

Most years, the denizens of City Hall and the upper echelons of law enforcement would manage to rig the grand jury with compliant jurors. Jurors who obediently followed the opinions of the investigators appointed by the district attorney's office, who by their reports, effectively controlled what the jury was allowed to see. But, every once in a while, there would be a jury that refused to toe the line, that rebelled from the control of its prosecutor-appointed investigators. A jury that became a real thorn in the side of the powers that be, probing into what was truly going on behind the revolving doors of City Hall, or in the closed investigation bureaus of the Halls of Justice. Such a grand jury would be termed a "runaway" jury. The 1949 grand jury was such a one.

The tone of the 1949 grand jury was set by a tough and distinguished foreman. Harry A. Lawson had been born in Nova Scotia. Later he had migrated to Idaho, where he had worked himself up from beat reporter on a Boise newspaper, through to city editor, and, finally, newspaper owner and publisher. But like so many others, Lawson soon felt the call of the West Coast. In 1931, he left the snowy peaks of Idaho for the Californian sun, with his wife in tow and $500 in his pocket. He settled northeast of Los Angeles, in the town of Eagle Rock—a cluster of houses at the foot of a red rock slashed by a jagged laceration that would, at certain times of the day, show the silhouette of an eagle in flight. It was only a stone's throw from where Robert "Red" Manley was arrested by the cops. In this northeastern suburb of the City of Angels, Harry Lawson began a new life as publisher of the local newspaper, the *Eagle Rock Sentinel*. But politics and campaigning ran in Lawson's blood: as newspaper owner and president of the Eagle Rock Chamber of Commerce, he was usually involved in some local crusade or another, cleaning up parts of town. Now in his late sixties, Harry was determined in his role as foreman of the 1949 grand jury to clean up the city as a whole. If that meant breaking up police-protected rackets such as those associated with Brenda Allen and Mickey Cohen, or indicting vice cops such as Elmer V. Jackson or even the likes of Thad or Finis Brown, so be it.

On October 18, 1949, at a closed session of the grand jury committee, Dr. Paul De River gave evidence on the Dahlia case, in secret, at Harry Lawson's invitation. Lawson did not consult the DA's office before inviting De River to attend the committee session, and the contents of the discussion were never divulged. It was an omission that would not be forgiven or forgotten by the DA's office. Lawson's secret session with the doctor gave a strong signal that this grand jury was prepared to take matters into its own hands. But even "runaway" grand juries determined to get to the truth, like this one, faced one big problem. They were dependent on the reports of the DA's investigators. And the DA's investigators, in their turn, were dependent on the primary police officers who were assigned to assist them on the case. The DA investigator allocated in this instance to assist the grand jury in its Dahlia investigation was a stolid, droopy-eyed prosecutor, Lieutenant Frank Jemison. Assigned to assist Jemison were an officer of the Homicide Division, Ed Barrett; an intelligence officer by the name of Sergeant Jack Smyre (apparently appointed "to investigate particularly the activities of psychiatrist Dr. Paul De River"); and Sergeant Finis Brown.

While the grand jury prepared to begin its investigation into the Dahlia case, Chief of Detectives Thad Brown sent one of his officers, Inspector Hugh Farnham of the Detective Bureau, on a secret mission.* This was to meet with Leslie Dillon and his ex-wife, Georgia, who were now back in Oklahoma. The purpose of the meeting was finally to eliminate Dillon as a suspect by establishing incontrovertibly that he was in San Francisco, as he claimed, on the night of the murder of Elizabeth Short.

When Hugh Farnham reported on his Oklahoma meeting with Dillon to Thad Brown, he wrote that he had trouble, at first, with Dillon's attorney. "But I finally convinced him," he continued, "that I was just as interested in clearing Dillon, if he was innocent, as he was." But the October meeting in Oklahoma failed to provide the corroboration of Dillon's alibi that Thad Brown was looking for. "Almost three years have passed, and their memory is pretty dim," wrote Farnham of the Dillons. Leslie Dillon could not, Farnham said, remember working anywhere after he left his job as bellhop at the Devonshire Hotel in San Francisco, on January 8, 1947.† Farnham also attached, to his letter to Thad, a statement of what Mrs. Dillon had to say about her ex-husband's whereabouts on the day.‡ "Nothing very concrete as you will notice, but has some possibilities," he wrote. The secret meeting with Dillon in Oklahoma was not revealed to the grand jury.

On the same day that Thad Brown received Farnham's letter confirming that Dillon could not establish his alibi in San Francisco at the time of the murder, Lieutenant Frank Jemison made a prelimi-

---

* Inspector Hugh Farnham was not infrequently entrusted by Thad Brown on sensitive missions. When the actress Jean Spangler "disappeared" in late 1949 in a possible mob-connected murder, Farnham was tasked with searching an area of Ferndell Park where the actress might have gone missing. Farnham was also called as a character witness by a police officer accused of mob connections in the convoluted "Seven Dwarves" affair, involving Mickey Cohen. When Detective Lieutenant William Harper was accused of accepting bribes by Worton's new Intelligence Division in 1950, he chose Hugh Farnham, along with two other LAPD officers, to hear his disciplinary case. Farnham took the exams for LAPD police chief to replace Clemence Horrall in 1950, coming out among the top five candidates.
† Contrast with the evidence of Tommy Harlow and Mrs. Pearl McCromber, that Leslie Dillon came to Los Angeles sporadically by bus to work for Harlow in January 1947 (page 135).
‡Georgia Dillon's account as to Leslie Dillon's whereabouts on the night of January 14, 1947—surely one of the most pertinent, since she was his wife at the time—has never been released.

nary report to his bosses at the DA's office. The report was based on the information given to him by Officers Finis Brown and Ed Barrett of Homicide. It was later read to the grand jury. The purpose of the report was manifestly obvious: to stave off any further inquiry into Leslie Dillon.

The report began by acknowledging that there were aspects of the Dahlia case that were problematic. There was controversy and uncertainty over the exact whereabouts of Leslie Dillon on the night of January 14/15, 1947. Witnesses claimed to have seen Elizabeth Short in a drugged state at the Aster Motel on South Flower Street in January, and yet, although Elizabeth's vital organs had been sent to the county chemist for analysis, they had apparently been thrown away in a laboratory cleanup, with no analysis having been done. Under Sergeant Brown's helpful supervision, Lieutenant Jemison had listened to selected extracts of the tape-recorded conversations between Leslie Dillon and Dr. De River.* Approximately half of what he heard was unintelligible. However, from what Jemison could make out from the little he could understand, there was no evidence that Dillon knew any "secret facts" relating to the murder. In particular, Jemison cited the following extract from the transcript of the recordings:

> *Dr. De River:* What do you think the killer did with the hair
> he shaved off the private parts of the body of Elizabeth Short?
> *Dillon:* I think the killer would probably have thrown that
> into a toilet and flushed it.
> *Dr. De River:* What do you think a killer such as he was
> would do with the piece of flesh with the tattoo on it after he
> cut it off her thigh?

---

* The originals of these recordings have, apparently, disappeared. For further discussion of the disappearance of physical evidence, see the preface of this book.

The corpse was decorously airbrushed for the newspapers to
remove the slashes to the mouth, and was shown covered with a blanket.
(Getty Images/Archive Photos)

Robert "Red" Manley
kisses his twenty-two-
year-old wife Harriette
for the photographers.
(Getty Images/
Bettmann)

Elizabeth Short, the black-haired Hollywood hopeful
from Massachusetts whose murder became one of the
most notorious unsolved cases in American history.
*(USC Los Angeles Examiner archive, Courtesy of University
of Southern California, on behalf of the USC
Libraries Special Collections)*

Jimmy Richardson
chaining Luckies.
*(UCLA/James Hugh
Richardson archive)*

Aggie Underwood.
(USC Los Angeles
Examiner *archive, Courtesy
of University of Southern
California, on behalf
of the USC Libraries
Special Collections)*

Evidence in the case including Elizabeth's address book
and the package addressed to the *Los Angeles Examiner*.
(Getty Images/Archive Photos)

Det. Sgt. Bill Cummings
inspects the contents of
Elizabeth's suitcase and
hatbox, checked into the
Greyhound bus station
when she was with
Robert "Red" Manley.
(Los Angeles Times *Photo-
graphic Archives [Collection
1429]. UCLA Library Special
Collections, Charles E. Young
Research Library, UCLA)*

Mark Hansen, the elusive Hollywood nightclub and movie theater owner and prime suspect for the murder of Elizabeth Short.

(Los Angeles Times Photographic Archives [Collection 1429]. UCLA Library Special Collections, Charles E. Young Research Library, UCLA)

Ann Toth, Hollywood bit-part player and close friend of Elizabeth, besieged by photographers.

(Los Angeles Times Photographic Archives [Collection 1429]. UCLA Library Special Collections, Charles E. Young Research Library, UCLA)

Leslie Dillon (center) is questioned by (from left to right): Dr. John Paul De River, Det. Lt. Willie Burns (head of the Gangster detail), LAPD chief Clemence Horrall, and Captain Francis Kearney (head of Homicide).

(USC Los Angeles Examiner archive, Courtesy of University of Southern California, on behalf of the USC Libraries Special Collections)

Hollywood madam Brenda Allen with her attorney Max Solomon. Brenda's evidence in 1949 about her connections with the LAPD through her boyfriend, Sgt. Elmer Jackson of the LAPD Vice Squad, were to help bring down the police department and lead to the biggest scandal in its history.

(USC Los Angeles Examiner archive, Courtesy of University of Southern California, on behalf of the USC Libraries Special Collections)

The entrance to the Aster Motel.

(loyaltyphoto)

Leslie Dillon ascends an ominously worded bus on his release, threatening
to sue the city authorities for false imprisonment in "at least six figures."
(USC Los Angeles Examiner *archive, Courtesy of University of Southern California,
on behalf of the USC Libraries Special Collections)*

Dillon: Well, I think he would probably have thrown that
down the toilet and flushed it.*

Jemison continued to state that, in the opinion of the "present
administrators of the police department," there "was an error made
on the part of the preceding administrators when they assigned the
gangster squad and Dr. Paul De River as psychiatrist to investigate
the Short murder. They appear to be of the opinion that the homicide division officers should have had control over it at all times."
There was, Jemison continued, evidence of "some stupidity and care-
lessness on the part of the more inexperienced officers who were
working on the case," but no indication of "payoff, misconduct, or
concealment of facts on the part of any officers." Jemison would, he
continued, be available to present all material evidence from the files
to the grand jury in November. However, Sergeant Finis Brown was
"thoroughly familiar with their contents and could no doubt convey
any desired information." Finally, Jemison concluded, he and Officers Jack Smyre, Ed Barrett, and Finis Brown were of the opinion
that there was "insufficient evidence" to date upon which "any suspect could now be brought to trial for the murder of Elizabeth Short."

The obvious problem with Jemison's report was that it was reli-
ant on information provided by the very police officers—those of the
Homicide Division—whose conduct in the case was being investigated by the grand jury. Would the 1949 grand jury be discouraged
from taking the case further, as was clearly the intention? The LAPD
had not reckoned on Harry Lawson and his colleagues. The jurors
ignored Frank Jemison's advice. They determined that they would
carry on with the probe into Leslie Dillon, Mark Hansen, and the

---

* The difficulty with this quoted "extract" is that the date of the recording is not given. If it
was made when Dillon was wised up to the fact he was a suspect, he would obviously not be
giving out knowledge of key facts at this stage. Contrast this innocuous "explanation" with
the detailed explanation of the mutilations that Dr. De River recorded Dillon giving at the
interviews in Banning, with JJ O'Mara listening in. (See page 102.)

Aster Motel. They ordered Frank Jemison to go up to San Francisco in order to establish incontrovertibly where Leslie Dillon was on the night of January 14/15, 1947. And they determined to call up members of the police department to testify as to what had really happened in the Dahlia case.

THE GLASS
ALIBI

On November 1, 1949, DA Investigator Frank Jemison went up to San Francisco on the grand jury's instructions. His brief was to interview the witnesses who, according to the LAPD, provided alibis for Leslie Dillon. They were not a confidence-inspiring bunch.

Dillon himself had said, in the secret meeting in Oklahoma with Hugh Farnham, that he could not remember working anywhere after January 8, 1947, when he left his job as a bellhop at the Devonshire Hotel in San Francisco.* He had been fired from the Devonshire on this date, possibly on a theft or pandering charge.† At that point, Dillon said, he was planning to move to Los Angeles. He had sold the furniture in his San Francisco apartment to a couple by the name of Anderson. Mrs. Shirley Anderson, when questioned, thought—but

---

* Dillon's claim that he did not work anywhere after January 8 was contradicted by the evidence of Tommy Harlow and Mrs. Pearl McCromber, who stated that he came up to Tommy Harlow's office by bus from San Francisco in January. (See page 135.)

† Dillon was invariably fired by the hotels he worked for as a bellhop. He was fired from the Lankershim Hotel in San Francisco for pandering in February 1946, and in 1949 from a Santa Monica hotel for robbing the safe. In Oklahoma, it appeared he indulged in bootlegging.

was not certain—that she met Dillon in San Francisco on January 16. She came to view the furniture with her mother and stepfather the next day. A receipt for payment for the furniture in Dillon's handwriting was dated January 21. The registration cards of the El Cortez Hotel in San Francisco showed that Dillon had registered there, with wife and child, on January 20. He had then moved his family to Los Angeles, where they stayed at his mother-in-law's house on Normandie Avenue. He spent a brief spell in Santa Monica in March, where he burgled the safe of the Carmel Hotel. From then on he had done various jobs for Tommy Harlow, moving his family to the Aster Motel in March. In June he headed off to Oklahoma, where he was arrested for bootlegging. Finally, by the end of the year, he wound up in Florida.

The burning question, therefore, was: Where was Leslie Dillon between the dates of January 8, when he was sacked from the Devonshire Hotel, and January 16, when Shirley Anderson had seen him back at his apartment in San Francisco? The first alibi witness was Woodrow J. Wood, a bellhop described by the police as "hot." Dillon, just as he had "borrowed" Jeff Connors's name on occasion, had also been known to adopt the alias of "Woodrow," presumably in honor of this friend. Wood originally told the police that after Dillon was sacked from the Devonshire, he had gone to Los Angeles for about a week before he went to the El Cortez Hotel on January 20. This would have put Dillon squarely in Los Angeles during the period of the "missing week." But when re-interviewed, Wood changed his story. Now he said that in fact Dillon had been in San Francisco after he left the Devonshire, and that he had seen him every day during this time. Phil Compoli, a jobber subsalesman and hotel manager, said that he had seen Dillon on the afternoon of January 15, 1947. Grant Robertson, a Mill Valley taxicab driver, and his wife recalled having dinner with the Dillons at Clifton's Cafeteria on January 16 and stated that they had seen Leslie Dillon four or five times in the preceding week, on different days, Grant could not remember which.

Dillon, Robertson recalled, drove a black Ford with purple-painted taillights.*

In truth, there was no clear-cut evidence of Dillon's whereabouts between January 8 (the day he was sacked from the Devonshire in San Francisco) and January 15 (the morning Elizabeth's body was found in Leimert Park). The Andersons did not see him in his San Francisco apartment to view his furniture until January 16, and his friend Phil Compoli could only testify as to his presence there on the *afternoon* of January 15. It would have been perfectly possible, if Dillon had been in Los Angeles on the night of January 14, to complete the six-and-a-half-hour drive up to San Francisco the following morning, in time to meet Compoli. All the Robertsons could say was that they had seen Dillon in San Francisco, on four or five unspecified occasions, in the week prior to January 16. In fact, the only evidence that Dillon had been consistently in San Francisco from January 8 to 15 was that of the "hot" bellhop Woody, who had changed his story. Most perturbingly, the person who would have been expected to have given the soundest alibi—Dillon's own wife, Georgia—could, according to Hugh Farnham's letter to Thad Brown, give no clear account of his whereabouts. There was no doubt, on the other hand, that Dillon was in Los Angeles at the time of the anonymous telephone call to Jimmy Richardson (January 23) and the posting of the package containing the Dahlia's belongings from a Los Angeles downtown mailbox (January 24).

Not surprisingly, the grand jury was not impressed with the "alibi" evidence for Leslie Dillon that was turned up by Frank Jemison in San Francisco. Of course, the jurors had no idea that Thad Brown

---

* Compare the eyewitness description of a 1936 or 1937 dark Ford sedan seen at the body dump site of Norton and Coliseum in the early hours of the morning of January 15, 1947 (page 47); the landlady of the Normandie Avenue address where Dillon's mother-in-law lived saying that Dillon had owned a black Ford coupe during the two months he had resided there, from January to February 1947 (page 115); and Tommy Harlow stating that Dillon drove an old 1936 two-door black sedan during this period (page 135). The 1936/7 Ford coupe and the two-door sedan models were virtually indistinguishable.

had already sent an officer in secret to interview Leslie Dillon personally, and that Dillon had been unable to establish his alibi. The jurors therefore pressed on with their investigation. They called up the police officers involved in the case to give an account of what had happened.

By the time the first police officers were called to give evidence in December, the 1949 grand jury was virtually at the end of its term of office. Harry Lawson and his co-jurors had already heard detailed evidence about the cop tie-up with the prostitution racket through the liaison between Brenda Allen and her boyfriend on the LAPD Vice Squad, Elmer Jackson. After the grand jury's indictments in that affair, Chief Clemence Horrall and his assistant, Joe Reed, had resigned that summer, and the LAPD had itself collapsed and been put into receivership in the hands of Worton, the Marine general. So Harry Lawson and his colleagues could have had no illusions about what they were about to hear when the police officers who were to testify on the Dahlia case took the stand in room 548 of the Hall of Justice.

Members of the Gangster Squad were first on the stand. They recounted the story of the strange cross-state odyssey with Leslie Dillon and Dr. De River, stopping off at seedy motels on the route from Vegas to Los Angeles. Tough and wiry Willie Burns had, in General Worton's reshuffle, been demoted to a lieutenant police officer on day watch at the Venice Division. He told the jury about his bugging of the motel rooms with the help of Francis Kearney. The recordings of the interviews with Dillon were of poor quality, and it was difficult to make out the words. But Burns did recall that Dillon spoke in a "very soft, well-modulated voice."* JJ O'Mara, the Irishman with the killer blue stare, had—unlike many of his Gangster Squad colleagues—escaped demotion. He had been transferred

---

* Compare the "sly, soft voice" of the person believed to be the killer who called the *Examiner* offices on January 23, 1947, as recounted by Jimmy Richardson (page 48).

from the now-disbanded squad to the new internal espionage department that Chief Worton had created to replace it, the Intelligence
Division. JJ recalled Dillon's bizarre behavior when they visited the
body dump site at Norton and Thirty-ninth. It was O'Mara's opinion
that Dillon was thoroughly familiar with the area of Leimert Park.

The Gangster Squad went on to relate their investigations at the
A1 Trailer Park in Long Beach. Loren Waggoner—now transferred
to the University Division—testified how both Jiggs Moore, the
manager of the A1 Trailer Park, and the old man who lived there,
Mr. Carriere, were adamant that Elizabeth Short had stayed at the
trailer park with Leslie Dillon late in 1949. James Ahern, who like
Willie Burns had been demoted and was now a patrol sergeant in
the Newton Division, confirmed Waggoner's account. He testified
that there had been a possible confusion of Elizabeth Short with a
dark-haired, much older woman called Mrs. Ashford, who had lived
at the park with her husband at the same time as Leslie Dillon. Jiggs
Moore, however, had refused to accept that he was wrong in his identification, and, after being shown a photograph of Elizabeth Short,
had steadfastly maintained that she was the girl who was at the park
with Dillon.*

The Gangster Squad officers also revealed to the grand jury that
they had interviewed Mark Hansen in February at his office next to
the Florentine Gardens. "Hansen recalled a tall man coming to visit
Elizabeth Short six or seven times," said Waggoner. "He identified a
picture of Leslie Dillon, from about 25 photos, as the person who had
come to visit her." Hansen had said to Waggoner and Ahern, "This is
the fellow here. . . . I remember the side view of his face, and that's
the way his hair was combed." Ahern had said to Hansen, did he
realize that by making a positive identification, he could be sending
the man to prison for life? Hansen said he had better not be positive,

---

* Mrs. Ashford, who resided at the trailer park in 1946, was a married woman in her forties.
It seems highly unlikely that Jiggs Moore or Mr. Carriere would have confused her with the
twenty-two-year-old Elizabeth Short.

then, without seeing the man in person. When Waggoner handed the report to Finis Brown, Willie Burns, and Dr. De River, the doctor in particular had seemed to be very pleased. Finis Brown had no special reaction at the time. However, Waggoner testified, "I believe that Mr. Brown found Mark Hansen, and it later turned up, they said that identification was just a big wild story, there was nothing to it."

Officer James Ahern confirmed Waggoner's account that Mark Hansen had identified a photograph of Leslie Dillon, saying, "This looks like the fellow who came six or seven times to pick her up," but he had said he would like to see Dillon in person to make a positive identification.* Asked who investigated Mark Hansen, Ahern stated that "at all points" it was Sergeant Brown.

"Wasn't Mark Hansen a friend of this sergeant?" a juryman asked Ahern.

"Pardon?"

"Wasn't Mark Hansen a friend of this sergeant? Sergeant Brown?"

"I wouldn't know whether he was or not. I know that Brown interrogated him in the primary investigation; as to whether or not they were personal friends, I don't know."

"In other words, you are more or less at liberty to question anyone, except to a certain point Mr. Hansen? Is he more or less Mr. Brown's private witness?" wondered another juror.

"Let me ask you this," said Harry Lawson. "Was it significant to you that a man of Mark Hansen's position and title by any chance would be down in a motel like that sometimes?"

"Well—"

"You ever draw any conclusions on that, or give it any thought?"

"Yes, I gave it thought. If the girl was there, and Hansen was there—he was directly concerned with this murder."

"Did you form any opinion, sergeant, as to who might be a strong likely suspect? Do you care to express any opinion on it?"

---

* Mark Hansen was never taken to see Dillon in person, in order to make a conclusive identification.

"In my opinion, until it is proven different, there are several people that are involved in the thing at the motel, and who withheld the evidence, which we had to drag out, who are suspects along with Hansen and Dillon."

"Hoffman?"

"Yes, sir, and his wife, Mrs. Sartain."

James Ahern's partner Archie Case confirmed that it was common knowledge among the Gangster Squad that Mark Hansen was friendly with Sergeant Finis Brown. Archie, like JJ O'Mara, had been transferred to the new Intelligence Division.

"I want to ask you this question," a juror asked Archie. "At any time in this investigation, did you ever hear it said, or was it talked among department members, that some certain police officer was on very friendly and cordial terms with Mark Hansen?"

"Oh yes, I've heard that said."

"Who was that officer?"

"Brown."

"Which Brown, please?"

"Sergeant Finis Brown."

A new revelation from the Gangster Squad was that they had investigated Mark Hansen not only in relation to the Dahlia case, but in connection with a jewelry scam involving a man called Bill Miller. Willie Burns told the jury that Miller ran a jewelry store on Frank Street, out Santa Monica way. He recently went bust. Before his creditors could get to his valuable jewelry stock, it had mysteriously disappeared. The stock had been replaced with worthless, low-grade stones. At the same time, there was talk of the jewelry going to Mark Hansen, and a $15,000 transfer from Hansen to Miller.* The Gangster Squad strongly suspected that Mark Hansen, with his known connections to organized crime through his friend Jimmy Utley, was somehow mixed up in the jewelry scam. There were also possible links to the Dahlia case: one witness had said that, after the

---

* $15,000: over $150,000 in today's money.

murder, Beth's old housemate Ann Toth had called up Bill Miller and told him, "We had better get together." The Moormans, too, had said that the man who stayed at the Aster Motel in January '47—with whom they had dined, and whom they identified as Mark Hansen—had driven with them to an unidentified location downtown, from which he had collected "a large suitcase."* A search was made of Mark Hansen's home, but the jewelry was never found. The Gangster Squad went to the LAPD chief to get Hansen's bank account checked for a transfer to Bill Miller, but nothing came of it as far as Burns knew. If there was an investigation into Hansen's bank account, he had never heard about it.

The Gangster Squad officers went on to recount the story of the blood-caked room at the Aster Motel. Waggoner told of how he and Officer Ward had painstakingly developed the confidence of the slippery old ex-con manager of the Aster, Henry Hoffman, leading to the explosive revelations by Hoffman that had been filed in Waggoner's final confidential report, leaked to the *Herald-Express*. According to Ahern, the Gangster Squad had attempted to find out whether Leslie Dillon had stayed at the motel in January 1947. The motel records established that Dillon had definitely lived there for a few days from April 5, 1947, but two witnesses—Dillon's real estate agent employer Tommy Harlow, and a woman who worked at his office, Mrs. Pearl McCromber—had stated he had come over on a bus from San Francisco in the early part of January. The question had been complicated by the fact that Mrs. Hoffman burned the motel's registration cards for that month.

"How did she happen to burn those cards?" Harry Lawson asked Ahern.

"Well, she said she was in a small apartment with her two children. The cards were getting in the way. She just threw them in the fire and burned them."

---

* Los Angeles' historic Jewelry District is located downtown, a stone's throw from the Aster Motel.

"That is rather strange, isn't it?"

"I thought so, yes."

All the Gangster Squad officers confirmed that they had been making "remarkable progress" in the Dahlia investigation when they were suddenly and inexplicably ordered off the case in the summer. At this point, the files were turned over to Homicide. In Waggoner's opinion, the transfer was baffling. "The case could have been solved if we had been allowed to carry on our investigation. I was suddenly taken off the case, and I never did learn the reason why."* Garth Ward, Waggoner's partner in the Aster Motel investigations with University Division, told the jury that he and Waggoner had asked to see the files on the case, but when the lieutenant at the University Division telephoned Homicide to ask for them, the request was denied. Garth himself had overheard the telephone conversation when the lieutenant asked for the file and was refused. He thought Thad Brown had been on the other end of the phone.

Archie Case agreed that this was the only instance where a Homicide case had been transferred to the Gangster detail, and then back to Homicide. He had no explanation for why this had happened. But even before the transfer, according to Willie Burns, from the moment that Dillon was booked and released, Sergeant Brown had been assigned to "assist" in evaluating the reports made by Burns's men. Finis Brown, Burns testified, read all the Gangster Squad reports on the case. Often he would go out and re-interview witnesses himself, if he thought the reports of Burns's men "were not specific enough. . . . Brown would say maybe, 'This is this fellow's opinion. Will he testify to that?' And the officer would say, 'I'm not sure about that.' So Brown would go out and see him and find out."

And somehow, when the witnesses were re-interviewed by Finis Brown, their stories would change. A picture that had seemed clear

---

* Waggoner's allegations were published by the intrepid *Long Beach Independent* crime reporter Chuck Cheatham. Chuck later said that he believed Finis Brown was a "bagman" for Mark Hansen. (See page 77.)

in the early Gangster Squad reports became, suddenly, confusing and riddled with contradictions.

"Do you remember," asked DA Arthur Veitch, when questioning Willie Burns, "Assistant Chief Reed ever talking to some officers and saying to them, 'Have you any serious doubt or if you don't believe this fellow Dillon is guilty, I wish you would come out and say so'? Do you recognize anything of that sort being said in front of Chief Reed, at a meeting you attended?"

"I attended a couple of conferences on the things. I am not going to say whether it was or not. I don't remember." Burns hedged the question. But he confirmed that he still considered Leslie Dillon very much a live suspect in the case: "He certainly hasn't been eliminated in my mind." The main problem, in Burns's view, was pinning Leslie Dillon down as to where he was at the time of the murder: "I sure would like to know what Dillon was doing between January 9 and 16. I have been unable to find him anywhere, either in San Francisco or here."

"He is a person whom it might transpire that evidence might tie him in definitely?"

"That is right. That is my opinion."

Like Willie Burns, all the Gangster Squad officers were convinced there were strong circumstances linking Leslie Dillon and Mark Hansen to the murder, and that the events at the Aster Motel demanded further inquiry. They agreed that they had seen most of Dr. De River's evidence in the case, and had confidence in him.

"Did you form your own opinion as to possible suspects?" Harry Lawson asked Garth Ward.

"Yes."

"Do you mind expressing them?"

"I feel that, from my investigation, there must be something more than just coincidence in this Dillon and Hansen deal out on Flower. I am firmly convinced in my own mind there is something there, or I would say, a good probability."

"Sergeant O'Mara, with your knowledge of police investigation and so forth, at the time you were with Dr. De River, with this here

Leslie Dillon, were you satisfied that he was a likely suspect in the Elizabeth Short case?"

"I would say I was."

Archie Case was even more categorical in his support of Dr. De River and suspicions of Dillon and Hansen.

"You are familiar, of course, with Dr. De River's analysis of this case?" a juror asked Case.

"Yes."

"What were your relations with Dr. De River? Were they friendly, co-operative?"

"Yes, I valued Dr. De River's part in this very much."

"Have you changed your attitude with regard to Dr. De River's analysis of the case?"

"No, I've got quite a lot of confidence in Dr. De River."

"You never changed your attitude with regard to De River's solution of the case?"

"No, I did not."

"You haven't now?"

"I haven't now."

"Do you have any opinion as to who the possible suspect in this case might be, in your investigation?"

"Yes sir, Dillon is a good suspect, and Mark Hansen."

Even the redheaded Iowan Con Keller, who had played a minor role in the investigation, said he believed all along—and still did—that Leslie Dillon was a "pretty good suspect." He was also sure that Mark Hansen was "mixed into it somewhere."*

At the end of their testimony, the grand jury congratulated the Gangster Squad, in particular Officer Ahern, on their frankness.

"I'd like to compliment Officer Ahern," said a juror.

"He's been cooperative and intelligent and helpful," said another.

"A fine witness," said Harry Lawson.

---

* Con Keller also said that he had checked for the presence of Leslie Dillon in San Diego and that, although not confirmed, he "looked familiar" to several people there.

—

So ended the testimony before the grand jury of the members of the Gangster Squad. Every one confirmed his strong suspicions about Leslie Dillon and Mark Hansen. Every one stated that he believed they had been on the verge of a breakthrough in the case. Not one could account for why the case had been taken away from them and the investigation terminated.

Another curious circumstance was that, as reported by Aggie's *Herald-Express* newspaper, there were in fact seven officers who testified before the grand jury on December 1, 1949. Six were listed by name: Ahern, O'Mara, Keller, Waggoner, Case, and Ward. But there was also listed in Aggie's report an unnamed "officer who went to Florida during one phase of the probe." That officer must have been Officer Jones, who tailed Leslie Dillon in Miami. His testimony was never released.*

In their testimony before the grand jury, all the members of the Gangster Squad had voiced their personal confidence in Dr. De River's "solution" of the case. And what was the doctor's solution? Incredibly—or perhaps not incredibly—it is not recorded. Because Dr. De River's grand jury testimony, given at Harry Lawson's invitation in October, was the only evidence of a witness, in the entire proceedings, that was not transcribed.† His words were registered only in the heads of the jurors themselves, now dead and buried— although a remarkable oral record of the doctor's "solution" was to surface, many years later.

For now, however, the baton passed from the Gangster Squad to the Homicide Division. Harry Hansen and Finis Brown were about to take the stand.

Harry "the Hat" stepped into the witness box in his trademark pin-striped suit and loud tie. If he had knocked out the dent in the fedora

---

* The grand jury record of Jones's evidence is not included with the transcripts of the other witness evidence and seems to have disappeared.

† With the possible exception of Officer Jones, whose witness evidence, as mentioned above, has disappeared.

he clutched in his hand, or given an extra spit and polish to his mellow brown oxfords, he wouldn't have admitted to it. Harry's long, lean, basset-hound face was as droopy-eyed and expressionless as usual. It was a face that would, in the ensuing years, become known in many American households as the LAPD spokesman for the Dahlia case. Harry "the Hat," smooth and charming on the surface, was invariably wheeled out whenever a sound bite from the cops was required.

Harry told the jury about his involvement in the early stages of the Dahlia investigation. He had been one of the first officers on the crime scene. He recalled the address book that had been mailed to the *Examiner* newspaper, and agreed that it was "safe to assume" that the package was from the killer. The police had tried to get finger-prints off the package, but there were "a lot of blurs and smudges." Harry had interviewed Mark Hansen a few times in the early stages of the investigation. Every time, he had been accompanied by Ser-geant Brown.

The first Harry had heard of Leslie Dillon was when Captain Kearney, chief of Homicide, telephoned him in January and told him to hightail it to Highland Park Police Station, where a "hot new suspect" was being questioned. Dillon had been interrogated exhaustively at Highland Park, then questioned at the police acad-emy by Deputy DA John Barnes. Harry had been present at some of the interviews, but not all. He was asked what he thought about Dillon as a suspect: "I actually felt in my own mind that the man had no connection with the murder." Harry then went on to proffer his own, layman's "little pet theory" about the case: "I think that a medical man committed the murder, a very fine surgeon. I base that conclusion on the way the body was bisected." He was asked if the Homicide Division actually had any current suspects in the medical profession. "No, we have not."

If there was one single, overall impression that came from the evi-dence of Harry "the Hat," it was how little he knew about the Dillon and Mark Hansen angles in the Dahlia case. Apart from the early questioning of Mark Hansen in 1947, and of Leslie Dillon in January 1949, Harry had never, as he himself admitted, been involved in those aspects of the investigation. He knew nothing about the Aster Motel; nothing about Dillon's movements in or around Los Angeles. Everything relating to Leslie Dillon and Mark Hansen had, it appeared, been the preserve of Sergeant Finis Brown. Nor was Harry involved in advising the DA's office, or any aspect of the grand jury investigation. That, also, was the preserve of Sergeant Brown. Many years later, Harry was to give in a newspaper interview what was, perhaps, his true opinion of Elizabeth Short. "She didn't have any standards. She had an obviously low IQ. She was a man-crazy tramp. There were all kinds of men in her life, but only three had any sexual experience with her.* She was a tease. She asked for trouble. There wasn't much to like about her."

The time had come for Sergeant Finis Brown to take the stand. Squat and scruffy in his usual rumpled suit, with his belligerent bulldog expression, Finis made a marked contrast to his dapper colleague.

Brown began by running through the early history of the case, as Hansen had done. The receipt of the package containing the Dahlia's purse contents, which he agreed must have come from the killer, who clearly had a "mania for publicity"; the surprise arrest of Leslie Dillon, about whom he was told for the first time while patrolling artworks at the Berlin exhibition; the subsequent release of Leslie Dillon and his friend Jeff Connors without charge, after interviewing by others including himself. The investigation of Dillon, Finis claimed, was not yet complete: he was still considered a suspect, along with some fifty other individuals. The crucial issue was where Dillon was on the night of the murder—if it could be established whether he was in Los Angeles or San Francisco. Dillon's alibi that he was in San Francisco at the time was established by witnesses,

---

* Three men who had sexual experience with her: presumably Robert "Red" Manley, Peter Vetcher, and Carl Balsiger. (See pages 26, 71, and 244.)

not by "actual work record or anything that you can bring in as facts."
And being Dillon, a known pimp and bootlegger, Brown conceded
that his associates were not necessarily to be considered reliable alibi
witnesses.

"What was your acquaintance—if you had any prior to the time
he appeared in the police station—with Mark Hansen?" Harry
Lawson asked.

"That is the first time I knew who he was at all."

"You had no prior contact with the man before that time?"

"No."*

But the intrepid Harry Lawson remained undaunted. How was
it, he asked, that, when Mark Hansen was shot by Lola Titus on July
15, he uttered the now notorious words, "Get me Brown"? Finis's
explanation for the incident was convoluted and obscure. According to Brown, Mark Hansen had offered to act as a "stool pigeon" or
police informant, reporting to the LAPD the various criminal activities going on in the Los Angeles underworld.† Finis had pretended
to agree to this, but what he really wanted to do was to check out
Hansen himself. Therefore, the police had bugged Hansen's house
at Carlos Avenue—*with Hansen's knowledge.* Hansen thought the
bug was to pick up evidence of criminal activity at his home. In
fact, it was to spy on him. (How the cops proposed to pick up any
incriminating admissions from Mark Hansen when he knew his
home was bugged remained a mystery: a discrepancy not lost on
the jurors.)

It was in pursuance of this informer's agreement with Mark
Hansen, Brown said, that Lola Titus's name had cropped up. Brown
had obtained a photograph of Lola in the nude. He had evidence that

---

* Given that Finis's big brother Thad was in charge of Patrol Division, monitoring Divisional
Vice, it is inconceivable that Finis Brown would not even have heard of Mark Hansen, a
major player in Los Angeles vice activities, prior to January 1947.

† It seems highly unlikely that Hansen, a successful businessman with known connections
to organized crime, would have proffered his services for this dangerous activity.

she was involved in a lewd photography ring* as a model, and also
in narcotics. The police, through Mark Hansen's help, were about
to jump on Lola. Hence her accusation of Hansen, that he was a
"damned cop lover." While Hansen was in the hospital, the LAPD
crime lab checked the Carlos Avenue house for blood, with negative
results. Not surprisingly, the bug also turned up no incriminating
admissions relating to Elizabeth Short. When Hansen's house was
searched, however, two photographs of Elizabeth Short were found.
One was the Santa Barbara police mug shot, the other a photograph
taken by a young man called Glenn Sterns. Mark Hansen explained
that he had obtained the photographs from the police to help him
check out a girl who claimed to have known the Dahlia.†

One of the jurors pointed out that this was a highly peculiar
situation. There was evidence that Mark Hansen had been seen at
a motel on Flower Street in January. Numerous police officers had
testified that they had gotten to a certain point in the case and then
been transferred. Wasn't it unusual, in Brown's opinion, that there
had not been more effort to tie in the "man from Batavia" with
Mark Hansen? Finis's response was evasive. The investigation at
the Aster Motel was not complete.‡ The statements of the Moormans and the Hoffmans, which had identified Hansen at the motel,
were confusing and contradictory. If "a man like that was placed
in the witness box—I think it would blow up." The jury remained
unconvinced.

"On the other hand, these people up in San Francisco who you

---

* Yet another reference to a friend of Elizabeth Short being involved in a lewd photography
ring. Short's other friend and apartment share partner, Lynn Martin, mentioned being photographed in the nude by photographer George Price, whose name was in Elizabeth's address
book. (See page 63.) The papers of the late John Gilmore, journalist and Dahlia researcher,
stored at UCLA, include an uncredited nude photograph of a woman described on the back
of the photo as Lola Titus.

† Again, strange that a suspect in a murder inquiry appeared to be taking on aspects of the
investigation himself.

‡ And yet, as we know, Thad Brown had already terminated the Aster investigations in June,
and had announced in September that the rumors of the murder taking place there were
unfounded.

think in court might develop an alibi for this man, most of them have questionable reputations, have they not?"

The jury then went on to question Finis Brown about the claims by members of the Gangster Squad that Mark Hansen had initially identified a picture of Leslie Dillon as resembling a man who visited Elizabeth Short, and that Hansen had then changed his mind after talking to Finis. Brown confirmed that both Mark Hansen and Ann Toth had talked about a man who had picked up Beth Short on several occasions, when she lived at Mark Hansen's home on Carlos Avenue. The man, they said, was about six feet tall, with light hair, and drove a light-colored Chevrolet coupe. Both Ann Toth and Mark Hansen identified a photograph of Leslie Dillon as the man they had seen with Short. Hansen called attention to Dillon's prominent Adam's apple, which he recalled the man he saw with Short as having, too. Later, Finis said, Hansen was shown a picture of one of Elizabeth's boyfriends, Lieutenant Stephen Wolak.* He thought this also looked like the man with the light-colored coupe who had visited her. Hansen wanted to see Leslie Dillon in person, to be sure of the identification. The meeting, as far as was known, never happened.

What, the jurors asked, could in Sergeant Brown's mind, finally resolve the question of Leslie Dillon's culpability for this crime? If the crucial issue was Dillon's whereabouts on January 14–15, DA Investigator Frank Jemison had already been up to San Francisco to re-interview the alibi witnesses. Was there anything else that could be done to clear up this point?

"I can't think of anything. It is Dillon that might be talked to. If the officers—the police officers of the city or some officer could get his cooperation and maybe establish beyond a doubt that he had anything to do with it—"

"Determine as to whether or not he was telling the truth as to his whereabouts in this period of the eight days? In other words, could Dillon bring to bear upon the proposition any corroboration, any cor-

---

* An Air Force officer based out in El Paso.

roboration of his declaration that he wasn't in Los Angeles at the time; that is what you come down with, isn't it?"

"That is what I mean."

Effectively, Sergeant Brown was saying that only a personal interview with Leslie Dillon himself could establish the issue of his whereabouts on the night of the murder. But what Finis omitted saying was that there had, in fact, already been such a meeting with Dillon: the secret meeting with Inspector Hugh Farnham in Oklahoma in October. The truth was that, by the time Finis Brown testified to the grand jury, the LAPD had already tracked Dillon down. They had carried out just such a personal interview with him and his wife that Brown, in his testimony, said would be necessary to obtain corroboration of his alibi. The Dillons had failed to establish that alibi. There was, in fact, no solid evidence to confirm that Leslie Dillon had been in San Francisco at the time of Elizabeth's murder. And yet Sergeant Brown said nothing of this to the grand jury.

It was a bald-faced lie.

The testimony of the police officers at the grand jury hearing was now complete. From what they had said, it was abundantly clear that there was a serious internal rift in the LAPD over the Dahlia case. The officers of the Gangster Squad were adamant that there was a strong prima facie case against Leslie Dillon and Mark Hansen; that great suspicion surrounded the events at the Aster Motel; and that they had been mysteriously pulled off the case. The officers of the Homicide detail, on the other hand, dismissed Hansen and Dillon as suspects. They glossed over the events at the Aster Motel. One glaring omission was the fact that Captain Francis Kearney—the head of the Homicide detail who actually went on the Dillon mission in January 1949—was not called to give testimony. This was especially strange because it was Captain Kearney who would have been in the best position to explain why he did not reveal the details of the secret mission to his own men. Captain Kearney was to continue in Homicide for two years, transferring back to the Narcotics detail in 1951.

Neither he nor anybody else in the LAPD ever publicly explained why the chief of the Homicide Division was not called to give testimony to the grand jury on the Dahlia investigation.

Meanwhile, the evidence having been heard, the grand jury, headed by Harry Lawson, retreated to deliberate. Aggie Underwood, Dr. Paul De River, and the public of Los Angeles waited expectantly for its judgment to be pronounced. Aggie, for one, fully expected indictments to come out of the jury's investigation of the Dahlia case. She was convinced that the full story was, after all her diligent digging, finally going to explode—and dynamite the rotten police department with it. But the grand jury's pronouncement, when it came—as with so much else in this case—was totally unexpected.

THE VERDICT

GRAND JURORS SHIFT DAHLIA PROBE TO 1950!

The morning's headlines rolled off the giant printing presses in the neo-Gothic downtown *Examiner* offices, steamrolling the hopes of Dr. De River, Aggie Underwood, and all who had set so much store by the grand jury investigation into the Dahlia case. So much for Harry Lawson's much-trumpeted crusade against corruption. Now he and his fellow jurors seemed to have capitulated to the very forces with which they had battled.

For Aggie Underwood and Dr. De River, the announcement that the Dahlia investigation was to be transferred to the 1950 grand jury beggared belief. How could the 1949 jury, the "runaway jury" that had virtually brought down the police department over the Brenda Allen affair, have handed off the task of giving indictments to its successor? Aggie and the doctor did not know about the battle then being played out in the corridors of the Hall of Justice. Harry Lawson hinted at the deadlock. On the morning of December 7, he gave a statement to the press. "We feel the evidence is strong enough," he told the newspapermen. "But there is not enough time left in our term to complete the inquiry." The grand jury, Lawson went on, was due to discuss the next steps with the ex-head of the Gangster Squad, Willie Burns, and Chief of Detectives Thad Brown, the next day.

On the same day that Harry Lawson made his statement to the press, Frank Jemison presented another report to the grand jury. It repeated the substance of his first report, in what was swiftly becoming the LAPD mantra on the Dahlia case. Based on his own investigations and the information provided to him by Barrett and Brown of LAPD Homicide, Jemison told the jury—just as he had done back in October—that there was "insufficient evidence to place Leslie Dillon in Los Angeles at the time of murder, and none whatsoever to connect him with it." Nothing was said to the grand jury of the secret meeting in Oklahoma, when Dillon had failed to establish his alibi. Nothing was said about key items of evidence that had been produced by Fred Witman to the DA, including the initials D and E that were purportedly carved into Elizabeth's body. Yet again, the jury was delivered the one clear message from the DA's office, channeled via Jemison's advisors in the Homicide Division: "drop Leslie Dillon."

Also on December 7, a curious article appeared in the *Los Angeles Examiner*. Reporting on Lawson's statement that the evidence was "strong enough" for an indictment, the paper quoted another, unnamed juryman as stating that the jurors were interested in reports that a "wealthy Hollywood nightclub and theater owner should be investigated in the case." The juror explained that the panel had been told that this "wealthy Hollywood nightclub owner" had stayed with the Dahlia at a motel on South Flower Street in January 1947. The article continued:

> Jury questioning of police officers, concluded yesterday, is understood to have concerned reports that the Hollywood man was "protected" by members of the police gangster squad during investigation of the Dahlia slaying.
>
> Early in the hunt for the slayer of Miss Short, whose

bisected body was found January 15, 1947, on a vacant lot in the 3800 block of South Norton avenue, it was established that the Hollywood man had known her.

Since then it has been persistently reported that because of his friendship for members of the gangster squad, investigation of the man's connection with Miss Short was shifted to that squad from homicide, with the result that he was dropped as a suspect.

From the evidence presented in secret to the grand jury, it was clear that the "wealthy Hollywood nightclub owner" suspected of being mixed up with the murder of Elizabeth Short was Mark Hansen. But it was also clear, from the transcript of the grand jury proceedings, that the police "cover-up" that the jury strongly suspected had taken place to protect Mark Hansen was not by the Gangster Squad. Rather, it was a cover-up by the Homicide Division, through the Brown brothers' links to Hansen. Once again, as with the earlier *Examiner* report about the Flower Street motel, Thad Brown's men seemed to have been twisting the story told to the newspapers. As to the events at Flower Street, the *Examiner* article went on to say that "witnesses familiar with the motel at that time are supposed to have identified the Hollywood man as one registered there and, at the time, supposed to have been connected with a foreign government."* The grand jury, the *Examiner* continued, was not satisfied that the witnesses at the motel had been given an opportunity to tell their full stories. Those stories, in the jury's opinion, should be heard.

On the next day, December 8, the grand jury held its secret meeting with Willie Burns of the Gangster Squad and Thad Brown, chief of detectives. The contents of the discussion were never divulged. However, the outcome of the meeting was that the grand jury was

---

* "Connected with a foreign government": i.e., the "man from Batavia" or the "Danish consulate." (See page 141.)

somehow persuaded by the senior police officers not to issue immediate indictments in the Dahlia case. Instead, the jury issued a final
assignment to Frank Jemison. He was to re-interview Mark Hansen
and Ann Toth, along with the witnesses at the Aster Motel.

DA Frank Jemison and Officer Ed Barrett re-interviewed Ann Toth
on December 13. The pale Danish actress, who had been Elizabeth's housemate at Mark Hansen's Carlos Avenue home, remained
as tight-lipped and cagey as when she had been questioned before
by Harry Hansen and Finis Brown. Elizabeth and Mark had had a
stormy relationship, Toth acknowledged. There was the fight over the
other girl who stayed at Carlos Avenue, and the row when Elizabeth
threw Mark's things out of the bathroom cupboard. Mark was given
to tantrums and explosive rages. He "had a yen" for Elizabeth, and
was jealously possessive of her. Asked about Mark's alibi for the evening, Ann hedged: Hansen was usually home by 11:00 p.m., but she
could not be sure he was home at that time on the night of January
14. She might have been partying herself that evening, so how was
she to know? Ann was also evasive over the question as to whether
Hansen might have seen Elizabeth over the "missing week": she had
been "occupied with her boyfriend practically all of the time," so she
"didn't keep up with things." The Danish actress did recall that when
she returned to Carlos Avenue from a visit to her parents on Friday,
January 10, Mark was acting "excited and strange." He told her that
Betty had called him from San Diego, and that he had told her she
could come and stay in the house at Carlos Avenue for a few days, if
she had no other place to go.

Ann also recalled a strange incident that had taken place at
the Carlos Avenue house around Sunday, January 12, 1947. Mark
Hansen had been at home at the time. At about midnight, the telephone started ringing. But when Ann picked up the receiver, there
was no answer on the line. The telephone must have rung every five
minutes for about thirty minutes, between midnight and one o'clock.
In the end, Ann had threatened to call the police. Then the calls

stopped. Neither Ann nor Mark could figure out from whom the calls had come.*

Three days after interviewing Ann Toth, Officers Jemison and Barrett interviewed Mark Hansen in his office next to the Florentine Gardens. Whether on the grand jury's instructions or by the decision of Frank Jemison, it had been decided that Finis Brown was not to be present at the interview.

No, Hansen claimed, he had never "tried to make" Elizabeth Short.

"Was she a pretty-looking gal?" Jemison asked.

"Well, I thought she was fair-looking, average. If it wasn't for her teeth. She had bad teeth. Other than that she would have been beautiful."

Mark repeated his recollection of the man who came to collect Elizabeth a few times, in a '35 or '39 Chevrolet or Ford coupe: "He didn't look too good." He denied that he had a "yen" for the Short girl. He had never kissed her, or even put his arm around her.

At first Hansen denied that he had spoken to Elizabeth after she left Los Angeles for San Diego in December '46. But Jemison pointed out that this was not true: they had evidence that Betty had called Mark from the Biltmore Hotel on the evening of Thursday, January 9, 1947. Hansen then backtracked. Yes, Betty had called him on Thursday night from the Biltmore. He had told her that she could not stay with him, as Ann Toth was not at home, and she would not like it. This did not tie in with what Ann Toth had said to the police. She had told Jemison and Barrett that Hansen had told her Betty could stay for a few days at his house when she got back from San Diego, if she had no other place to stay.

And so it transpired that Elizabeth Short had called Mark Hansen in one of her last known phone calls, on Thursday, January 9, from

---

* The mysterious calls, if they did indeed happen on Sunday, January 12, would have taken place in the middle of the "missing week," when Elizabeth Short was likely held trapped or captive. The caller and possible motive are discussed later on page 246.

the phone booth at the Biltmore Hotel. Had she, in fact, stayed at Hansen's home on Carlos Avenue on that Thursday night? There was nobody to offer an alibi for Mark on that evening. Ann Toth was away, and did not return until the next day. If Elizabeth had stayed with Mark on that Thursday night, had she been removed, out of the way, to another location when Ann returned the next day? Could that location have been the motel on Flower Street?

In the dying days of the year, on the grand jury's final instructions, Jemison and Barrett re-interviewed the people at the Aster Motel. The second anniversary of Elizabeth Short's murder was fast approaching. The interviews took place in Mark Hansen's office, next to the Marcal Theatre: a green and purple neon strip-lighted Art Deco extravaganza, set back from the arc lamps of Hollywood Boulevard where the hookers and hustlers patrolled the sidewalks.*

Closeted with Jemison and Barrett in Mark Hansen's office, and confronted by the Hollywood millionaire in person on his own premises, the Hoffmans now completely changed their story from what they had told Officers Waggoner, Case, and Ahern the previous summer. No, they said, the "man from Batavia" who had stayed at the motel was not Mark Hansen.

Clora Hoffman's brother and sister-in-law Burt and Betty-Jo Moorman, on the other hand, stood firm on their story. A middle-aged man with a foreign accent had definitely stayed at the Aster Motel sometime during their stay there, between January 11 and 18, 1947.† The man had asked the Moormans to drive him to a location downtown, where he had collected a large suitcase. Afterward, the man had invited them to his motel room for a drink. They had then gone out for dinner together at a Mexican restaurant on Slau-

---

* The fact that these key witnesses were re-interviewed in the offices of Mark Hansen, one of the prime suspects in the case, was peculiar to say the least. Regular practice would have been to interview them at the DA's office or their own homes and arrange a police lineup or a separate meeting for the purpose of identifying Mark Hansen as the "man from Batavia."
† For the Moormans' earlier account of this man given to the Gangster Squad, see page 142.

son Avenue. The man was left-handed and "wolfed" his food down greedily. The Moormans could not now recall exactly if he was the "man from Batavia," but they were certain of one thing. The man who stayed at the motel, who collected a suitcase from downtown, and who took them out to dinner, was Mark Hansen. They were even more positive of this fact now that they saw him in person.

Jemison made Mrs. Moorman stand face-to-face with Mark Hansen.

"Are you ready to go into court or not, and testify that this is the man that you went out that day for dinner with, and with whom you went down town and spent six hours? Are you ready to go in and testify, and answer yes or no? We are not kidding."

"I know you are not."

"It is serious."

"Yes, it was him."

Burt Moorman was just as certain as his wife that Mark Hansen was the man at the motel.

"And even though it might mean the gas chamber for Mark Hansen for this murder, you will still go into court and testify he was the man who took you to dinner?" Jemison said to Burt.

"Yes, I will."*

"Did you ever tell anybody that you thought there was probably a payoff on this?"

"Well yes, I told the officers that."

"Which officers?"

"Case and Ahern."

"What do you mean by that?"

"I mean that the squabbling in the department and all was a put-up job. In fact, everywhere Case and Ahern went, they so much as told me their hands were tied. When they began to hit a sore spot they were warded off in another direction. They were limited in what they could do, and what they could investigate."

---

* It is difficult to see how one could obtain more unshakable identifications than these by the Moormans.

As the Moormans left Mark Hansen's office, Mrs. Moorman was overhead muttering something about a "payoff." She was immediately recalled by Frank Jemison.

"I heard you make a remark when you went down the hall a moment ago about a payoff."

"Did I?"

"You never made the remark that you thought there had been a payoff?"

"Not a payoff, no. I think that Brown stopped the case because he is a friend of Mr. Hansen's."

"How do you know he is a friend of his?"

"He told us he had dinner with him."

"From that you gather he was a friend of Mark Hansen?"

"That is right."

On January 12, 1950, the grand jury issued its final report. The section that dealt with the jury's investigation into the Dahlia affair ran as follows:

Something is radically wrong with the present system of apprehending the guilty. The alarming increase in the number of unsolved murders reflects ineffectiveness in law enforcement agencies and the courts that should not be tolerated. . . .

In addition to the sadistic murder and mutilation of Elizabeth Short, the record shows that other victims of unsolved murders included Mary Tate, Mrs. Jeanne French, Evelyn Winters, Rosenda [Mondragon], Mrs. Laura Trelstad, Gladys Kern and Louise Springer. "Mysterious disappearances" are involved in other cases, to which strict law enforcement demands a solution, such as those of Mimi Boomhower and Jean Spangler. This record reveals, in the opinion of the 1949 grand jury, conditions that are appalling and fearsome. Criminals are using varied techniques in writing a record of crime that includes murders, mysterious disappearances of persons and loathsome sex crimes. The criminals, in many cases, have gone unpunished. Because of the character of these murders and sex crimes, women and children are constantly placed in jeopardy and are not safe from attack.

If the 1949 grand jury has done little else during its term of office, it has, we believe, stirred the public conscience to recognize the seriousness of this situation, which is sapping the moral strength of law-abiding citizens.

The grand jury also noted the "apparent evasiveness" of some police officers called to give testimony, and the "deplorable conditions indicating corrupt practices and misconduct by some members of the law enforcement agencies of this county." In many cases, it concluded, "jurisdictional disputes and jealousies among law-enforcement agencies were indicated. In other cases, especially where one or more departments were involved, there seems to have been manifested a lack of co-operation in presenting evidence to the grand jury and a reluctance to investigate or prosecute." The report concluded with the recommendation that the investigation into the Dahlia murder be continued by the next year's grand jury.

On the very day the grand jury's final report was read to Superior Judge Robert H. Scott, there was a retirement banquet at the police academy "in grateful tribute" to the demoted chief, Clemence Horrall, and his assistant, Joe Reed. In attendance were over five hundred police officers and city luminaries, including Mayor Fletcher Bowron, District Attorney William E. Simpson, Sheriff Eugene W. Biscailuz, and the interim LAPD chief, William Worton. Whatever scathing criticisms Harry Lawson's jury was making, it was "business as usual" for law enforcement in the City of Angels.

The final report of Harry Lawson's "runaway" jury was both an indictment of law enforcement and an admission of defeat. Through its exposure of the Brenda Allen scandal, the jury had succeeded in partially toppling the hierarchy of the LAPD. It had scratched the surface layers of corruption in a police department that was rotten to the core. But the canker at the heart of the department, the blight that crippled the Dahlia case, had withstood the jury's best efforts to root it out. That task, now, had passed to the grand jury's successor. Would the 1950 grand jury take up the challenge?

DETOUR

T he day the 1949 grand jury left the Hall of Justice forever, all further inquiries into Leslie Dillon stopped. As did the investigation into the Aster Motel. It was as if Dillon, De River, Jeff Connors, the saga of Palm Springs, and the Aster Motel had never existed; they had gone with the hot, dry Santa Ana winds.

Nevertheless, the mandate from the 1949 grand jury to continue investigation of the Dahlia murder meant that Frank Jemison was obliged to prolong, in some form, his task of research and reporting on the case. And so he continued his review into 1950. This time, still guided by his trusty advisors at the LAPD, Jemison was led to focus on various other, sundry suspects: a medical student named Marvin Margolis, who had dated Elizabeth Short in her final months; a Mexican dishwasher at Brittingham's Restaurant, who might, or might not, have known her; the shady manager of the Chancellor Apartments. None of these suspects had much in the way of evidence to connect them to the murder. Then, in the fall of 1949, came the perfect sideshow for the LAPD Homicide Division. A drama that would send Jemison off on a wild goose chase to keep him busy, and off Dillon for the rest of his investigation.

Dr. George Hill Hodel was a brilliant and fashionable Hollywood physician who ran a venereal disease clinic on East First Street in Alameda. He dabbled in mystic Eastern religions, Surrealist art, and the occult. When not performing illegal abortions at his First Street clinic, Hodel held court at his Hollywood residence, a monolithic Frank Lloyd Wright, Jr., construction on Franklin Avenue with a front entrance resembling the open jaws of a shark. Here he would hold nude parties and hedonistic orgies under the impassive gaze of statues of nymphs and satyrs, with a bevy of girls in attendance.

It was at one of George Hodel's sex parties at the house on Franklin Avenue that his teenage daughter, Tamar, accused her father of molesting her. The resulting trial, which started in October 1949, was a cause célèbre of Tinseltown. "Doctor Faces Accusation in Morals Case," ran the banner headline of the *Los Angeles Times* on October 7. Deputy DA William L. Ritzi was quoted as describing how both men and women attended the bizarre sex parties at Hodel's home, at one of which Tamar had been assaulted. Hodel was also said to be a photography enthusiast, with many "questionable" photographs and pornographic art objects being seized in his home.

George Hodel's trial for incest began on December 8, 1949. To defend him, the doctor hired Robert A. Neeb, partner to the celebrity lawyer Jerry "Get Me" Giesler. During his cross-examination of Hodel's daughter Tamar, Neeb put the following question to the teenage girl:

"Tamar, do you recall a conversation you had with a roommate at the Franklin House by the name of Joe Barrett? And do you recall, in that conversation, making the following statement to him: 'This house has secret passages. My father is the murderer of the Black Dahlia. My father is going to kill me and all the rest of the members of this household because he has a lust for blood. He is insane'?"

The courtroom fell into stunned silence as all eyes focused on Tamar's response.

"I don't remember saying that to Joe."

The next day, the newspapers had a field day. "Girl Accused of

Trying to Pin Dahlia Murder on Dad," reported the *Daily News* on December 17. "Girl's Story Is Fantasy, Court Hears," ran the headline in the *Los Angeles Mirror*. On December 24, the jury acquitted George Hodel on all counts of incest, after less than four hours' deliberation.

After Hodel's acquittal on the incest charges, rumors persisted of a payoff arranged by Jerry Giesler on the doctor's behalf, to members of the DA's office. The evidence against Hodel in relation to the charges of molesting his daughter had been compelling, and yet he was set free. Other members of the DA's office, it was whispered, were not happy with the result. Two DA officers had been demoted because of the trial. People at the DA's office wanted revenge. Meanwhile, George Hodel was beset with other problems: charges of tax evasion; allegations that he had killed his secretary in order to stop her from blowing the whistle on illegal abortions that he was performing; accusations of being a closet Communist. To add to Hodel's woes, his attorney Robert Neeb's "clever" strategy—to allude in court to the allegation that Hodel was somehow involved in the Dahlia killing, as an example of his daughter Tamar's fantastical imagination—now backfired. Even though it had been made as a joke, Neeb's reference to the Dahlia case during the molestation trial had linked George Hodel, for the first time, to Elizabeth Short's murder. The DA's office now had a way to get its revenge on the doctor.

Throughout the early part of 1950, Frank Jemison and his men diligently pursued George Hodel. They tailed his Packard car around visits to sundry art galleries. They wired the doctor's Franklin Avenue home, placing a bug in the basement. For a month and a half, from mid-February to the end of March 1950, Jemison's men listened in on the activities in the Hodel house through the wires placed in the basement. They heard a great deal of noisy sex, loud music on the radio, erotic poetry readings, and the flushing of many lavatories. It was patently clear that George Hodel was fully aware of—even obsessed with—the fact that his house was bugged. His home was under siege, with journalists from the *Hollywood Citizen-News* parked outside his front door. Every day, the investigators listened in on banging in the basement, the opening and closing of drawers, and Hodel's loudly barked orders to his harassed housekeeper to keep trying to find the bug that the doctor was rightly convinced was hidden somewhere.

Of George Hodel's acquaintances, two women believed the doctor had known Elizabeth Short. The rest of his associates, including his ex-wife, swore that he had not known her. None of Elizabeth Short's own friends or relatives—her mother, sister, close friend Ann Toth, her roommates at the Hawthorne or the Chancellor, or indeed Mark Hansen—identified any doctor among the dead girl's acquaintances or boyfriends. There was no evidence to link the doctor to the body dump site in Leimert Park, the Aster Motel, the trash can in which Elizabeth's shoe and purse had been found, the *D* and *E* that had purportedly been carved onto the body, the telephone call that had been placed to Jimmy Richardson at the *Examiner*, or the sending of the package containing the victim's belongings. Hodel, in fact, showed decidedly secretive as opposed to exhibitionist tendencies in his behavior. All his dubious antics took place discreetly, behind the heavy doors of his monolithic private mansion. The idea of him dumping a body in full view in an area of Los Angeles that he never visited, sending misspelled messages to the press, or telephoning a city editor anonymously, were not far short of absurd.

From the secret recordings of the DA's office at Hodel's home, it was clear that the doctor was increasingly panicked, aware of the investigators closing in on him. Even though he had eluded them in the incest trial, there was, after all, plenty more for them to get him on: his taxes, the illegal abortions, the mysterious death of his secretary, his clandestine Communist connections. Finally, the doctor decided to hightail it out of trouble. He sold off his statues of nymphs and satyrs, divested himself of his house and Packard car, and ran off to the Philippines by way of Hawaii. But he had given the DA investigators a good run for their money, and many years later he would become an even longer-running distraction in the Dahlia case.*

In February 1951, Frank Jemison filed his last report on the Dahlia investigation. In it, he gave his final list of possible suspects. Many were individuals with barely a link to the Dahlia. Some did not even have a name. "Madam Chang," the "queer woman surgeon," was still featured. So was the now quasi-mythical "Sergeant Chuck," the Army sergeant with whom the Dahlia was supposed to have quarreled during her time at Camp Cooke. The "queer woman surgeon" was in fact a certain Dr. Margaret Chung, the first Chinese-American female physician and a local celebrity in San Francisco. She had gained national fame during the war when she took under her wing thousands of soldiers, sailors, and flyboys, including Ronald Reagan. But there was nothing suspicious about Mom Chung, apart from her being a female physician, Chinese, and a lesbian.† Dr. George Hodel was also featured, although low on Jemison's list.‡ Mark Hansen was at the bottom. There was no reference to Leslie Dillon. In the report, Jemison stated that the 1950 grand jury had shown no interest in the Dahlia murder. Therefore, it had been agreed with the Deputy Chief Thad Brown that the case would "never be assumed by the DA" again. All files were to be turned over to Homicide, and the DA investigation terminated.

Once more, the waters closed over Elizabeth Short.

---

* The amplification of George Hodel's minor role in the Dahlia affair after his death is discussed later, on page 241.

† Dr. Margaret Chung (1889–1959), also known as "Mom Chung," was a colorful and flamboyant Chinese-American physician who founded one of the first Western medical clinics in San Francisco's Chinatown in the 1920s. Over the war she adopted thousands of soldiers, whom she called her "fair haired bastards." She was also a prominent celebrity and behind-the-scenes broker in World War II.

‡ George Hodel was never listed as a primary suspect for the Dahlia killing, although this has been claimed, as discussed later on page 241.

FALL GUY

The LAPD had succeeded, finally, in burying the Dahlia case. Now the knives came out for Dr. De River. The doctor had testified before the grand jury against members of the police department. He was, therefore, a rat and a whistle-blower. He would not be forgiven.

On March 2, 1950, Dr. De River spoke at a luncheon meeting for the Parkview Women's Club, on the subject of "Juvenile Delinquency and the Home's Influence in Its Prevention." That afternoon he was asked to stop by the city attorney's office on an undisclosed matter. When he got there, the doctor was greeted by officers of the State Division of Narcotic Enforcement. They were investigating him for a series of prescriptions for marijuana, written out during the period December 1949–January 1950. The doctor explained to the agents that the prescriptions were used as painkillers to help his wife, who had been in severe pain after spinal surgery had gone wrong in November of that year.

Misdemeanor charges were filed against De River by the state narcotics agency on March 22, 1950. Nobody was under any illusion as to who was behind the charges. As Aggie's newspaper the *Herald-Express* reported, the LAPD had pushed the city attorney's office to prosecute the case, after "the District Attorney's office refused to issue the complaint." According to the doctor's lawyers, "the case against Dr. De River was pressed by the Police Department in retaliation for the psychiatrist's appearance before the County Grand Jury in an investigation last year into the unsolved murder of Elizabeth 'Black Dahlia' Short."

Not content to rest with the trumped-up narcotics charges, the police department also began investigating the doctor in relation to a book he had published the previous October. *The Sexual Criminal: A Psychoanalytical Study* was a textbook of forensic psychiatry. Despite its undoubtedly voyeuristic content, it was and is still widely considered a pioneering book on the subject. The introduction to the textbook was written by Eugene Williams, former chief deputy district attorney of Los Angeles County, and investigator on the Babes of Inglewood case. Williams had bonded with De River, Aggie Underwood, and Judge White during the trial of Albert Dyer back in 1937. The lawyer, the doctor, the journalist, and the judge had remained close friends ever since.* Further chapters in *The Sexual Criminal* were contributed by the distinguished Los Angeles public defender Ellery E. Cuff,† Judge Joseph Call,‡ and Inspector Roy Blick of the Washington metropolitan police Vice Squad.§

While primarily a textbook of psychiatry, *The Sexual Criminal* was influenced by the yellow press "true crime" paperbacks of the day. It was written in the doctor's usual dramatic style, with rhetorical flourishes and a liberal sprinkling of lurid crime-scene photographs from famous cases. The identities of the killers and victims were ill-concealed by bars superimposed across their eyes, in a half-hearted attempt to anonymize the well-known "case studies." The assorted

---

* For the Babes of Inglewood case, Albert Dyer, and the roles of Aggie Underwood, De River, Judge White, and Eugene Williams in the investigation, see page 84.

† For more on Ellery E. Cuff, see page 223.

‡ Judge Joseph Call was a distinguished municipal court judge who, among other things, called for a grand jury inquiry into the "Bloody Christmas" beatings of Christmas Eve 1951, when members of the LAPD seriously assaulted a group of Latinos in the city jail on an erroneous pretext (see page 218).

§ Inspector Roy E. Blick was notorious for his crackdowns on lascivious displays in the burlesque clubs of the Washington area.

accounts of rape, pederasty, and murder told a story of postwar Los Angeles at its most grimly noir. Incensed by the unauthorized use of crime scene photographs, the LAPD referred the book to the Police Commission. An unnamed member of the commission handed a copy of the book to the City Council.

Councilman Ernest E. Debs—De River's old enemy who had challenged his professional credentials previously—was quick to jump on *The Sexual Criminal.* "The book is filthy and shocking," boomed the outraged city worthy. "There's no question about it, that De River, who calls himself a crime psychologist and sexologist, is using the pictures just to sell the book." Debs demanded an immediate vote by the City Council to abolish De River's position as police psychiatrist, on the basis that the doctor had used crime scene photographs "without permission of the department." The final council vote was split seven to six in favor of the motion. Because the vote was required to be unanimous, the doctor had escaped. But not for long.

De River had already been suspended from his position without pay by the LAPD, pending the outcome of his drugs trial. That trial began on July 3, 1950, before Municipal Judge Vernon W. Hunt. Five witnesses, mainly the doctor's relatives, were called to the stand. Three testified that they did not use the drugs prescribed in their name by the doctor. Two could not recall whether they had ever done so. The next day, the doctor himself took the stand. He admitted obtaining the painkillers for his sick wife, because "I adore her, next to God." According to the *Los Angeles Times*, the doctor blamed his prosecution on a "factional fight within the Police Department, centering about the infamous and as yet unsolved 'Black Dahlia' case." He maintained that he was "caught in the middle" of the factional difficulties. The doctor called three judges to stand as character witnesses, all of whom testified that he was known to them as a man of honesty and good repute. The prosecution took the unusual step of requesting the dismissal of three of the four charges. It then rested its case.

On July 7, a jury of nine women and three men found Dr. De River guilty of improperly maintaining prescription records. Judge Hunt sentenced him to thirty days' probation, "with the sole condition that he not violate narcotics laws of the state." The judge continued:

"The defendant in this case is a reputable physician who, rather than impose on his professional colleagues, undertook to personally administer pain-killing narcotics to his suffering wife—and resorted to ill-advised means of obtaining narcotics for her. There can be no doubt that his wife was and is suffering. This is not a case where narcotics were obtained for improper purposes, but rather it is a case where they were obtained for perfectly proper and humane purposes. . . . The defendant, a highly respected professional man, has already suffered far greater punishment than is justified by the purely technical nature of the charges in this case and this court is not disposed to impose any further penalty."

On August 9, 1950, Chief William Worton resigned from his post and took up office as a police commissioner. The retired Marine general, who had been made interim police chief following the Brenda Allen fiasco, had fulfilled the function for which he was appointed. He had presided over the LAPD during the greatest scandal of its history. During his term of office, he had attempted to reorganize the police department and impose some order. Now it was time to hand the responsibility over to a successor.

The battle for the new chief of the Los Angeles Police Department was a bitter one. Pitted against each other were the popular chief of detectives Thad Brown, the preferred choice of the Protestants, Freemasons, and the underworld; and Thad Brown's polar opposite, the cold and calculating William Parker, the candidate preferred by the Catholic contingent of the city. Widely considered the dark horse, Parker had been placed in charge of the Intelligence Division that Worton created to replace the disbanded Gangster Squad.

The campaign for the appointment of a new chief was characterized by the usual LAPD opacity and intrigue. Mickey Cohen and his underworld cronies were certain that they had Thad Brown's appointment in the bag. That is, until the sudden death of one of Thad's supporters on the appointments commission, Agnes Albro, from breast cancer. The loss of that key vote propelled Parker into the top job. "I know I'm supposedly coming in with a life expectancy of two weeks," Parker told the press corps when he was selected. "We'll see." He lasted sixteen years.

With the appointment of Bill Parker as chief, the LAPD entered a new era. Gone were the old days of the "gangster cops," the cozy relationship played out in downtown bars between police and mobsters, the wads of dough traded at the doors of the gambling dens and whorehouses as a price for being left alone. In came a superficially sanitized police force: an army of tanned, cookie-cutter motorcycle cops with inscrutable features hidden by dark sunglasses. They were Bill Parker's elite squad, the "New Centurions." Under Parker, the cops on the streets turned clean and the backroom deals went right to the top: to the now-supreme Intelligence Division, the department formed from the old vestiges of the Gangster Squad, which became the all-powerful, all-seeing, all snooping organ through which Bill Parker ruled the department and the city with a rod of iron and secret phone taps. It was the era of the "thin blue line," a new type of policing that swiftly identified and targeted a new type of enemy. Not the old-time gangsters of the likes of Bugsy Siegel or Mickey Cohen; they were swiftly fading into the nostalgic recesses of collective memory. Rather, the new enemy was hinted at in the first signs of rebellion and restlessness coming from the simmering black areas of the city, the run-down streets of Compton and Boyle Heights. A new war to be waged against a new foe, one that was to erupt with violence in the carnage of Watts and the turbulence of the civil rights era. But that was, and is, another story.

The immediate consequence of Bill Parker's appointment and Chief Worton's transfer to the Police Commission, as far as Dr. De

River was concerned, was that he was fired. On August 23, Worton instructed Chief Parker to sack the doctor and abolish the position of LAPD police psychiatrist. According to the *Los Angeles Examiner*, Worton said that "in the 13 months he was chief of police, he decided a full-time psychiatrist was not needed, and that the city could hire a qualified medical expert at a saving to the taxpayers when one was needed." Because he was not protected by any civil service provisions, the doctor received no pension. Nor, in the opinion of the city attorneys, was he entitled to compensation for the lack of pay during his period of suspension pending trial on the narcotics charges.

By now the doctor was living in Beachwood Canyon, in a red-roofed Spanish villa crouching beneath the tall, jagged white capitals of the Hollywood sign. It was fall, and the ginkgo trees and Japanese maples were streaks of flaming color. The doctor's eldest daughter, Jacqueline, was home on a visit from campus at UCLA. She was explaining to her parents how it was hard to make friends, as the university was so big.

Suddenly there was a loud knock at the door. Jacqueline went to open it.

"Who is it?"

"Lieutenant Hamilton from the LAPD Intelligence Unit." The man was tall and lean. He was not smiling. "Is your father in?"

"Yes, but . . ."

"I take it you're his daughter."

"Yes. . . ."

"You'd better invite me in."

The man brushed past the girl and went straight to the living room. He clearly knew the layout of the house.

The doctor rose to greet him, and introduced his wife. The men shook hands. What followed, according to Jacqueline, was a long diatribe. And a clear warning. "People have disappeared," said the lieutenant. "They've been killed. Whole families have suffered. And these were good people." He paused. "But they insisted on sticking their nose into someone else's business."

Finally, the man stopped talking. He looked directly at De River. "Do you have any questions, doctor?"

The doctor shook his head and moved to the door. His face was grave, his voice calm. "Good evening, Lieutenant." He nodded good-bye.

"What the Lieutenant warned us about," recalled Jacqueline many years later, "was the murder of Elizabeth Short, the Black Dahlia, and any possible interest my father still had in the case."*

De River's curt dismissal of the Intelligence chief's warning was to have consequences. Already, the doctor had been subject to a campaign of harassment. Back in March that year, his adopted daughter, Margaret, had been frightened by two men trespassing outside her bedroom window. The doctor had fired two shots, and the men had run away unharmed. Now the campaign of harassment intensified. When the doctor's other daughters, Jacqueline and Gloria, got off the bus and walked up the hill to their home, a police patrol car would be waiting to follow them. One day, Gloria was stopped by one of the officers in the car.

"Aren't you doing some modeling in the garment district?"

"Yes. Why do you ask?"

"I thought I'd seen you around. What does your father think about that?"

"It's none of your business."

The doctor still had his .45, and a license to carry it. One evening, when he and Jacqueline were in the house, they heard noises on the side of the hill outside. The doctor got his daughter to call the Hollywood Division. They promised to send someone around.

---

* Lieutenant James Hamilton was an officer of the LAPD Intelligence Division and Chief Parker's right-hand man, charged with spying on members of the police department and others whom the chief wished to place under surveillance. He was later to become a close confidant of Robert Kennedy and was seen at the Brentwood home of Marilyn Monroe, on the day of her death by ostensible suicide in August 1962. Hamilton later left the LAPD to work as a private security advisor to the National Football League, to assist the league in dealing with interference by the mob. He was appointed to the position because of his inside knowledge of organized crime.

The pair returned to the living room to read. Again, the same noises. The doctor ventured outside, and fired a couple of shots. There was silence. The doctor and his daughter waited all night for the promised visit by the cops. Nobody showed up. "We came to the conclusion," said Jacqueline, "that we could call and call and no one on the department would help us." One of De River's granddaughters, now a successful attorney, also recalled the campaign of police harassment to which the family was subjected. "They were followed constantly," she said. "One day, they opened the front door and there was a dead fish on the doorstep."

Throughout the doctor's misfortunes, his old friend Aggie Underwood tried to help him. Aggie offered De River's daughter Jacqueline a job at the *Herald-Express*, to tide the family over. The only opening available was a part-time job in classifieds on Saturdays. But Aggie, too, was very afraid. Her daughter-in-law, Rilla Underwood, recalled how, in the early 1950s, she "seemed to behave differently, nervous, and took to carrying a gun. She warned me to watch the children and be extra careful." Aggie's own statements about her beliefs as to the identity of the Dahlia killer were telling. "There were grave suspicions about one guy who was questioned. Evidence was almost conclusive," she said, years later. "The police had him, and they let him go. He was no one of much importance."

Who could the police have "had, and let go," but Leslie Dillon? The fact that Dillon was Aggie's prime suspect for the Dahlia murder was later confirmed by her daughter-in-law, Rilla, in a letter to Jacqueline De River. "Aggie and your father worked closely on the case, and she said they believed they knew who killed Elizabeth Short," wrote Rilla to Jacqueline. "If my memory serves me, about that time or shortly thereafter, your father was let go from the department."

A dramatic change in Aggie's journalistic approach at this point also suggests that, like the doctor, she had been threatened or harassed. On Christmas morning of 1951, six (mainly Chicano) prisoners in the Los Angeles Central City Jail were severely beaten by LAPD officers at a drunken Christmas party after (incorrect) rumors that they had blinded an LAPD officer in a brawl. As many as fifty police officers—including Dahlia investigator Harry Fremont—participated in the beatings, in what was to become known as the infamous "Bloody Christmas" case.* All the prisoners received major injuries, including punctured organs and broken facial bones. At least a hundred people knew of or witnessed the beatings. But Chief Parker still managed to keep the events out of the press for almost three months.

One of the people who witnessed the "Bloody Christmas" beatings was the distinguished crime journalist Nieson Himmel, then a junior reporter working for the *Herald-Express*.† When Himmel was subpoenaed to give evidence to a grand jury about the beatings, he asked for Aggie's advice as city editor. She told him to keep out of it. It was a stunning reversal in approach from her go-get-'em exposure of the police cover-ups relating to the Brenda Allen scandal and the Dahlia case just two years beforehand. Himmel, the junior reporter, was fearful of the wrath of the LAPD. He had no support from his city editor. So he lied to the grand jury and testified that he saw nothing.‡

The doctor therefore now stood alone in his defiance of the police department. In a final irony, even as he was being humiliated by the LAPD, De River was featured with a drumroll as a great scientific detective in *12 Against Crime*, a book by the journalist Edward D. Radin. The acid-yellow dust jacket promised that the book would reveal the "smashing, inside story of the Deadly Dozen, the experts

---

* For Harry Fremont's role in the early Dahlia investigation, see page 28.
† For more on Nieson Himmel and his suspicions about Finis Brown and the Dahlia murder, see page 246.
‡ The "Bloody Christmas" beatings—which were immortalized by the writer James Ellroy in his L.A. Quartet novels and featured in the movie *Hollywood Confidential*—ended with a public inquiry and grand jury investigation in which eight LAPD officers were indicted for assault. The inquiry was precipitated by the pioneering judge Joseph Call, a friend of Dr. De River who contributed a chapter to his textbook *The Sexual Criminal*. (See page 212.) The beatings marked a turning point in the previously cozy relationship between the police and press, with the latter subsequently becoming more hostile and critical of the LAPD.

the police call in to solve America's toughest and most notorious cases in the fight against crime." Radin had this to say about the doctor:

> In Los Angeles, where glamour is largely manufactured, Dr. De River's genuine glamour is conspicuous. Claiming to be a descendant of Jean La Fitte, the pirate of the bayous of Louisiana who is credited with saving New Orleans, he has a swashbuckling air about him, accented by his lengthy dashing side-burns, his thin sweeping mustache, and a wing worn in the lapel of his jacket, a reminder of the days when he was a flying doctor for the Navy. Tall, immaculately dressed, with a pair of shoulders developed by working as a lumberjack during his youth, his appearance outdoes even a movie director's conception of a man about town. But behind the smooth-appearing façade there is an inquiring mind always seeking the cause behind the effect, and it has led him into a pioneering study of the modern sex criminal.

Radin went on to describe the psychiatrist's uncanny ability to spot a culprit, an ability that had left many police officers unable to "fathom how he reaches certain conclusions." He concluded with some remarks on the doctor's most notorious case to date, that of the Black Dahlia:

> Without realizing it, the Black Dahlia killer, like other sex criminals, left a message that Dr. De River has read. From it he has furnished police with enough information about the type of man they should look for. Enough officers have committed the description to memory to recognize the murderer if he is picked up. Even if he manages to elude all the traps set for him, Dr. De River still predicts that he will be caught because he says that the Black Dahlia killer is a man who some day will have to talk about it, and once he confides to somebody, he is on the road to capture.

What Radin did not say was that the doctor had, in fact, already identified to the police the man whom he believed to be the Dahlia killer. They had let that man go. They were now bent on destroying the doctor. They were determined to shut him up. But the doctor would not shut up. He continued to tell his story, to anybody who would listen. A few years later, somebody did.

VOICE IN
THE WIND

I t was late 1953, the climax of a long, hot summer that ended in
October with the hottest day of the year. Up the winding path
to the doctor's Beachwood Canyon home toiled the figures of two
men. One was middle-aged, but a good six feet five inches tall, with
the powerful physique of a heavyweight boxer. The other was much
younger—barely twenty-one years old, with piercing eyes and a tight
thatch of curly black hair.

The pair arrived at the doctor's front door and knocked. Through
the frosted pane, a shadow could be seen, peering out suspiciously.
Finally, the door opened a crack. Then there was the heavy sound of
bolts being unshot and chains released. When the door opened fully,
the doctor was revealed, standing in the doorway. He wore a thick
velvet dressing gown over his shirt and tie. From the folds of the dressing gown could be seen the dark glint of a gun. Dr. Paul De River had
been expecting the visitors. He ushered them in immediately.

The middle-aged, powerfully built man was Wally Klein, a well-
known Hollywood screenwriter with a number of credits to his name,*

---

* Wally Klein (1904–78) was a Hollywood writer and producer. Writing credits include *Oklahoma Kid* (1939), *They Died with their Boots On* (1941), *Hard to Get* (1938), and *Indianapolis
Speedway* (1939). He was the brother-in-law of legendary film producer Hal B. Wallis (*Casablanca, The Maltese Falcon*).

mainly historical westerns like *They Died with Their Boots On*, an early pairing of Errol Flynn with Olivia de Havilland, and *The Oklahoma Kid*, a movie that pitted a gunslinging James Cagney against his villainous nemesis in the form of Humphrey Bogart. Klein was a friend of John Huston and a fully paid-up member of the hard-drinking, hard-living, fast Hollywood set.

The younger man was Wally Klein's nephew, Donald Freed. Freed was then an aspiring actor/director/writer who had been studying in New York. The young Donald was staying at the Kleins' home on Fountain Avenue while he tried to break into the movie business. Many years later, he was himself to become a distinguished playwright in the tradition of Arthur Miller and a close associate of Harold Pinter.* But for the moment the young man followed his uncle around, picking up what he could of the tools of the screenwriter's trade and rubbing shoulders with Klein's extensive network of Hollywood contacts.

Wally Klein was interested in making a movie about the Dahlia case. The LAPD had been extremely helpful when he approached them. Perhaps they were too helpful. Klein was not convinced by what the LAPD told him. He wanted to find out more. He had heard that there was a doctor who had worked for the police department who knew the true story. So Klein had arranged to interview De River. His young nephew Donald Freed came along for the ride, mainly from curiosity.

The interior of the doctor's house was stifling in the late summer heat. The doctor himself sat hunched in a stuffed armchair, drawing long puffs from his black pipe. With the doctor was an eagle-like, bespectacled man. To the best of Donald's recollection, this was Ellery E. Cuff, public defender of Los Angeles. A Northern California farm boy, Cuff had grown up to become a passionate defense

---

* Donald Freed (b. 1933) is an American playwright, novelist, and screenwriter. He has been writer-in-residence at USCLA, the Old Vic, the York Theatre Royal, and the University of Leeds.

lawyer. He was to lead the Los Angeles Public Defender's Office for fifteen years, the first and biggest such office in the country, famously defending more than four thousand accused criminals in a thirty-five-year career.* Ellery Cuff and Dr. De River went back a long way, to the trial of Albert Dyer, whom Cuff had defended.† The pair remained close friends throughout their lives. Cuff had contributed a chapter to De River's textbook *The Sexual Criminal*. It was entitled "The Criminal Attorney Views Mental Disease as a Factor in Crime." He attended the meetings with Klein and Freed to lend his quiet support. Occasionally De River's eldest daughter, Jacqueline, would come into the room. The pair were clearly close: when they talked to each other, De River would speak softly to her in the old dialect of the South.

Donald Freed would never forget the half dozen or so interviews he and Wally Klein had with De River during the long, dark nights of that California fall. Many years later, he recalled the physical presence of the doctor with clarity: the sleek sartorial image of the well-dressed man from 1940s New Orleans; mustache, pipe, tie, velvet dressing gown. Having been fired from the LAPD, De River was now working for the Veterans Administration. "He had to live secretly. He withdrew, he was suspicious, his wife was very sick," recalled Freed. "It was a besieged household. It was dark, and it was sad." But the doctor himself spoke "in a resonant voice, with a natural sense of drama." Clearly, he had powerful friends to help him, as he had managed to get a job with the federal government and had avoided the blacklist. Donald Freed at that time had no knowledge of the Los Angeles Police Department. Many years later, he was to become an expert in its secret workings, in particular its Intelligence Division,

---

* Ellery E. Cuff (1896–1988) was the distinguished head of the Los Angeles Public Defender's Office from 1949 to 1963, the first public defender's office in the country. He was a long-standing campaigner against the death penalty.

† For more on Albert Dyer and the Babes of Inglewood case, see page 84.

the "Glass House."* But then, as a young man in the fall of 1953, he was hearing the names of Aggie Underwood, Mark Hansen, and Thaddeus Brown for the first time.

"Gradually, over the course of the interviews, I became familiar with the patois, the *lingua franca* that develops between people versed in a case, and so little by little I began to make out what was being said. I could see the doctor was beleaguered, and that this was his narrative, the story he had to tell. He was a natural dramatist, able to tell that story in a way that I never forgot. I carried it with me for the rest of my life."

The doctor told Klein and Freed that his analysis of the Black Dahlia murder had led him to a conviction about the type of "schizothymic"† personality that, he believed, had committed the crime. He had drawn up a detailed psychological profile of the killer. He would be, in the doctor's view, someone extremely sharp, an amateur deeply interested in crime and psychology. He would likely be an aficionado of true crime and detective stories, and had clearly followed the case in the newspapers. He would be likely to boast about his crime. He was exactly the type of personality who, like Albert Dyer before him, was likely to put himself onto center stage in the police investigation. Therefore, the doctor had deliberately made speculations as to the psychology of the Dahlia killer in true crime magazines such as *True Detective*. Eventually, he got the response for which he was looking—from one Leslie Dillon in Florida. And so the doctor started an epistolary exchange, finally culminating in the meeting between Dillon and himself in Banning. Dillon and the doctor met and talked and he—De River—could see at once that Dillon was the man. Dillon, the doctor explained, knew intimate details of the crime—including key facts such as what had happened

---

* In 1973, Freed was to edit *The Glass House Tapes*, an account of the inner workings of the LAPD and FBI based on interviews with a former spy and informer, Louis E. Tackwood.
† Schizothymia is an introverted psychiatric condition resembling a milder form of schizophrenia.

to the rose tattoo.* He gave detailed explanations of the mutilations. He told the doctor the killing had taken place in a motel, before police had even interviewed the witnesses at the Aster.

It was on the basis of what Dillon had revealed in Banning that the then-chief of the LAPD, Clemence Horrall, had stated to the press that "this is the man": the best suspect by far in the entire case. Aggie Underwood at the *Herald-Express* had been mercilessly listing the number of days that there had been no breakthrough in the case. Now the police finally had the break. The LAPD was categorical, in the press conference, that they had a suspect who had made statements that only the perpetrator of the crime could have made. That Dillon knew facts about the killing that the police did not even know themselves. That he had been in Los Angeles at the time of the murder. And yet, within a day of Leslie Dillon being re-interviewed by the Homicide detectives, he was let go. Why?

The doctor's explanation of the sudden and mystifying release of Leslie Dillon was powerful and succinct. Here, finally, was the last piece of the puzzle that connected Mark Hansen, Leslie Dillon, and the Brown brothers. "The doctor told us that Leslie Dillon, with his connections to the prostitution network, was a pimp and errand boy for Mark Hansen," said Freed. "Elizabeth Short was part of the Hansen entourage. But Hansen was getting tired of the Short girl. He was jealous of her many boyfriends, had enough of her pestering him for money. So one day, Hansen said words to the effect of, 'Get rid of her.' Hansen, not knowing or caring that his functionary was a dangerous and murderous psychopath, was stunned when she turned up as she did, all cut up. Although he didn't care what happened to her, he hadn't imagined *that* happening, particularly. Dillon was simply a runner, a messenger, a small-time hood running errands for Hansen and his friend, NTG. But he knew where the bodies were

---

* For the two "secret facts" relating to the mutilations that were withheld from the public and which De River and the LAPD initially said that Dillon knew, see page 105.

buried, and who at the LAPD was on the cuff for betting, bookmaking, prostitution, et cetera. . . ."

Leslie Dillon, De River told Freed and Klein, had played a dangerous game with the cops. A game that only a narcissistic, psychopathic egoist would dare to play. He had revealed, during the confidential interviews in the desert, that he was the killer. And then, when under arrest, he had threatened to blow the cover off the whole den of vice and corruption at the heart of the LAPD. "We were absolutely certain that Paul De River had solved the case," Freed said. "He had brought in the murderer, Leslie Dillon. But in order to cover up small-time vice on the part of Thaddeus Brown and his brother Finis—NTG, Mark Hansen, the organized vice of the day, which had the LAPD on the pad—to cover that up, they let a dangerous psychopath on the loose. In that interview with homicide, Leslie Dillon took them on. He told them that he wouldn't say a word, if they let him go. But if they arrested him, he knew plenty: and he mentioned Hansen and NTG, and he mentioned the Brown brothers, and he said he knew where the bodies were buried in terms of organized vice. And then, he was gone."

The doctor's voice droned on as he puffed on his black pipe. Occasionally, he would play extracts from the wax cylinder recordings of the interviews with Leslie Dillon, and Dillon's soft, mellifluous voice would float out of the phonograph. "I met the doctor at a time of deep depression in his life," Freed remembered. "He had lost a battle of savage infighting which only a police department can have, and after the collapse of his career and his job, and the police department itself, he had retreated—to his home, daughters, son, and very ill wife. He had been through a traumatic event, and he just had a few people who weren't afraid to be seen with him. One of them was the public defender, a very well-known and respected man. He was present at the interviews, and seemed very familiar with the case. It was clear that he fully supported the doctor. There were others, like Aggie Underwood, to whom the doctor referred all the time. She was his great friend and ally. De River had been wrecked by the Dahlia case. Aggie had not been wrecked, but she had played a dangerous game. She was the doctor's last hope—not that she herself had any overriding power—but she had a circle, she was highly respected, she was an influential figure, and as long as she believed in him and had gone to the lengths she went to, despite the fact she had been ordered off the case, the doctor clung to her. So he made Aggie an unforgettable character, the way he talked about her, and pinned his hopes on her. And I don't believe she ever abandoned him. She kept it alive, she was the keeper of the flame, and as long as she believed in him he could believe in himself and have some hope." The doctor's interviews with Klein and Freed were an extension of that hope. "He thought, in talking to someone like Wally Klein—a screenwriter of some prestige—that, while it could no longer be adjudicated legally, the full story might emerge. He, Paul De River, would then be seen to be a conscientious and creative officer of the justice system, the Los Angeles Police Department, who had been on the way to solving the case. At least, that is what might have been. We now know, of course, that it never happened."

Donald Freed himself has never been in any doubt as to what did happen in the Dahlia case. "There was a tremendous cover up. And it went far beyond this case. It was symbolic of the situation in Los Angeles: the nexus of political power, the newspapers, and the police." In the end, Wally Klein never did make his Black Dahlia movie. It was a story that, in the 1950s, was too dangerous to tell.

In his chapter about Dr. De River in 12 Against Crime, the journalist Edward Radin said about the Dahlia killer: "Even if he manages to elude all the traps set for him, Dr. De River still predicts that he will be caught because he says that the Black Dahlia killer is a man who someday will have to talk about it, and once he confides to somebody, he is on the road to capture."

Time and again, the Dahlia killer had demonstrated a compulsion for glory through grotesque theatricality. There had been the public display of Elizabeth's body next to the sidewalk; the sending in of the package to the newspapers; the phone call to Jimmy Richardson; the purported carving of initials in the victim's body. These were acts that this particular killer was psychologically compelled to do. They constituted a unique element of his pathology.* It was this key exhibitionist trait, a component of the Dahlia killer's distinctive "signature," that Dr. De River identified as potentially leading to his downfall. It was what he had in mind when he stated that whoever committed this crime would effectively come to the police himself, because he would be "compelled to boast about it." It was the reason why the doctor decreed that all the "confessing Sams" must be interviewed. But the Dahlia killer was more cunning and insidious than the "confessing Sams." For—in contrast to them—his self-identification with the crime was never direct. It was taunting and elusive. Time and again, he would thrust himself into the picture with a hint—a phone call, a letter—but never in such a way as to definitively be pinned down. It was a teasing game of cat-and-mouse with the authorities. A game that had something to do with self-publicity, but more to do with power. Leslie Dillon's initial approach to Dr. De River claiming knowledge of a third-party culprit, the offer to help in tracking the killer down, the revelation of secret facts, and then his ultimate escape from charges—all these facts fitted in with this signature behavior. It was a signature that would recur in Dillon's subsequent actions, years after he disappeared from public view upon his surprise release in January 1949. But these were not to be revealed until more than sixty years later, to a different writer, in a new century.

---

* The "signature" element of a killer's behavior—i.e., what is done as a result of a deep-seated psychological compulsion, and does not change across his or her crimes—is to be contrasted with the "M.O." or "modus operandi," i.e., behavior that evolves and changes as a result of expediency and/or learned experiences. So, for example, if a killer uses a knife to kill a victim in one crime and a hammer in another, depending on what is readily available at the crime scene, this would be a part of the M.O. But if he or she always decapitates the victims after death, this would constitute an element of the "signature." Distinguishing the M.O. in order to identify the "signature" elements of a crime is one of the major tasks of the forensic profiler.

PART 4

OUT OF THE PAST

"Heavy. What is it?"
"The, uh, stuff that dreams are made of."

—THE MALTESE FALCON (1941),

QUOTING WILLIAM SHAKESPEARE

22

THE NAME OF THE ROSE

"**W**hy did he call me Elizabeth, Mrs. Eatwell?"

The woman stared at me. She shook her long, dark hair in disbelief.

For a moment I also was shaken by disbelief. Here I was, in a neat suburban home. The wall clock ticked cozily. The room was spotless. Ranged on the tidy bookshelves were brightly colored children's books. The woman herself, although not young, had a childlike innocence about her, as if she were trying, subconsciously, to reclaim a childhood that had never been her own.

I did not reply to her question. After all, what was there to say?

It was a bright spring morning in 2016. By now I had been researching a book on the Dahlia case for two years. To a writer of historical true crime, the story was compelling. It held the dark allure of L.A. noir: a period synonymous with the golden age of Hollywood, yet riddled with the cynicism and savagery of postwar America. I was fascinated not only by the murder—with its many riddles and paradoxes—but also by the snapshot it revealed of Los Angeles at the time. A city of bright lights and darker shadows, where cops fraternized with mobsters and girls sold themselves for the promise of a bit part in a movie. The twists and turns of researching the case had led me to many surprising places, but none more so than this. Leslie Dillon, after the public furor and frenzy of the Dahlia debacle, had remarried several times. He had had another daughter. He had called her Elizabeth.*

And here she was. Elizabeth. After a painstaking trawl through the available records, I had finally traced and contacted her. I had written to her, briefly referring to her father's connection with the Dahlia investigation, and tentatively requesting an interview. Her initial reply was brusque. She had never heard of any connection between her father and the Dahlia murder. She could not believe he had been connected with the case. But then she relented, and agreed to a meeting.

There was not much that Elizabeth could tell me about her father, Leslie Dillon. The two were not close. She had decided to cut off ties with him when she was young. He and her mother had divorced. (Dillon married four times in all.) He had drifted around from job to job—music teacher, bartender, bookseller. He had spent time in Las Vegas in the 1970s. Finally, he had settled down in San Francisco, where he had died in February 1988. He had gone by the name of "Jack," not "Leslie." Elizabeth had not been proud of her father, but she never imagined he was capable of carrying out such an act as the Dahlia murder. He was not, she said, a violent man.

"I read the reports that the killer was a surgeon," she said to me hopefully. "That doesn't sound like my father."

"He is believed to have worked in a morgue."

"A . . . morgue?" Her shock and horror were apparent.

"Didn't you know that?"

"No."

But then, Elizabeth knew almost nothing. She had been told almost nothing.

Why, I asked, had she decided to cut off close contact with her father?

Oh, he was just not around much, that was all.

---

* Full name withheld.

Why had her mother divorced Leslie Dillon?

A pause. Finally: "Probably because he was still married when he married her. Also, maybe because he just stopped coming home."

Was that what happened, I wondered, on the night of January 14, 1947? Leslie Dillon had just "not come home"? Was that why Georgia Dillon, his first wife, was unable to provide an alibi for him that night? And then there was the baffling question that the daughter herself posed, with a dawning realization of shock:

"Why did he call me Elizabeth?"

I was now even more perplexed than before. I could think of no explanation for Leslie Dillon's bizarre choice of the first name "Elizabeth" for his daughter. After all the noise and sensation of the arrest and subsequent court proceedings, it was a provocative and perverse choice. Was it yet another indirect allusion to a woman with whom Dillon felt compelled to connect himself? To me, this seemed potentially yet another manifestation of the "signature" behavior that Dr. De River had identified: another move in the cat-and-mouse game with investigators; a further veiled, teasing allusion to the crime. In my experience as a writer and researcher of historical crime, I had already encountered several killers with a compulsion to draw attention to themselves, without actually admitting culpability, by communicating with the media or somehow getting mixed up in the police investigation. The infamous Zodiac and BTK killers had both sent cryptic communications and clues to the police and the press. The notorious British murderer John Reginald Christie had acted as a star witness in the trial of his tenant for murders that it is now believed he himself committed.* And, of course, Albert Dyer, the Inglewood killer, had come forward to the police investigating the murders of the three little girls, to proffer his assistance.†

---

* Zodiac, BTK, John Reginald Christie: for summary information on these killers and their crimes, see the endnote on page 330.

† For more on Albert Dyer, the Inglewood killer, see page 85.

If the killer had indeed inscribed his initial on the victim's body, this—like the naming of his daughter after the victim—would have constituted another instance of his both appropriating the victim, and indirectly drawing attention to himself. It would fit in with the pattern of "signature" behavior that had been demonstrated already. In this context, the crime scene photographs purportedly showing the initials *D* and either *E* or *F* were a crucial piece of evidence—if they could be found. The photographs had been exhibited at the secret hearing between Fred Witman and the DA's Officers Veitch and Stanley. During that hearing, as recorded in the official transcript, the investigators had agreed that the initials appeared to be carved over the postmortem lacerations on the pubic area. And yet, despite my repeated requests, both the LAPD and the DA's office refused to release any crime scene photographs.* This blanket refusal was deeply frustrating. After all, the presence of the initial *D* on the body would be telling evidence against Leslie Dillon. Not one of the other primary suspects in the Dahlia case had the initial *D*.

While the Los Angeles District Attorney's Office refused to release the crime scene photographs, it did release a large number of documents relating to the case. They included two samples of "creative writing" purportedly written by Leslie Dillon, and discovered by Officer Jones of the Gangster Squad in Dillon's lodgings in Florida. The fragments were unsigned and typed on the letter paper of the Greystone Hotel on Collins Avenue in Miami Beach. They appeared to be submissions of synopses for stories to a newspaper editor called "Mr. Stern."† They made intriguing reading:‡

---

* The LAPD has consistently refused to release the Dahlia case file, despite repeated requests by many researchers. A limited number of documents was released to this author by the LAPD as a result of a legal demand, but these did not include the crime scene photographs. The district attorney's office disclosed a large number of documents to the author but also refused to disclose the crime scene photographs.

† Possibly J. David Stern (1886–1971), a well-known newspaper publisher.

‡ The fragments are reproduced here exactly as in the originals and include all errors of spelling, grammar, and syntax.

FIRST FRAGMENT:

The Greystone Hotel
Collins Avenue at Twentieth
Miami Beach—Florida

Tell you about Tinas big time gambler who took over the gap after you surrendered.

He was rooming with the doorman from the Blackamoor Room which is now the 5-Oclock Club.

Doorboy had a very beautiful Jewish girl who was a clerk at Saks. Youve seen her around may know her. He was nuts about her, but her living right in the next room, for a whole year or more. and him working so late at night. She decided she liked his roomates nuts better. So she started to unravel the doorman slowly. The roomate would move in with her one shoe at a time. It began to get on the dorman's nerves. When he would come home so late after work, and get ready for the doorman's double deep dive. He would almost drown. The BTO* had stretched that little old thing so. So the next morning at 10 AM The bastard who parks the cars went in to alter the situation but he failed to look at the calender. It was no less Friday August the 13th.

Resenting his ungentlemanly acquasitions the pump† went to the front office to call up the high roller. Who was at the local bookshop.‡

Realizing this as the climax, Little boy park your car went back to his room and retrieved a role of cabbage§ big enough

---

* "BTO": acronym for big-time operator, referring to the "big time gambler" of the first sentence. The inference is that the gambler has so "stretched" the woman's (Tina's) vagina that the doorman "would almost drown" when he tried to have sex with her.
† "Pump": possibly derived from the verb "pump," gambling slang from poker referring to increasing another player's bet.
‡ "Bookshop": bookies, betting parlor.
§ "Cabbage": slang word for roll of (green) banknotes.

to stuff her. and gashed right back to the front office to offer
the stuffing which was one kind peter boy did not have. She
refused the bribe so he made another digging and came back
with some thing she couldnt refuse.

He pulled his trigger finger all over the place. Passed the
light so fast behind her eyes the balls shot out of the sock-
ets. Resenting either the sight or his poor workmanship, He
gunned himself twice in the same place and fell dead over
her unconscious body.

She is still alive the last I heard, But doesn't feel so good.
She will probably be blind or [nuts]. Which goes to show he
should have been satisfied with Tina. What good is a wife
with her eyeballs hanging out.

You wouldn't have shot Tina, Would you?

The fragment gave an illuminating insight into the writer's psychological complexes. In the story, the protagonist, the "doorman,"
was shown to be impotent, his inferior member "drowned" by that of
his rival, the "high roller" gambler. The doorman's revenge was to find
a roll of "cabbage" (cash) big enough to "stuff" the victim. While the
overt scenario was one of bribery/paying for sex, the imagery—"stuff
her," "gashed"—also evoked the forcible use of an object to penetrate
the victim, where the protagonist's own member was inadequate to
the task.

The second fragment was also revealing:

SECOND FRAGMENT:

The Greystone Hotel
Collins Avenue at Twentieth
Miami Beach—Florida

Have you ever killed a man? Do you know what it is
to hide from fear? Fear of your own fear. Surely you have

considered such a venture. Not even the landlord? Well now
that we understand each other. If the rascal in question is
laid away without any serious planning. In just maybe a fit
of anger. With a brick or something. then no body gets really
mad at you. They will probably just put you up with some of
Uncle Sam's chosen guests until all is forgotten.

But on the other hand. If you are a very thoughtful sort
of a person, and really give the matter serious thought. Does
this guy really deserve to go, so young? And if you decide he
does. and if you make elaborate plans to that end. For his
end. Then you did it in the first degree, no less. You have
done it up so cleverly (except for the knife in the back) that
the boys in blue get real upset. That is no rose they are trying
to pin on you. They are trying to gas or electrocute you.
Depending on who has the most votes the gas or the electric
company. On the other hand if you are just a poor Chinaman
and live in China. Where the basket weavers union is affili-
ated. They will chop off your hair just below the adams-apple
and let the unsmiling remnants drop into one of their little
hand-woven baskets,

That they so smilingly weave.

Don't do it.

She isn't worth it.

In this fragment, the "hypothetical" scenario of a hotheaded killing
was contrasted with that of a thoughtful, cold-blooded, and calculated
murder. The protagonist was shown considering the consequences of
one versus the other: the gas chamber or electric chair, as opposed
to a mere spell in one of "Uncle Sam's" jails. The substitution of the
word "he" for "she" in the final sentence—"*She* isn't worth it"—was
especially significant. It implied that the use of the masculine gender
in the opening sentence of the fragment—"Have you ever killed a
man?"—was a cover or displacement for the real scenario underlying

the piece: that of killing a *woman*.* This slip obviously struck Dr. De River as it was pointed out by his representative, Fred Witman, to Veitch and Stanley at the secret hearing. Witman also told the DA investigators that multiple drafts of the fragments had been discovered, suggesting intensive and careful reworking and rewriting.

Both fragments exhibited errors of grammar and syntax similar to those in the letters Leslie Dillon wrote to De River, and similar also to those in some of the communications sent to the police in 1947 purportedly by the Dahlia killer. The note in the original Dahlia package, for example, read, "Here *is* Dahlia's possessions . . . ," and the subsequent postcard that might have been the promised "letter to follow" stated, "Had my fun *at* the police."† Most significantly, the first fragment in particular manifested an extreme insecurity about the writer's masculinity and ability to satisfy a woman, a pathology that boiled over into a climax of violence in which an orgasm appeared to have been achieved, not by normal sexual intercourse, but by an orgy of brutality in which the protagonist shot his "trigger finger all over the place" and shot out his girlfriend's eyeballs. Similar themes of sexual insecurity and violence against women were reflected in the news clipping Leslie Dillon had preserved, about the man who shot out a schoolgirl's tooth because she had mocked him. It was also the motive Dillon had hypothesized to Dr. De River for the Dahlia murder. Was it not possible, he had written, that an associate of Elizabeth, after an affair "not considered proper by the average person," had been "mocked or threatened exposure by her to his friends?" He therefore might, out of revenge, inflict "pain of some nature on her and experience a new sensation by accident. . . . Thus leading to the complete annihilation of her and other victims."‡

If Dr. De River's observation that Dillon had a "juvenile penis" was

---

* Interestingly, in the 1946 movie *Blue Dahlia*, a husband comes home from the Navy to find his wife kissing another man. He pulls a gun on her and then changes his mind, with the comment, "You're not worth it."
† My italics.
‡ See page 104.

true, this fact would proffer an explanation for such a deep-rooted insecurity. It would validate Dillon's explanation of the motive for the killing. It would explain some of the details of the actual crime: for example, why the victim was not raped, but sodomized with a foreign object; and the killer's many postmortem acts of "piquerism," or cutting with a knife. The criminal psychologist and signature killer expert Robert Keppel has written: "Acts of piquerism—jabbing, stabbing, cutting, and gouging through the use of a knife or other sharp-pointed instrument for the purposes of sexual gratification—strike terror in living victims. Knives are fearsome and unyielding and their phallic nature as weapons supersedes any harm the predator can inflict with his penis. Knives are therefore sexual weapons psychologically as well as weapons of combat."

In addition to the fragments of Dillon's writing, in the course of my research, I also came across an intriguing photograph. The picture had been posted on one of the major Black Dahlia case Internet discussion forums. It depicted a young woman in profile, with a mass of dark, curly hair. She was sitting bent over in a chair, semi-nude in her panties, brushing her hair. The background of the photograph showed a sparse bedroom with a single bed draped in a candlewick coverlet. A polka-dot blouse that might have been made of silk lay tossed aside, crumpled carelessly on the floor. Beside the blouse was a pair of black, open-toed, high-heeled shoes. A small snapshot of a serviceman in a peaked cap was pinned to the wall. The woman was the very double of Elizabeth Short.

According to the person who placed the photograph on the Black Dahlia site, the picture had originally been posted on the popular image hosting site Flickr, credited to "George Price." However, upon inquiry as to the provenance of the photograph, the picture was mysteriously taken off Flickr. The resemblance of the semi-nude woman in the picture to Elizabeth Short was striking. Could this be a photograph of Elizabeth taken by George Price, the photographer listed in her address book? If it were, this would establish without a doubt that she had been caught up in the porno ring described by her friend Lynn Martin and in which Lola Titus had also been involved. In order to try to establish whether the photograph was indeed of Short, I decided to consult an expert. I therefore sent the semi-nude picture—along with a selection of known photographs of Elizabeth Short, including the only known profile shot of her (which was taken by the Santa Barbara police)—to retired police sergeant Michael Streed, a leading forensic facial recognition expert based in Corona, California. Michael's long and distinguished career has included stints working as a forensic artist/consultant to the Los Angeles and Baltimore City police departments. Was it possible, I asked him, that the semi-nude woman in the photograph was the same woman depicted in the known pictures of Elizabeth Short?

In the meantime, I again looked at the list of suspects in Frank Jemison's final report. From my exhaustive examination of the available case files, not one of them had the weight of circumstantial evidence against him that had been gathered against the suspects Leslie Dillon and Mark Hansen. The case against the Hollywood physician George Hodel was notably weak. Despite this, I was surprised to find that George Hodel's son, Steve Hodel, an ex-member of the LAPD, had written many books claiming that his father was the Dahlia killer. Steve's case for this contention was based on an accumulation of assertions and evidence, set out in his various books. To me, the two potentially most compelling facts were these:

- That two women had said George Hodel knew Elizabeth Short.
- A purported "confession" to the crime by George Hodel in a
  telephone conversation recorded when the DA's office bugged
  the doctor's house in the early part of 1950.

Ultimately, after careful consideration, I was not convinced that either of these amounted to a case that George Hodel had committed the Dahlia murder.

As to the first contention, it was true that two people did claim that George Hodel knew Elizabeth Short. However, there were many more witnesses who asserted that he did not; and, more tellingly, none of Elizabeth's own close friends or acquaintances—Ann Toth, Marjorie Graham, Lynn Martin, or the victim's own relatives— mentioned George Hodel, or indeed any doctor, among her numerous boyfriends. In any event, the mere fact that the doctor might have been acquainted with Short or in her circle did not amount to evidence that he killed her.*

The second key item of evidence was a statement supposedly made by George Hodel during the secret recordings that DA Frank Jemison made in his home on Franklin Avenue in February/March 1950:

> *Supposin' I did kill the Black Dahlia. They couldn't prove it now. They can't talk to my secretary any more because she's dead.*

According to George's son Steve, this statement amounted to a "confession" by his father that he was the Dahlia killer. But there were difficulties with this contention. At the time of the recordings, George Hodel knew that he was being investigated on many fronts by both the DA and the FBI: tax evasion, performing illegal abortions, the possible murder of his secretary, alleged Communist sympathies. He was also in the newspaper headlines as the latest suspect in the Dahlia killing. It would therefore be natural for the doctor to allude to these various allegations in his telephone conversations. It was also obvious, from the transcripts of the recordings, that Hodel was perfectly aware that he was being bugged. The transcripts recorded him banging about the house, digging in the basement for bugs, and exhorting his housekeeper to search for the concealed device that he

---

* It is perfectly possible that George Hodel might have met Elizabeth at one of his louche sex parties, or through his interest in nude photography. He would certainly have heard of Mark Hansen and NTG.

knew was hidden somewhere. It was highly improbable, therefore, that he would have made a telephone "confession" to a sensational murder which he knew would be relayed straight to the listening ears of Frank Jemison. In any case, if there had been any real likelihood that Dr. George Hodel had been the Dahlia killer, it beggared belief that his own attorney would have brought up that fact in court during the doctor's trial for molesting his daughter Tamar.* Neeb, it was clear, alluded to Tamar's accusation as a joke, an illustration of her allegedly hysterical behavior and outlandish accusations. It was a courtroom tactic that seriously backfired, because it turned the doctor into a suspect for a murder for which he had never even been considered until that date.

Most significantly of all, there was no circumstantial evidence that I could see to link George Hodel to the actual crime. The Hollywood physician did not have any connection to the body dump site in the working-class neighborhood of Leimert Park, over thirty minutes' drive from his Hollywood home; nor to the spot on Crenshaw where Elizabeth's shoes and purse were found. He had no known connection to the Aster Motel, nor was he referred to by any of the witnesses there. The doctor drove a black Packard car, not a Ford. Moreover, he had returned from China in September 1946 because he had suffered a serious heart attack. He had spent September and October in the hospital. It was highly implausible that he would have had the strength to carry out the Dahlia murder.

Dr. George Hodel was, in fact, never high on the Dahlia suspect list. As he himself said in one of the recorded telephone conversations, he was probably only being investigated because he had angered the DA's office by bribing his way out of molestation charges. Two members of the DA's office, the doctor claimed, had been demoted because of him. They wanted revenge. That, and the foolish cross-examination ploy of his attorney, put him on the Dahlia suspect list.

From my exhaustive examination of the case files available, the

---

* The incident with Neeb and Tamar at the trial is discussed on page 207.

only suspect on the DA's list who appeared to have any credible evidence against him, other than Leslie Dillon and Mark Hansen, was a somewhat mysterious Army sergeant called Carl Balsiger. Balsiger was a known boyfriend of Elizabeth Short and had visited Camarillo with her in December, before her trip to San Diego. He told police that he had stayed overnight with Short at a motel on Yucca Street on December 7 and then had put her on the bus to San Diego, where she was found at the Aztec Theatre the next night by Dorothy French. Balsiger claimed that nothing had happened between Elizabeth and himself during their motel tryst, but the police—not surprisingly—did not believe him. He had been stationed at Camp Cooke at the same time Short was there, although he denied knowing her at this point.* Frank Jemison noted that Balsiger had a propensity for violence. He had attended the University of Kansas City at the same time as a beautiful socialite, Dorothy Welsh, who was brutally murdered in 1941.† In December 1949, Balsiger had married Jane Ellen Moyer, daughter of a prominent family in Lincoln, Nebraska and an assistant attorney general of Nebraska. He therefore had connections in high places. He would have been in a position to cover up a crime.‡

But there were other, compelling facts that made it unlikely that Carl Balsiger had killed Elizabeth Short. He had agreed to and passed a lie detector test. More significantly, his name was included in Elizabeth's address book that had been mailed by the killer to the

---

* The police reports note that Carl Balsiger denied he was the "Sergeant Chuck" who had allegedly had an affair with Elizabeth at Camp Cooke and subsequently been court-martialed. Balsiger's Army record contains no reference to a court-martial.

† Leila Adele Welsh, known as Dorothy Welsh, was a beautiful twenty-four-year-old heiress who was murdered in Kansas in March 1941. Her mother discovered her dead in her bedroom: she had suffered blows to the head, had her throat slit, and a piece of flesh had been removed from her thigh/buttock. Leila's brother George was prosecuted for the murder but subsequently acquitted. The killer was never found.

‡ Jane Moyer Balsiger died in a car accident in January 1952. Carl Balsiger was investigated in relation to various insurance frauds, including as vice president of a company underwriting high-risk car insurance, in the late 1960s and early 1970s. (See the *Kansas City Times*, January 25, 1952; March 22, 1968; *St. Louis Post-Dispatch*, February 1, 1970.)

Examiner newspaper, and from which several pages had been cut. If Balsiger was indeed the killer, why had his name not been removed from the book? Moreover, the extravagantly exhibitionist behavior of the Dahlia killer—the phone call to Jimmy Richardson, the sending in of the package with Elizabeth's belongings—did not tally with the character or behavior of Carl Balsiger, who was extremely discreet and circumspect.

Elizabeth's censored address book—which did not include an entry for Leslie Dillon, but did feature Mark Hansen's name on the cover—was another puzzle. If Mark Hansen was mixed up with the Dahlia murder, as Dr. De River and the Gangster Squad believed, why did the killer incriminate him by sending a book with his name on the cover to the newspapers? The sending in of the address book implied that the killer was deliberately attempting to implicate, threaten, or bribe Mark Hansen. This fit with other events in the story. In particular, it fit with the mysterious calls to Mark Hansen's home telephone on the Sunday before Short was murdered, and with Dr. De River's claim that Leslie Dillon used his inside knowledge about Mark Hansen's underworld activities and police connections as a means to threaten the homicide detectives that he would "tell all," thus securing his release.

In fact, it was Dr. De River's account of events—as relayed to Donald Freed in 1953—that finally tied the scattered pieces of the puzzle together. Mark Hansen had the motive to "get rid" of Elizabeth Short. He was obsessive and possessive of her and furiously jealous of her many boyfriends. He was fed up with her pestering him for money. According to Dr. De River, Mark Hansen said, "Someone get rid of that girl." Like Henry II when he exclaimed, "Who will rid me of this pestilent priest?" he had not expected the response he got. Leslie Dillon, who was part of Hansen's entourage of pimps, went out and, literally, performed an overkill. Hansen was then obliged to take action. Relying on his contacts with the Brown brothers, he got the matter hushed up. At least three distinguished Los Angeles crime reporters—Tony Valdez of Fox News, Chuck Cheatham of the *Long*

Beach Independent, and Nieson Himmel of the *Los Angeles Times*—
all stated, on the record, that Finis Brown was a bagman for Mark
Hansen.* Harry Lawson and other members of the grand jury shared
that suspicion. The Moormans were convinced Hansen was thick
with Finis Brown and told Frank Jemison that Officers Case and
Ahern had said to them that "their hands were tied." Somehow, the
cops always seemed to be at Mark Hansen's beck and call. According
to Finis Brown, Hansen was a police informant; when Jeff Connors
split from his wife Grace Allen, policemen were there to escort her to
Hansen's home; on being shot by Lola Titus, he called immediately,
"Get me Brown." In what would appear to be yet another stunning
conflict of interest, Walter Morgan of the DA's office—one of the
assistant DA investigators on the Dahlia case—was married to Tanya
"Sugar" Geise, a featured dancer in the floor show at the Florentine
Gardens and a close friend of Mark Hansen's. Effectively, Morgan
was investigating his wife's friend and employer. Many years later,
reporter Nieson Himmel gave an interview in which he summarized
what had always been suspected among the newspapermen but never
openly acknowledged. It was a story that came startlingly close to Dr.
De River's account as related to Donald Freed. "Mark Hansen was
rumored to be Finis's layoff man. The story goes that Finis was into
Mark for $5,000. A lot of money in those days.† Mark Hansen had
supposedly been after Elizabeth Short for months, wanting to get her
into the sack. She wouldn't come across. Mark became infuriated
and killed her. Finis Brown supposedly covered up for Mark Hansen,
cajoling his brother Thad Brown, Chief of Detectives, to protect
Finis and destroy some evidence. Hansen then, supposedly, forgave
Finis Brown's debt." Himmel went on to say that Aggie Underwood
frequently hinted that she knew what had happened, although she
never revealed it.

Mark Hansen had known ties with the Los Angeles underworld,

*See discussion of Finis Brown on page 78.
† Worth $55,000 today.

in particular the notorious local gangster Jimmy Utley, who had police connections and who ran a secret gambling parlor in Hansen's nightclub, the Florentine Gardens.* According to Ann Toth, Hansen was also linked to the illegal abortion racket. The Gangster Squad had investigated him in relation to a jewelry scam, but got nowhere once the information was passed up the line in the police department. Hansen lied to the DA investigators about receiving a telephone call from Elizabeth on the night of Thursday, January 9, the last night she was seen alive. He lied about the fact that he had told her she could stay at his house if she had no other place to go. In fact, there was evidence that Mark Hansen did see Elizabeth during the "missing week." The Moormans, in what appeared to be an unshakable identification, said he was at the Aster Motel during the period that Elizabeth Short was seen there, drugged and naked on a bed in a cabin of the motel. But Mark Hansen, fanatically discreet about his private life, was not the type to leave a body sprawled beside a sidewalk in full view. Nor to send packages with his address book in them to the press. Mark Hansen, it seemed, was mixed up in the Dahlia murder, and the reason for the subsequent cover-up. But Mark Hansen did not commit the murder.

Alone of all the suspects in the Dahlia case, the weight of circumstantial evidence against Leslie Dillon as the actual killer was compelling. There was the testimony that Dillon, even when living in San Francisco, visited Los Angeles in January 1947, as stated by his former employer Jimmy Harlow and Mrs. Pearl McCromber; that the body dump site at Leimert Park was close to an address that he used when in Los Angeles, namely his wife's aunt Nellie Hinshaw's house on Crenshaw Boulevard; that he demonstrated thorough knowledge of the area when traveling to the scene with Officer JJ O'Mara; that Elizabeth's shoes and empty purse were dumped in a trash can less

---

* Mark Hansen admitted knowing Jimmy Utley when questioned by the DA. The Florentine Gardens was to go through successive co-ownerships in the period 1947–49. Co-owners with Mark Hansen in 1949 were Barney Van Der Steen and Eddie Allen, both connected to the Las Vegas gambling casino El Rancho (*Billboard*, July 23, 1949).

than a couple of blocks from Dillon's Crenshaw Boulevard address; that nobody could establish a firm alibi for Dillon on the night of the murder, not even his own wife; that he drove, according to three witnesses, an older-model dark Ford at the time of the murder, similar to the car seen by eyewitnesses at the murder scene; that he was identified as one of Elizabeth's boyfriends by her close friend Ann Toth, Mark Hansen, and the actress Ardis Green; that he had been seen in Elizabeth's company at the A1 Trailer Park by Jiggs Moore and the old man Carriere in autumn 1946, and at the Aster Motel in January 1947. Not to mention Dillon's admitted interest in sexual sadism and the fact that both Dr. Paul De River and the LAPD asserted that he knew details about the mutilations that had been kept secret, including some that even the police did not know.

Then there was Leslie Dillon's patently exhibitionist and narcissistic behavior, fitting the identified signature pathology of the Dahlia killer. In particular, he reached out to Dr. De River, offering to help track down the killer; he bizarrely turned himself in to the FBI in Florida; he chose to pack razors, a dog leash, and phenobarbital pills in his suitcase when he clearly suspected he was under surveillance for murder; and he perversely chose "Elizabeth" for his daughter's name. The actions of the actual killer similarly reflected a deep narcissism and thirst for attention: the package sent to the press; the phone call to Jimmy Richardson (and indeed, the "soft, well-modulated voice" of Dillon would correspond with the "sly, soft voice" that Jimmy Richardson recalled); and the carving of the letter D, and possibly E, into the victim's body, corresponding to D for "Dillon" and E for "Elizabeth." There was, in addition, Dillon's own explanation of the motive for the crime: that of rage at being "mocked" and "threatened exposure." This tied in both with a personal sexual inferiority complex—explained by De River as the result of a physical abnormality—and details of what had been done to the victim. Not to mention the intimation of other sexual paraphilias evoked by the discovery of the man's-size female shoes at Briargate Lodge in Banning—a hint of a possible transvestite fetishism that found an echo in the fact that on Elizabeth's body, according to Aggie Underwood's early newspaper reports, each large toenail had been painted red.

Then there was the fact of Dillon's known connections to prostitution and the procurement of women, rackets in which Mark Hansen was involved. Dillon had told investigators that he liked to drug women by sprinkling powdered phenobarbital pills on their ice cream when on dates, to "knock them out"; some seven hundred phenobarbital pills had been found in his luggage when he was arrested. Witnesses had described seeing Elizabeth Short naked and apparently in a drugged state during the "missing week," although— astonishingly—the LAPD claimed to have "lost" the contents of her stomach, which had supposedly been sent off for chemical analysis.* Most significant of all, Dillon had stated that the murder was committed in a motel. Not only this, he was proved to have stayed at the very motel in which five people testified that, on the morning of January 15, 1947, the most hideous carnage had been discovered.

The evidence of the bloody room at the Aster Motel was perhaps the most compelling of all. Five witnesses—the motel owners Mr. and Mrs. Hoffman, the guests Mr. and Mrs. Moorman, and the cleaning lady, Lila Durant—all testified to the discovery of a room covered in blood and feces at the Aster on the morning of January 15, 1947. The state of the room was so bad that Mr. Hoffman cleaned it out personally, although this was not his usual habit. The laundry bill at the Aster confirmed an unusually large washing load in the week of January 15. And yet, the LAPD had tested the cabins at the motel for blood two years later, and supposedly turned up negative results.

In the course of my research, I managed to track down a grand-

---

* In a memorandum to Leo Stanley of the DA's office, Frank Jemison stated that officers asked the coroner and the county chemist to analyze the vital organs of Elizabeth Short chemically to find out whether, for one thing, they contained narcotics. "At a later date when the officers requested the results they were informed that these vital organs had been misplaced and had probably been thrown out at the time they were cleaning up the laboratory and further that they had made no analysis." For a discussion of the disappearance of contemproary evidence, see the preface to this book.

daughter of the Hoffmans.* Her mother had been Pamela Hoffman, daughter of Henry and Clora Hoffman. As a ten-year-old girl, Pamela had been present at the Aster Motel when the carnage was discovered on the morning of January 15, 1947. Pamela's daughter told me that her mother had died of pancreatic cancer in 2013. However, before Pamela died, she had recorded a filmed interview for posterity in which she related the events of that morning on January 15, 1947. In the course of the interview, Pamela—then seventy-five years old and close to death—confirmed the discovery by her parents of the bloody room. She also confirmed that—however much Henry Hoffman and his wife backtracked in Mark Hansen's office in 1949 on their identification of Elizabeth Short as being the dark-haired girl who stayed at the motel—the Hoffmans were, in fact, in no doubt that Elizabeth had been murdered there. Pale and drawn, Pamela was clearly terminally ill. Yet she retained her mental acuity and vividly recalled the horror of that morning:

> We were living at the Aster Motel then. And one night
> a couple came in, [my father] didn't pay any attention to
> them, he didn't have his glasses on, didn't require the proper
> registration. The next day my mother found the room com-
> pletely destroyed, all the bedding was bloody. They burned
> the sheets and pillows and bedspread and spent the whole
> day washing down that room. And when they read about the
> [Dahlia] murder, my mother was horrified, because she real-
> ized that she had destroyed evidence.

So—in addition to the five contemporary witnesses that I already knew about—here was yet another witness, giving a firsthand account before she died, of the carnage that had been discovered at the motel. What motive could Pamela, a dying woman, possibly have, other than to tell the truth?

* Name withheld.

Given the compelling witness testimony of a serious crime committed at the Aster Motel on the night of January 14/15, 1947, the total failure of the LAPD's forensic tests to trace *any blood at all* in the motel cabins was bizarre. A further strange fact was that—while earlier forensic evidence had been passed to the FBI for testing*—the tests at the Aster Motel had not been handled by the FBI, but internally by the LAPD. In fact, all forensic testing relating to Leslie Dillon, including tests on the dog leash found in his luggage, had been handled by the LAPD, and not sent to the FBI. The LAPD's forensic reports on the Aster motel rooms and the dog leash have never been released. I could find only one brief allusion to the tests at the motel, in one of the police reports released to me by the DA's office:†

On March 15, 1949, Lee Jones, Crime Lab, made a benzedine‡ test in unit No. 3, [address redacted] S. Flower St. . . . This check showed a pseudo reaction. Samples were taken to the lab and the second blood test, which was a kastelmeir test made in the crime laboratory, was given with a negative result. Tests were made on all of the cabins at the Aster Motel, S. Flower, on August 2nd, 1949. In making the tests, Officers removed the baseboards and thresholds of all the cabins at this address at which time chemist Ray Pinker found pseudo reactions in all the cabins, by means of the benzedine test. If there had been any blood in these cabins, there would have been a positive true blood reaction. In cabin no. 6 the benzedine test was used on the asphalt tile on a spot in the floor in front of the

---

* For example, all fingerprint testing and forensic tests on the brush bristles found on Elizabeth's body were passed to the FBI's Forensic Department.

† There was also one brief reference in a police report that the LAPD had tested the dog leash and "found no blood." Again, the original test report has never been released.

‡ Benzidine is an organic compound that in the past was used to test for blood. An enzyme in blood causes the oxidation of benzidine to a distinctively blue-colored derivative.

bed, about a foot away from the wall, where in the crevices
between the asphalt tile there was found a blood reaction.
The manager of the motel stated at the time that a woman
living in there a few days before had menstruated on the
sheet and that there was a few drops on the floor. That was
the only place where there was any true blood reaction in
any of the cabins.

This extract was the only information available as to the nature of
the forensic tests conducted at Flower Street by the LAPD. According to the extract, the tests showed a "pseudo reaction" for blood in
cabin 3—the very cabin which, according to the Gangster Squad
officers, was discovered smeared with blood, feces, and bloody footprints on the morning of January 15, 1947. But, the LAPD claimed,
this was not a "true" blood reaction. The only "true" reaction was,
allegedly, a small amount of menstrual blood in cabin 6, dating from
after the killing.

The first question that obviously arose was: How reliable were
these tests, carried out two years after the killing and almost seventy
years ago, when forensic science was as yet in its infancy? Could it
be that, as Fred Witman and Dr. De River had claimed, the results
had been voided or rendered unreliable by the presence of chemicals
used for cleaning up the scene, which had caused "pseudo-reactions"?
The fact that there had been a significant "pseudo-reaction" in cabin
3, indicating a large presence of chemical agents in that particular
room, was itself a cause for suspicion. Mr. and Mrs. Hoffman and
Lila Durant had testified that the bloody cabin had been thoroughly
cleaned on discovery of the carnage.

In order to attempt to answer these troubling questions, I decided
to send all the information I had to a modern forensic scientist.
Suzanna Ryan is a leading DNA analyst and forensic serologist based
in Carlsbad, California, with extensive experience in crime scene
investigation and reporting on cold cases. She kindly agreed to examine what documentary evidence there was, to attempt to establish

the reliability of the LAPD's forensic testing at the motel. I sent what I could find off to her and waited for her response.

In the meantime, I decided to collect and scrutinize every available copy of the crime scene photographs. Although the original photographs have never been officially released by the authorities, some of them have been reproduced from time to time in books and magazine articles, where an author or journalist has managed to obtain access to them by unofficial means. I was leafing through one such book about the case, originally published in 1994, when I made a discovery. A picture of the victim's bisected body lying supine on the table of the morgue as though on a butcher's slab, the hacked out section of the left leg and lacerations on the pubic region clearly visible. The reference of the photograph was exactly as noted by Veitch and Stanley during the secret hearing with Witman: photograph #295-771, 1-15-47 G.L. Across the slashes on the pubic region was—to me, it seemed unmistakably—the letter *D*, and what might have been an *E*, or an *F*.

The police photograph showed precisely what Veitch and Stanley had seen.

23

SPECTER OF
THE ROSE

n an outlandish case, this was the most outlandish discovery yet. I had spent so much effort, so many hours, attempting to locate a photograph that would show what Veitch and Stanley had seen at the secret DA hearing. I had subjected the LAPD and DA's office to a barrage of disclosure requests. And yet here was a photograph that revealed what they had been shown, for all to see. The second letter—the E or the F—was, as observed by Veitch, Stanley, and Witman at the hearing, difficult to discern. It might have been a letter carved over the crisscross lacerations. Or it might simply have been a part of the lacerations themselves. The *D*, on the other hand, was remarkably distinct. The two strokes of which it was composed—the vertical stem and the curved bowl—were in marked contrast to the diagonal slashing that underlay it, crisscrossing the pubic region. And there was only one suspect that I knew of in the case with the initial *D*.

One of the police reports I had seen referred to the fact that "experts in handwriting have stated that it would be impossible to determine any type of handwriting from the so-called 'D' cut into the pubic region of Elizabeth Short's body." It was, therefore, clear that the LAPD had subjected the crime scene photographs to analysis by more than one graphologist, and that they had been of the opinion that it was impossible to identify the handwriting characteristics of whoever had carved the "so-called 'D.'" But the report was silent as to whether the graphologists who studied the crime scene photographs were of the opinion that there was a *D* carved into the body in the first place.

What would a modern graphologist think about the issue? To find out, I sent the photograph to a modern handwriting expert. Caroline Murray is a British graphologist and director of the British Academy of Graphology. After a close examination of the photograph, her opinion was that, while the quality of the print was too poor to be certain, there did appear to be a *D* inscribed on the pubic region. "It is difficult to make a fluid curved movement like that," she wrote. "Therefore it looks deliberately curved, as opposed to the straight slashes surrounding it."

Looking at the photograph, it was also not surprising that the initials had not, apparently, been picked up in Professor Newbarr's autopsy report. Their significance as letters as opposed to random scrawlings could easily have been overlooked, unless pointed out by somebody, as Fred Witman had pointed out to Veitch and Stanley. Witman, I mused, must have received his intelligence from Dr. De River. And where had Dr. De River obtained the information? There could only be one answer: Leslie Dillon himself. Suddenly the cryptic statements made by Clemence Horrall and Dr. De River when Dillon was apprehended in early 1949—that Leslie Dillon knew "more about the Dahlia murder than the police did," and gave information explaining the mutilations on the body that they did not know—seemed, finally, to make sense. Surely, it was Leslie Dillon who had told Dr. De River and the LAPD about the initials that were carved on the body.

The inscribing on the victim's body of the initial *D*—and the possible *E*—were an egotistical appropriation that fit with everything I had seen in the behavior of both the Dahlia killer and of Leslie

Dillon. Like the naming of Dillon's daughter "Elizabeth," these were acts that asserted ownership and control. From time immemorial, the act of naming has been equated with proprietorship, starting from Jehovah giving man the prerogative to name all the animals, and thus implicitly the right to dominion over them. Yet, like Leslie Dillon's own first approach to the police, these acts fell short of a full "confession." They manifested a supremely egotistical need to be identified with, control, and boast about the murder and the victim, but a simultaneous counter-impulse to conceal, hide, and run away from it. It was a game, above all, of power: power over the victim, the press, the cops. The power game of a supreme egotist who knew he had gotten away. Robert Keppel, the leading expert on "signature" killers, has said that "inasmuch as most of these killers exert little or no control over their own existences or perceive themselves deep down inside as being life's losers and the victims of society, they gratify their sexual urges by demonstrating control over their murder victims. Whether that control manifests itself as necrophilia, bondage, humiliation, the torture of victims, or the posing of dead victims, it is the control itself that supplies the killer with his gratification."

A further strange "coincidence" that now became apparent to me was the fact that, barely three weeks after the Dahlia murder, there had been another killing in which initials had been found on the body of the victim—that of aviatrix Jeanne French, who was found stomped to death on the street with the words "FUCK YOU, BD" written on her body in lipstick. Initially, the LAPD had treated the two cases as linked. Then it had unaccountably separated them. Leslie Dillon had referred to the French killing when he was brought to the Dahlia body dump site by JJ O'Mara and Dr. De River. There was no doubt he was in Los Angeles at the time of the French murder. The fact of two violent lone female killings occurring in the same city, so close in time, linked by the highly unusual characteristic of inscribing initials on the body, and with the second even referencing the first with the initials *BD*, cried out for further investigation. The

LAPD, it seems, was determined to ignore the parallels.* And then there was the fact that Aggie Underwood—who had insisted on linking the murders—had been mysteriously "kicked upstairs" at the point when she attempted to make the connection, way back in 1947. Had she been getting too close to a truth that the police department didn't want people to know?

Reluctantly, I snapped shut my laptop computer. I had an appointment to go to. At this point, I was staying in downtown Los Angeles, at the old Los Angeles Athletic Club, on the intersection of Seventh and Olive and a stone's throw from the Biltmore Hotel. The club overlooked Raymond Chandler's old offices at the Dabney Oil Syndicate, just visible through the tall windows of the wood-paneled bar. Like much of downtown Los Angeles, the club seemed trapped in a time warp from the days of Philip Marlowe. The library, as in Marlowe's day, shelved rows of books behind glass doors, magazines on the tables, and lighted portraits of club dignitaries of the past, below which club dignitaries of the present snoozed peacefully in high-backed leather armchairs. The ancient bellhops spoke in whispers, respectfully wheeling trolley-loads of antique-looking baggage down corridors dimly lit by Art Deco lamps.

Leaving the club, I drove down Spring Street and past City Hall. In the time of Mayor Bowron, City Hall was the tallest building in Los Angeles. Now it was dwarfed by the jagged silhouette of skyscrapers on Bunker Hill. On the southwest corner of Broadway and Eleventh was the Spanish Colonial extravaganza of the old Los Angeles *Examiner* building. In Jimmy Richardson's heyday, the cast-iron presses had rolled into the small hours and the lights had blazed around the clock. Today the windows were dark and vacant. Pieces of chipboard were tacked onto the missing panes. On Pershing Square, steel skyscrapers glinted behind the red brick Spanish-Italian façade of the Biltmore Hotel. Perhaps ironically, the Biltmore—the last place

---

* The circumstances of the French case are discussed on page 65.

Elizabeth Short was seen alive—was itself built on the site of the old Salvation Army hostel where Aggie Underwood had washed up as a teenager alone in the world, back in the 1910s. Aggie and Elizabeth: two statistics in the vortex of Los Angeles' early twentieth century "female migrant problem." One had risen to dazzling success; the other had been propelled to equally spectacular destruction.

Some minutes later I reached my destination: two narrow strips of concrete cabins framing a parking lot, rattled day and night by the thunderous traffic that pelted down the adjoining Harbor Freeway. At the entrance a large sign read "Vacancies," and below it, "Cash Only." Small architectural details mapped accretions of time for those who could read them: the rounded Art Moderne corner of one strip of cabins; a fragment of old terra-cotta tile screen; a vintage neon sign. I had arrived at the Aster Motel.*

The Aster Motel had no website. When I tried to call the number given for it in the directory, the line was disconnected. The motel does not normally take advance bookings. It charges by the hour, in cash. Cars pass in and out of the parking lot silently, day and night. After each visit, rooms are cleaned and bed linens changed. The washing machines hum permanently in the laundry room.

At the front office I was met by a woman who worked the reception. The motel workers had heard vague rumors of the Aster's connections with a long-ago murder, but nothing in detail. The woman took me to the cabin that I had asked to visit—cabin 3. It was very sparse. A double bed, cupboard, TV enclosed in a wood-veneered cabinet. Adjoining it, a shower room with toilet and washbasin. The room smelled of cigarette smoke and Aqua Velva. It probably always had. So this, I thought, was it. The room that was discovered soaked in blood and feces on the morning of January 15, 1947, with bloody footprints tracked across the floor. A door slammed shut in the wind. In the background, the traffic hummed on the Harbor Freeway.

---

* The Aster Motel has changed ownership several times since the 1940s. The current management has no connection with the historical events described in this book.

The historic property records of the Aster Motel at the Los Angeles County Assessor's Office showed that the original strip of ten cabins remained intact, virtually unchanged since 1947. Many years later, in the 1980s, a new strip of cabins had been constructed facing the old, on the far side of the courtyard. The motel's checkered history weaved through the fabric of the city's past. It had been a mid-century gangster hangout, but also, for two decades, a place of refuge for African-American travelers during the segregation years.* A place of historical shoot-ups but also a haven; a mottled hybrid of the city's black and white story. And what a strange coincidence, I thought, that the *dahlia* happened to be a member of the *aster* family of flowers. According to *America's Garden Book*, a subgroup of *Astereraceae*, cultivated as an "ornamental plant for the cut flower industry."

I was waiting for my forensic scientist Suzanna Ryan, with whom I had arranged to meet at the motel. I held in my hand her report on the tests that had been conducted at the motel by the LAPD. The key section of the report read as follows:

> First, some background on chemical tests for blood. Both tests mentioned in the LAPD police report, the Benzidine test and the Kastle-Meyer (KM), or Phenolphthalein test, are presumptive blood tests. This means that substances other than blood can yield positive results. Therefore, in order to confirm the presence of blood a second, confirmatory test (which would be specific to blood) must be conducted.
>
> In regards to the testing performed by the police in 1949 in cabin 3 of the Aster Motel, it is possible that a dilute bloodstain was detected with the Benzidine test, but when a second swab or cutting was collected for laboratory testing, the stain was simply too dilute for the KM test to detect. Alternatively, what was termed in the police report as a

---

* The Aster Motel was one of a few motels in Los Angeles that accepted African-American travelers during segregation, and was listed in the *Negro Motorist Green Book*.

"pseudo-reaction" could have been a reaction to a cleaning product, like bleach. It is not completely clear to me what the term "pseudo-reaction" means in this instance. It may mean a false positive reaction or it may mean a weak reaction.

In the circumstances, Suzanna Ryan's view was that reliance could not safely be placed on the results of the blood tests carried out by the LAPD in cabin 3. The negative readings could have been due either to the lack of sensitivity of the tests, or to interference by cleaning agents. The question now was, could those forensic tests be re-performed in cabin 3?

In a few minutes, the forensic scientist's car swung into the parking lot. Suzanna herself emerged shortly afterward, a neat figure with a blond bob and deep California tan. We shook hands and I led her to the cabin. She pulled on white gloves and a lab coat. Within minutes she was on her knees, spraying luminol on the doorframes and scraping pieces of unidentifiable matter from obscure nooks and crannies in a business-like fashion. She spread the samples of dust and paint on a sheet of paper and subjected them to various tests. I held my breath. She shook her head. I breathed out. There was not enough to go on. It would be impossible, seventy years after the events, to come up with meaningful results without taking up the floorboards and shower tray. While I had known, deep down, that this must be the outcome all along, I also knew that to take the motel bathroom apart would not be feasible. Not, at least, without a court order, pursuant to a wholesale re-investigation of the case. And the LAPD had given every indication that it had no intention of reopening this particular can of worms.

In the meantime, while waiting for the motel test results, I had also received Michael Streed's report on his comparison between the photograph of the semi-nude woman posted on Flickr with the known photographs of Elizabeth Short. Streed's view was that the comparison between the profile of the woman in the semi-nude photo and the Santa Barbara police profile shot showed that both images shared "similar morphological traits," in particular:

1.   Forehead Height/Slope
2.   Eyebrow Shape/Height
3.   Nose Bridge Projection
4.   Angle/Shape of Upper Lip
5.   Chin Shape/Crease below Upper Lip
6.   Cheek/Nasolabial Fold

In the circumstances, Streed's conclusion was that, while an identification could not be made with 100 percent certainty through photographic comparison alone, it was his expert opinion that the female in the semi-nude photograph was "highly likely" to be Elizabeth Short.

Susanna and I were in the process of clearing away the test materials when the woman from the front desk of the motel came running up to us. She had with her one of the men who worked night shifts at the motel reception desk.

"We want to show you this," she said. She held out a cell phone. On it was a video taken from the phone of footage running on the motel security camera. The video had been taken earlier that year. The woman explained that her colleague had been sitting, as usual, at the front desk in the early hours of the morning. The screen at the front desk relayed footage taken from a security camera placed to overlook the motel parking lot. Suddenly what appeared to be a female figure could be seen on the security footage. The figure exited cabin 3 and hurried away, finally disappearing out in the street. As the security footage was showing the image of the figure crossing the parking lot, the cell phone video panned across the actual lot. It was empty. The security footage therefore appeared to be showing a figure hurrying from cabin 3 when in reality there was nobody there.

"He has seen this happening before, always about the same time, early in the morning," the woman explained to me, translating from her colleague's Spanish. "But this time he took a film of it."

I replayed the video, nonplussed. It was indeed difficult to explain.

"This place," the woman said, "has too much history."

24

THE WOMAN IN
THE WINDOW

The old videotape jumped and flickered. As I peered in the semidarkness, a woman's face appeared on the library computer screen. She was old and wizened, with frizzy hair and steel spectacles. She had a cracked, frail voice, but her eyes gleamed like a hawk's. When she spoke, it was in the language of the old City of Angels. She pronounced "Los Angeles" with a hard g.

I was in the library of the journalism archives at California State University, Northridge. The film was of Aggie Underwood. It had been shot in 1974, when Aggie was seventy-two years old. She was giving an interview in the living room of her home to a journalism major at the university.* The room overflowed with the clutter of old age: china, knickknacks, framed family photographs. Memories from the past jostled for space. The student asked Aggie many questions: about life as a female journalist in the 1940s; working on the *Herald-Express*; her memories of being a city editor. Aggie told many stories. She recalled when Stanley Bruce, the police reporter, got

---

* Interview by Natalie Holtzman, 1974, housed in the Agness Underwood collection at California State University, Northridge.

married in the *Herald-Express* offices. Police Chief Bill Parker was the best man. "They didn't stay married very long, but it was a blast. In the city room. We had the damnedest wedding you ever saw. Judge White performed the ceremony. The police band played the wedding march."* The student asked Aggie about her many cases as a crime reporter. She recalled them in detail. There was the mysterious death, ostensibly from carbon monoxide poisoning, of the beautiful actress Thelma Todd; the Overell yacht murder case, when a daughter was accused of murdering her millionaire parents; the unsolved killing of Mickey Cohen's smooth-talking henchman, Johnny Stompanato. The student asked Aggie about the Black Dahlia murder. Her face changed. For a moment, she faltered. For the first and only time, she looked afraid. "The Dahlia case . . . well . . . there was no solving there," she said. Then the interview cut out. Whatever Aggie had to say about the Dahlia case had been removed. Only one fragment was preserved: a short section in which she stated, for the record, that she had been the first journalist to discover the body at Leimert Park. Clearly, this was all Aggie wanted history to know about her role in the Dahlia investigation.

Heading back to Los Angeles from the vast suburban expanse of Northridge, I mused on the Dahlia case. All the key protagonists—Aggie Underwood, Paul De River, Leslie Dillon, JJ O'Mara, Willie Burns, the Brown brothers, and the rest—had now passed away. The physical evidence relating to the case—the Dahlia's address book, the shoes, the purse, the coconut brush hairs on the body, the dog leash, the stomach contents of the victim—all had, apparently, disappeared.† Most of the documents had been destroyed or locked away in the vaults of the LAPD. All that was left were fragments: a precious cache of documents left by the grand jury at the L.A. District

---

* For more on Bill Parker, see page 214. For more on Judge White and his friendship with Aggie Underwood and Paul De River, see page 88.

† For a discussion on the lack of evidence, see the preface of this book.

Attorney's Office; faded newspaper clippings on reels of microfilm; the personal archives of Aggie Underwood and Jimmy Richardson; echoes of long-dead voices reaching from the void on the other side of the din on the freeway. And yet, by painstakingly piecing together these hundreds of scattered fragments, I had managed to reconstruct a picture of what had happened. A picture that, while lacking in some details, was on the whole remarkably clear. How could that picture have remained buried for so long? Partly this was no doubt due to the difficulty in accessing the source materials. There was also the fact that, in the immediate aftermath of the 1949 grand jury investigation, there had clearly been a willful campaign to suppress the facts of the case, and to discredit and harass key witnesses such as Dr. De River. But also there seemed to be an unwillingness, on the part of some recent writers and researchers, simply to let the facts—as they appeared—speak for themselves. People seemed all too eager to shoehorn the case into some exotic, preconceived theory of who the culprit was, too often persons with little or no credible connection to the crime: Bugsy Siegel, Jack Dragna, Orson Welles, the glamorous and sinister Dr. George Hodel. They ignored the evidence, plain on the face of the contemporary documents, which pointed an unequivocal finger at an insignificant, sloop-shouldered man in glasses. A man who had, by conventional wisdom, been treated as a bizarre footnote in the case.

That Leslie Dillon was—according to my research—not a sideshow in the Dahlia drama but, in reality, its centerpiece was perhaps, in a case full of paradoxes, the ultimate irony. An irony that Dillon, complex and contradictory a character as he was, might well have appreciated. Dillon's appearance and personality resonates with the modern image of the psychopath—the bland, bespectacled, deceptively innocuous exterior—far more than it resonates with the gory monsters of movies from the war era, the blood-slobbering vampires played by the likes of Bela Lugosi. Here we have evil not with a European accent, but personified in a native boy from the Southern plains. An evil begotten in the maelstrom of postwar America. For once, the American public had no "Other" to blame: no homosexuals, Chinese, Communists, or Mexicans. The darkness came from within.

Today, the Dahlia case has entered the annals of Los Angeles lore and legend as one of the most infamous "unsolved" mysteries in California history. There is a room devoted to the Dahlia in the macabre collection of memorabilia at the Los Angeles Museum of Death; a heavy metal band with the name "the Black Dahlia Murder"; a cocktail called the Black Dahlia martini at the Biltmore Hotel. (One of the signature drinks at the hotel's Millennium Bar, the cocktail calls for Absolut Citron, not Blavod; it gets its dark color from a combination of Chambord and Kahlúa.) Fletcher Bowron and Thaddeus Brown have become immortalized as characters in the detective video game *L.A. Noire*, in which Bowron, as mayor, discusses a vice scandal over a woman called "Brenda," with "Chief William Worrell." One of the most famous books about the Dahlia case is James Ellroy's novel *The Black Dahlia*—a fantastic fictional account of the story, in which a crazed gardener commits the murder and keeps jars of preserved organs, including Betty's tattoo, in a Silver Lake bungalow.

And yet, the true facts of the Dahlia case—the facts buried in the contemporary newspaper reports, court documents, the memories of the few witnesses left to tell the tale—are so much more extraordinary and compelling than any of the "alternate facts." And perhaps more compelling still is the woman at the center of it all. The woman about whom there is so much speculation, but whom nobody really knows. We know that she was young, beautiful, complex, elusive, contradictory. That in her real life she occupied a territory as uncharted and controversial as the film noir heroines whom, in some ways, she resembled, and with whom she became equated. That for her contemporaries, her story became a morality tale, a fable illustrating the dangers posed to women by early twentieth century "Hollywood": a space of adventure and freedom, glamour, ruthless commercialism, and dangerously uncircumscribed female sexuality. Perhaps, in the end, all that matters for the purposes of her legend living on is that she was young, and beautiful. It means that she will always be a cipher, a blank board upon which we can write our own story. Elizabeth, Betty, Bette, Beth, Gilda, the martyr, the angel, the whore, the icon. Elizabeth Short. Every so often, we catch a glimpse of her—a hazy figure crossing a motel parking lot. But when we look again, there is nothing there.

POSTSCRIPT

Aggie Underwood, after being "kicked upstairs" off the Dahlia story to the post of city editor of the *Herald-Express* in 1947, remained in that position for seventeen years. She was one of the most popular, distinguished, and longest-serving city editors of a Los Angeles newspaper. She died in 1984, at eighty-one years old. In 2015, the Los Angeles Public Library ran an exhibition about her life and work.

Dr. Paul De River was fired from his position as police psychiatrist for the LAPD in 1950. He continued to work for the Veterans Administration. He died in 1977 at the Good Samaritan Hospital in Anaheim, California. There was no obituary or death notice in any newspaper.

Mark Hansen remained on the suspect list for the murder of Elizabeth Short for the rest of his life, although he was never charged. He died at his home on Carlos Avenue in 1964, at the age of seventy-four. At his death, he left an estate with an officially declared value of some $2 million ($15 million today). The Carlos Avenue house was razed to the ground in the 1970s to form a parking lot.

Leslie Dillon disappeared from the public eye after his release from police custody in 1949. He passed the rest of his life under the alias of "Jack." He died in obscurity in San Francisco in 1988, at the age of sixty-seven.

Jimmy Richardson continued as city editor of the *Los Angeles Examiner* until his retirement in 1957. He never touched a drop of alcohol for the rest of his life, although he continued to chain Luckies and pop his little white pills. He died in Boulder City, Nevada, in 1963.

Jimmy "Little Giant" Utley, Mark Hansen's gambling associate at the Florentine Gardens, was finally taken out of circulation in August 1955. Authorities arrested him when they raided a storefront in Long Beach that turned out to be one of his abortion clinics, turning over $500,000 a year ($4 million today). Utley waived a jury trial and received ten-year sentences for conspiracy and illegal surgery. He finally gave up the ghost while incarcerated at Folsom in 1962.

Clemence Horrall retired from the LAPD after the Brenda Allen scandal and went home to milk his cows in the Valley. He died in 1960 from a heart attack and is buried in the Forest Lawn Memorial Park, by the Hollywood Hills.

Thaddeus Brown continued to serve as chief of detectives under Bill Parker. After Parker's death in 1966, he was briefly appointed interim chief of the Los Angeles Police Department, before the appointment of Thomas Reddin in 1967. He died in 1970.

Finis Brown continued to serve in the Los Angeles Police Department. He died in Texas in 1990, at eighty-four years old. Rumor has it that he "lost his marbles" and died insane.

Harry "the Hat" Hansen also continued with the Los Angeles Police Department. He became a familiar face on television newsreels and documentaries as the LAPD spokesman on the Dahlia case. He retired to Palm Desert with his wife and pet spaniel, Cookie, and died in 1983.

John J. O'Mara, or "JJ," continued to serve in the LAPD's Intelligence Division. He died in 2003, at the age of eighty-six. O'Mara and his Gangster Squad colleagues, and their battles with Mickey Cohen and others in the L.A. underworld, were immortalized in the 2012 Hollywood movie *Gangster Squad*.

Frank Jemison continued to serve in the Los Angeles District Attorney's Office until his retirement. He died in Beverley Hills in 1967. At the time of his death he was an extremely wealthy man, bequeathing money to various organizations, including the Los Angeles District Attorney's Office.

Bill Parker continued, after his appointment as chief of the Los Angeles Police Department in 1950, to rule the department with a rod of iron. He presided over the department in some of its most turbulent times, including the Watts race riots of 1965. He died of a heart attack in 1966, the same year as his chief aide, Captain James Hamilton.

In 1962, the *Los Angeles Examiner* and the *Herald-Express* were merged to form the *Herald-Examiner*. This in turn folded in 1989, leaving the *Los Angeles Times* as the sole citywide daily newspaper. The old offices of the *Los Angeles Examiner* are now derelict, scheduled for redevelopment as a commercial complex. The Los Angeles Police Department moved from City Hall to new quarters in 1955. The Hall of Justice remained abandoned for many years, but has recently been restored.

The Aster Motel remains open for business.

AFTERWORD TO THE
PAPERBACK EDITION

was expecting a certain amount of controversy on the publication of *Black Dahlia, Red Rose*. After all, a British writer having the temerity to posit a solution to America's most famous "unsolved" murder was bound to raise eyebrows on either side of the Atlantic. However, I had not—perhaps naively—expected quite the storm of reaction that the book generated, especially in the United States. In particular, I was taken aback by the vicious trolling and abuse that I received from a self-appointed "expert" on the Dahlia case who wasn't even mentioned in the book (because he has produced no scholarship of his own) and his apparently rabid followers. All the trolls, without exception, were white males; a coincidence, perhaps, but nevertheless one that caused me to ponder the question of what it is about this tragic case that continues to trigger aggressive instincts in certain men, a desire to control and manipulate the narrative of what happened to one poor, lone woman, over seventy years ago.

Nevertheless, amidst the storm of controversy, there were also some helpful and interesting responses from members of the public, including a few that brought genuinely new and exciting information related to the case. In particular, there was the account given to me by Buz Williams. Buz is a retired member of the Long Beach police department. His father, Richard F. "Dick" Williams, and grandfather,

Lawrence E. "Bennie" Williams, were both members of the LAPD gangster squad. Buz's father served on the squad at the time of the Dahlia murder, and was a close friend of Con Keller,* one of the original gangster squad officers sent to tail Leslie Dillon in Banning and who gave evidence before the 1949 grand jury.

Over a course of conversations and correspondence, Buz told me that he had, as a child and young man, gone on many weekend fishing trips with his father and Con in the eastern High Sierra. After a day's fishing, Con, Dick, and Buz would gather round a campfire and the older men would tell tales of their gangster squad adventures. As a grown man, Buz became a close friend and confidante of Con, and he interviewed the older police officer before his death about his recollections of working on the Dahlia case.

Buz's father, Dick Williams, maintained that Leslie Dillon was the killer of Elizabeth Short. Con, on the other hand, leaned toward the opinion that the actual killer was Mark Hansen, with Leslie Dillon closely involved or actively assisting in the murder. Con told Buz that Dr. De River was convinced that Dillon was the killer. The doctor was, in fact, so afraid of Dillon, that at one point when he was interviewing Dillon in Banning, De River ran out of the room in terror, even though he knew police officers were in the adjoining room. Con told Buz that Leslie Dillon had an associate called "Wolf," and that both were members of a gang that robbed hotel safes. Elizabeth Short apparently knew about this gang, and therefore she had to be eliminated.

Buz sent me photographs from the gangster squad files of the man he believed was "Wolf." The photographs were of Dillon's friend Jeff Conners. According to Con, Leslie Dillon knew Mark Hansen and frequented the parties held at the Carlos Avenue house. Con also told Buz that blood corresponding to Elizabeth Short's blood type had been found under the tiles of a bathroom at a downtown Los Angeles motel owned by one Henry Hoffman. However, no action was taken. Con

---

* Buz told me that, although the court clerk spelled Con's second name as "Keller" in the grand jury transcript, Con in fact always spelled his name as "Keeler."

also said that both Harry Hansen and Finis Brown were friendly with Mark Hansen, who had a car dealership on Hollywood Boulevard. After the cover-up, Harry and Finis were seen driving around in flashy new cars provided by Hansen. Con also told Buz that the gangster squad had researched Mark Hansen's background and discovered that Hansen had some medical training in Denmark before he came to the U.S.

After extensive research into Mark Hansen's movements in Denmark, I could not find confirmation of his having had formal medical training. Hansen was the son of poor Danish farmers and had worked as a laborer prior to his arrival in America. It was highly unlikely, therefore, that he would have trained to be a doctor. He was a wheeler-dealer, a sharp-suited businessman, not an intellectual. However, given the large gaps in Hansen's Danish records, such training could not be ruled out, and some low-level work in a medical facility, hospital, or morgue—like Dillon—was entirely possible. It could have been such work that Con had in mind. Further research established that Mark Hansen did in fact own a car dealership in Hollywood, just as Con had told Buz.

Con also told Buz that the gangster squad made extensive efforts to extradite Dillon, but that the governor of Oklahoma refused to do so because of Dillon's "high connections" to someone that Buz could only recall as "Alfafa or something." Dillon was, in fact, related by marriage to the well-known Illinois politician Adlai Stevenson II: his first wife, Georgia, was Adlai's second cousin. A police report noted that Georgia's brother, Ted Stevenson, was excessively concerned about preserving the family reputation. Could Dillon's connections with the high-profile Stevenson family have been another factor in his evading capture?

Another significant piece of information came from a man who told me that his mother, Nannette, had been a dancer at Mark Hansen's nightclub, the Florentine Gardens. Nannette, he said, had been one of Earl Carroll's "golden girls," a leading cabaret dancer who worked all the major shows on the West Coast and in Vegas, and had known Joe

DiMaggio. Nannette's son told me that, on an evening in January 1947, his mother had been at a late-night party at Mark Hansen's home on Carlos Avenue. At one point during the party, she had gone upstairs to find the restroom. However, she opened the wrong door and instead found herself in a bedroom. Mark Hansen and a dark-haired girl were making love on the bed. Mark Hansen shooed her out of the room and, when she later asked him who the girl was, he gave her name—Beth Short—and told her she was an aspiring actress who needed a place to crash for the night. A week later, the girl was all over the newspapers as the woman whose corpse had been found tossed on the sidewalk in Leimert Park. Nannette told her son that Mark Hansen called all the girls who had been at the party that night and ordered them not to say a word about that evening. If any of them spoke about it, her career in Hollywood would be over.

If this account is correct, it is consistent with what I surmise in my book—namely, that Elizabeth Short spent the night of Thursday, January 9, at Mark Hansen's home. In his statement to the police, Mark Hansen claimed he had not seen Elizabeth Short since she left Los Angeles for San Diego in early December 1946. This evidence, however, would suggest otherwise, and that he was with her on the very night she disappeared.

How many afterwords are there to write on this case? An indefinite number, it would seem, since the fascination of the general public with this murder shows no sign of dimming. Like Prospero's book, every attempt to drown the story with an ending merely results in a resurfacing, a reworking, an addition to the already multilayered narrative that weaves its bright thread through this, one of the darkest episodes in the history of the city of Los Angeles. But it is precisely in this endless iteration that—for the writer as well as the reader—lie the seeds of madness, of an endless obsession. It is a danger that must at all costs be avoided, and for this reason, this is the one and only afterword to this book. Except—and I can say confidently that the chances of this happening are virtually nil—in the event that the LAPD does, finally, release its full file on the Dahlia case. That would indeed be worth another afterword: one that might even be the final word.

Piu Eatwell, May 2018

ACKNOWLEDGMENTS

Any list of acknowledgments to a book of this kind is inevitably going to be a long one.

First and foremost, I should thank the public institutions and archive holders that made the vast amount of primary documentation that I requested available. In particular, the Los Angeles County District Attorney's Office, which, through the medium of Deputy District Attorney Natalie Adomian, made available as much of its file on the Dahlia grand jury proceedings as possible; the FBI, which—albeit after many months—finally removed the redactions from its Black Dahlia file on my demand; the UCLA Special Collections Department, which made available the archives of James "Jimmy" Richardson, and those of the Dahlia writer and journalist the late John Gilmore; the archives of California State University, Northridge, which house the papers of Agness Underwood; the University of California, Berkeley, and Rabbi Patricia Fenton of the American Jewish University, for copies of the rare 1949 Los Angeles grand jury report; Cornell University Library; the Los Angeles Public Library; the British Library, London; and the U.S. Library of Congress. I should also thank the Huntington Library for providing papers relating to the Black Dahlia case in the collection of the late *Los Angeles Times* columnist Jack Smith.

The documentation that I did finally manage to obtain from the Los Angeles Police Department was extracted by means of a legal challenge, for which I have to thank Peter Scheer and the First Amendment Coalition. Other members of different police departments have assisted with documents on a confidential basis in different ways, and will (at their request) remain nameless.

The formidable task of obtaining the newspaper archives relating to the case, almost entirely on microfilm, could not have been achieved without the assistance of Miriam Amico and Margaret Posehn. In addition I was assisted in researching U.S. military records by David Goerss and Lori Miller. Sid Bloomberg assisted with archive film research, and Leisa Johnson-Kalin helped with picture research. Further research assistance came from Anthony Cosgrave, George Fogelson, Larry Pumphrey, Christina McKillip, and Johann Hammer. Molly Haigh at UCLA Special Collections and Louise Smith at USC Digital Imaging Lab were particularly helpful with researching archive newspaper photographs. Carlos Loya assisted with photography and field research in Los Angeles. Dave Kindy provided many useful contacts for the purposes of copyright clearances. Further extensive backup research after publication of the hardback edition and prior to publication of the paperback was carried out by Kim Aldridge, to whom I am truly grateful.

Two individuals to whom I owe perhaps more than any others are Donald and Patty Freed. Donald for both his tireless advice and his frank and honest recollections of his meetings with Dr. De River in the 1950s; and Patty for her enthusiastic guidance through the streets of Los Angeles, with the intimate knowledge that only a real Angeleno (with a hard g) can possess. It is through Patty that I began to see the city not as a modern suburban sprawl, but as an accretion of time.

Thanks are due to Christopher Coleridge, who kindly escorted me on an enlightening tour of Black Dahlia sites in Los Angeles. Lord and Lady Eatwell introduced me to some relevant and helpful contacts in Los Angeles. Michael J. Armijo reviewed the manuscript for accuracy of local detail. I should also thank the descendants of persons involved in the Dahlia case who gave interviews, and who at their own request remain anonymous. For the paperback edition, I am particularly indebted to Buz Williams, who came forth with startling evidence corroborating my theory of the case.

Of the many professionals and experts who gave so generously of their time and advice, I must in particular thank Suzanna Ryan of Ryan Forensic, Carlsbad, California; (Ret.) Police Sergeant Michael W. Streed, certified forensic artist, of SketchCop Solutions, Corona, California; Professor Michael Woodworth of the University of British Columbia, Okanagan; Caroline Murray of the British Academy of Graphology; Mark E. Safarik, Supervisory Special Agent, FBI (ret.); and ex–forensic scene of crime officer turned writer Larry Henderson. Other people who gave up time for personal interviews or correspondence on various topics of relevance include Tony Valdez of Fox News; Joe Domanick, the leading authority on the history of the LAPD; the late Kevin Starr, the foremost social historian of California; leading Los Angeles attorney John H. Welborne; and the chronicler of L.A. noir, John Buntin. I am also grateful to Stephen Karadjis for first pointing me towards a closer scrutiny of the Dahlia autopsy photographs.

Of the nonfiction books on the Black Dahlia case, I found particularly valuable Mary Pacios's memoir of early childhood in Medford with Elizabeth Short, *Childhood Shadows: The Hidden Story of the Black Dahlia Murders* (AuthorHouse, 2007), and Jacque Daniel's personal recollections of the Dahlia case as lived by the De River family, *The Curse of the Black Dahlia* (Digital Data Werks, 2004). I am indebted to both these books for firsthand accounts of events and records of interviews with people who have long since passed away. I am also indebted, for useful background information on Dr. De River, to Brian King's helpful introduction to his reissue of De River's textbook *The Sexual Criminal: A Psychoanalytical Study* (Bloat Books, second edition, 2000). All the aforementioned books are indispensable to a serious study of the Dahlia case.

I am fortunate in having one of the best of literary agents in Andrew Lownie, a tireless and stalwart exponent of my writing, despite his own heavy writing commitments. I should also like to thank my meticulous editor, Katie Adams, Gina Iaquinta, and all at my U.S. publishers, Liveright/Norton, as well as Mark Booth and

Oliver Johnson at my UK publishers, Coronet/Hodder & Stoughton. Dave Cole did a superlative job on the complex task of copyediting the book. Thanks are also due to my website designer, David Taylor of Black Horse Design, and my publicity agent, Ruth Killick.

Finally, no acknowledgments would be complete without a thank-you to my enormously dedicated and patient family: my husband, Nikolai, and children, Alek, Oscar, and Noah. The last three will not be allowed to read this book for a while, but when they do, I hope they find it worth the wait.

FULL DRAMATIS PERSONAE

AHERN, JAMES
Officer of the Gangster Squad charged with investigating Leslie Duane Dillon. Partner of Archie Case.

ALLEN, BRENDA
Notorious Hollywood madam. Girlfriend of Elmer V. Jackson of the LAPD Vice Squad, found to have been paying him protection money. Gave evidence to the Los Angeles grand jury in 1949 of a police protection racket centering on her activities.

ALLEN, GRACE
Former wife of Jeff Connors. Friends with Mark Hansen and stayed at his Carlos Avenue home when she divorced Connors.

BARNES, JOHN
Assistant District Attorney, known as the "Rottweiler." Interviewed Leslie Duane Dillon in custody in January 1949.

BERSINGER, BETTY
Housewife who discovered the bisected body of Elizabeth Short in Leimert Park on January 15, 1947.

BOWRON, FLETCHER
Mayor of Los Angeles from 1938 to 1953.

BROWN, SERGEANT FINIS ALBANIA
Sergeant in LAPD homicide division, jointly in charge of the Dahlia case with Harry "the Hat" Hansen. Younger brother of Thad Brown.

BROWN, THADDEUS FRANKLIN; "THAD"
Head of the LAPD Patrol Division, in charge of divisional vice, then chief of detectives from 1949. Elder brother to Finis Brown.

BURNS, WILLIAM; "WILLIE"
Head of the Gangster Squad, the elite police division created by Chief Horrall to investigate organized crime and police corruption.

CASE, ARCHIE
Officer of the Gangster Squad charged with investigating Leslie Duane Dillon. Partner to James Ahern.

COHEN, MEYER HARRIS; "MICKEY"
Leading gangster based in Los Angeles, with ties to the Jewish and Italian crime families. Major rival of Jimmy Utley.

CONNORS, JEFF
Friend of Leslie Dillon, allegedly met Dillon in 1948 in San Francisco. Accused by Dillon of committing the Dahlia murder. Linked to Mark Hansen via his wife, Grace Allen, who was a friend of Hansen's and stayed with him when she separated from Connors.

CUFF, ELLERY E.
Head of the Los Angeles Public Defender's Office from 1949 to 1963. A celebrated campaigner against the death penalty. Close friend of Dr. De River.

DEBS, COUNCILMAN ERNEST EUGENE
Los Angeles city councilman from 1947 to 1958.

DE RIVER, DR. PAUL
Police psychiatrist of the Los Angeles Police Department from 1937 to 1950. Credited with the second case of criminal profiling—that of Albert Dyer, the Inglewood killer. (See below.)

DE RIVER, JACQUELINE
Eldest daughter of Dr. Paul De River. Acted as his personal assistant and later wrote a memoir recording her recollections of the Dahlia case.

DILLON, GEORGIA
First wife of Leslie Duane Dillon.

DILLON, LESLIE DUANE
A hotel bellhop, among other casual occupations. Arrested in 1949 for the Dahlia murder, and then released.

DONAHOE, CAPTAIN JACK
In charge of the Dahlia case for a short period (January–September 1947), when he was transferred off the case to Robbery. His place was taken by Captain Francis Kearney.

DUMAIS, CORPORAL JOSEPH
One of over five hundred "confessing Sams" who (falsely) confessed to the Black Dahlia murder.

DYER, ALBERT
Killer of the three little "Babes of Inglewood." Tried, found guilty of murder, and hanged at San Quentin in 1938.

FARNHAM, INSPECTOR HUGH
Officer of the LAPD Detective Division sent by Thad Brown on a secret mission to interview Leslie Dillon and his wife in Oklahoma in 1949.

FREED, DONALD
Author, director, and screenwriter. Associate of the playwright Harold Pinter. Interviewed Dr. Paul De River about the Dahlia case in 1953, along with his uncle Wally Klein.

FRENCH, DOROTHY
Assistant at the Aztec cinema theater, San Diego. Found Elizabeth Short crashed out at the theater in December 1946 and invited her to stay at her family home at Pacific Beach. Daughter of Elvera French.

FRENCH, ELVERA
Mother of Dorothy French. Elizabeth Short stayed at the family home in Pacific Beach, San Diego, for a month, from December 1946 to January 1947.

GRAHAM, MARJORIE
Friend of Elizabeth Short, also from Massachusetts. Returned to Massachusetts from Los Angeles in late 1946.

GRANLUND, NILS THOR; "NTG" OR "GRANNY"
Famous nightclub host/compere. Of Swedish origin. Originally founded nightclubs in New York, then came to Hollywood in the 1940s and hosted the floor shows at the Florentine Gardens nightclub. A close associate of Mark Hansen.

HANSEN, LIEUTENANT HARRY; "THE HAT"
Lieutenant in the LAPD homicide division, jointly in charge of the Dahlia case with Finis Brown. Not related to Mark Hansen.

HANSEN, MARK MARINUS
Danish businessman and millionaire theater/nightclub owner in Los Angeles. Born in Aalborg, Denmark. Owner of the Florentine Gardens nightclub and a close associate of "NTG," with ties to the underworld via Jimmy "Little Giant" Utley. Elizabeth Short stayed in his house on Carlos Avenue on two occasions in 1946 and had a stormy relationship with him.

HINSHAW, NELLIE
The aunt of Leslie Dillon's first wife, Georgia Dillon. Lived on Crenshaw Boulevard in Los Angeles. Leslie Dillon used her address on several occasions when he visited Los Angeles, parking his trailer in front of the house.

HODEL, DR. GEORGE HILL
Celebrity Hollywood physician. A minor suspect in the Dahlia case.

HOFFMAN, CLORA
Co-owner of the Aster Motel from December 1946 to the latter half of April 1947. Wife of Henry Hoffman. Later remarried to become Mrs. Sartain.

HOFFMAN, HENRY
Co-owner of the Aster Motel from December 1946 to the latter half of April 1947.

HOFFMAN, PAMELA
Daughter of Henry and Clora Hoffman.

HORRALL, CHIEF CLEMENCE B.
Chief of the Los Angeles Police Department from 1941 to 1949. Resigned over the Brenda Allen scandal, in favor of General William Worton. Set up the Gangster Squad to investigate organized crime and police corruption.

INGLEWOOD, BABES OF, CASE
The notorious murder in June 1937 of three little girls—Madeline Everett, seven, her sister Melba, nine, and their playmate, Jeanette Stephens, eight. The girls were sexually assaulted and killed in the Baldwin Hills. Albert Dyer was later tried and convicted of the crime. (See Albert Dyer entry.)

JACKSON, SERGEANT ELMER V.
Officer of LAPD administrative Vice Squad. Boyfriend of the Hollywood madam Brenda Allen. Accused of taking protection money in a police department scandal arising from Allen's activities in 1949.

JEMISON, LIEUTENANT FRANK B.
Investigator at the District Attorney's Office. The principal DA investigator placed in charge of the 1949 grand jury's Dahlia case investigation.

JONES, OFFICER (FIRST NAME UNKNOWN)
Unidentified officer of the Gangster Squad sent to monitor the activities of Leslie Dillon in Florida in 1948. Testified before the 1949 grand jury, but his evidence has never been released.

KEARNEY, CAPTAIN FRANCIS
Head of the LAPD Homicide Division from 1947 to 1951. Sent on the Leslie Dillon mission to Palm Springs in 1949. Subsequently transferred to Narcotics.

KELLER, CONWELL
Member of the Gangster Squad sent on the mission to apprehend Leslie Dillon in December 1948.

KLEIN, WALLY

Hollywood writer and producer. Writing credits include *Oklahoma Kid* (1939), *They Died with Their Boots On* (1941), *Hard to Get* (1938), and *Indianapolis Speedway* (1939). Brother-in-law of legendary film producer Hal B. Wallis (*Casablanca, The Maltese Falcon*). Interviewed Dr. De River in 1953, along with his nephew, the writer Donald Freed.

LAWSON, HARRY

Publisher of the *Eagle Rock Sentinel*. Foreman of the 1949 grand jury that investigated a number of allegations of police corruption in Los Angeles, including in the Dahlia case and the Brenda Allen scandal.

MANLEY, ROBERT; "RED"

First serious suspect on the Dahlia case. A married man who had an affair with Elizabeth Short, and was the last person to see her alive—apart from the doorman at the Biltmore—on January 9, 1947. Later completely exonerated from suspicion.

MARTIN, LYNN

Real name Norma Lee Meyer, a sixteen-year-old runaway who was among the associates of Elizabeth Short. Implicated Short in a pornographic photography ring in which she was involved, run by a man called George Price.

MOORMAN, BETTY-JO

Wife of Burt Moorman. Stayed at the Aster Motel in the period January 7–18, 1947.

MOORMAN, BURT

Brother of Clora Hoffman, co-owner of the Aster Motel. Stayed at the Aster with his wife Betty-Jo over the period January 7–18, 1947.

NEWBARR, DR. FREDERICK

Well-known Los Angeles County autopsy surgeon. Performed the autopsy on Elizabeth Short.

O'MARA, JOHN J.; "JJ"
Officer in the Gangster Squad. Given the job by Willie Burns of chauffeuring Dr. Paul De River around on his covert mission to investigate Leslie Dillon.

PARKER, WILLIAM; "BILL"
Rival of Thad Brown for the post of chief of the LAPD after the resignation of Clemence Horrall. Won due to the death of one of the members of the appointments commission. Chief of the LAPD from 1950 to 1966.

REED, JOE
Assistant chief of the LAPD under Clemence Horrall. (See his entry.) Widely suspected of running the show while Horrall napped.

RICHARDSON, JAMES H.; "JIMMY"
City editor of the *Los Angeles Examiner*. A rival of Agness Underwood (see her entry), although both worked for papers owned by Randolph Hearst.

SHORT, ELIZABETH
Born July 29, 1924, Medford, Massachusetts; died January 15, 1947, Los Angeles, California. Her bisected body was found in the Leimert Park area of Los Angeles, leading to her being dubbed the "Black Dahlia" in one of the most notorious murder cases of the century.

SHORT, PHOEBE MAE
Mother of Elizabeth Short.

STANLEY, LEO
Chief of the Los Angeles DA's Bureau of Investigation.

TOTH, ANN
Danish actress, a friend of Elizabeth Short and Mark Hansen. Lived with Hansen and Short in Hansen's Carlos Avenue apartment in 1946.

UNDERWOOD, AGNESS; "AGGIE"
City editor of the *Evening Herald & Express* newspaper. One of the first female and most influential city editors of the twentieth century. A close friend of Dr. Paul De River.

UTLEY, JIMMY; "LITTLE GIANT"
Los Angeles gangster of Irish descent involved in abortion, gambling, and prostitution rackets. Major rival of Mickey Cohen. Close associate of Mark Hansen and had a secret gambling den in the Florentine Gardens nightclub.

VEITCH, ARTHUR
Deputy district attorney. Involved in 1949 grand jury investigation of the Dahlia case.

WAGGONER, LOREN K.
Member of the Gangster Squad. Investigated the activities of Leslie Dillon with officer James Ahern and Patrolman Garth Ward.

WARD, GARTH
Police patrolman with the LAPD University Division. Jointly investigated events at the Aster Motel with Loren K. Waggoner.

WHITE, JUDGE THOMAS P.
Distinguished member of the Los Angeles appellate court. Among his rulings as an appeal court judge was the successful appeal of the Latino defendants in the notorious "Sleepy Lagoon" case. Close friend of Aggie Underwood and Dr. Paul De River.

WITMAN, FRED
Private investigator. Close friend of Dr. De River. Presented evidence relating to the Dahlia investigation before the Los Angeles DA at De River's request.

WORTON, GENERAL WILLIAM A.
Interim chief of the LAPD from June 1949 to 1950. Appointed by Mayor Fletcher Bowron to bridge the gap between the resignation of Chief Clemence Horrall, pursuant to the Brenda Allen scandal, and the appointment of William Parker.

NOTES

ABBREVIATIONS:

- Documents released to the author by the L.A. County District Attorney's Office in June 2015 (not catalogued) are prefixed by DA and followed by the title of the document, author, and date (if known).
- Documents relating to the Dahlia case, disclosed by the U.S. Federal Bureau of Investigation to the author for the first time in unredacted form in September 2015 (not catalogued), are prefixed by FBI and followed by the title of document, author, and date (if known).
- Documents released to the author by the Los Angeles Police Department in September 2015 (not catalogued) are prefixed by LAPD and followed by the title of the document, author, and date (if known).

PART 1. FALLEN ANGEL

Chapter 1: Farewell My Lovely

3 **Sunrise was at 6:58 a.m.:** Calculated from the Spectral Calculator provided by GATS, Inc., on http://www.spectralcalc .com.

3 **Dense fog had descended:** The extreme weather conditions on the coast at Long Beach and Redondo Beach in January 1947 are described in the police interviews with several witnesses questioned on the Black Dahlia case, including Mark Hansen and Bernard H. Van Der Steen.

3 **Black smoke . . . smudge pots:** The LAX weather station reported smoke in the sky in the early hours of January 15, 1947; Robert Meyer, a neighbor who lived one block from Norton, recalled the smoke and surmised it was likely from the smudge pots on the orange groves (interview recounted in Pacios, Mary, *Childhood Shadows: The Hidden Story of the Black Dahlia Murders*,

AuthorHouse, 2007, p. 101). The *Los Angeles Herald-Express* reported the coldest temperatures since 1942 and a battle with fires to save the citrus groves (January 16, 1947).

3   **waning moon:** The moon on January 14, 1947, was in its last quarter: data from meteorological information collected at the LAX weather station and reported by Weather Underground.

4   **Bob Hope's words:** Simon, Richard, "Hollywood Freeway Spans Magic and Might of L.A.," *Los Angeles Times*, December 19, 1994.

4   **Leimert Park:** Background history of Leimert Park is extracted from Exum, Cynthia E., and Maty Guiza-Leimert, *Images of America: Leimert Park*, Arcadia Publishing, 2012.

5   **Betty Bersinger packed:** The account of Betty Bersinger's discovery is taken from: Harnisch, Larry, "A Slaying Cloaked in Mystery and Myths," *Los Angeles Times*, January 6, 1997; recorded telephone interview with Betty Bersinger in 1996 by documentary producer Kyle J. Wood (*Medford Girl: The Black Dahlia Murder*).

6   **police complaint board:** The details of the scene of the crime in the following pages are taken from: LAPD Dead Body Report by S. J. Lambert; and DA report by Lieutenant Frank B. Jemison, titled "Summary of the Elizabeth (Beth) Short Murder Investigation," both contained in the DA and LAPD files; the account by the city editor of the *Los Angeles Herald-Express*, Agness Underwood, in her memoir *Newspaperwoman*, New York: Harper & Brothers, 1949, pp. 6–7.

6   **Frank Perkins and Will Fitzgerald:** *Los Angeles Evening Herald-Express*, January 15, 1947.

6   **"female drunk passed out sans clothes" . . . bottle of bourbon:** Letter from journalist Will Fowler to *Los Angeles Times* columnist Jack Smith dated January 23, 1975, Huntington Library Jack Smith papers, folder "Black Dahlia", box S3.

6   **One of the first to arrive:** As with so many other facts in this case, there is dispute as to who arrived first at the crime scene. In his autobiography *Reporters: Memoirs of a Young Newspaperman* (Roundtable, 1991), and also in a letter to *Los Angeles Times* columnist Jack Smith, *Los Angeles Examiner* reporter Will Fowler claims to have arrived first on the scene, and photographer Felix Paegel did take a picture of Fowler kneeling alone beside the dead body. But *Herald-Express* city editor Agness Underwood insisted until the end of her life that she arrived first. (See final

chapter of this book on page 263.) Also, Jimmy Richardson, the *Los Angeles Examiner* editor, makes no mention of Fowler when he describes the events of January 15 in his memoir *For the Life of Me*. Whatever the truth of the matter, it is certain that both Fowler and Underwood arrived early at the crime scene.

6   **Agness, known to all as "Aggie":** Background information from Underwood, Agness, *Newspaperwoman*, New York: Harper & Brothers, 1949.

7   **short, sturdy woman:** See Cairns, Kathleen A., *Front-Page Women Journalists, 1920–50*, University of Nebraska Press, 2003, p. 108.

7   **"gogettum reporter":** See write-up on Underwood in the twenty-fifth anniversary edition of the *Los Angeles Herald-Express*, October 27, 1936.

7   **sob-sister line of reporting:** See Cairns, Kathleen A., *Front-Page Women Journalists*, p. 108 et seq.

8   **one of the first women to be appointed:** It is often stated (even in her obituary) that Aggie Underwood was the first woman city editor of a national newspaper. This is not correct. Predecessors in her position include Laura Vitray (*New York Evening Graphic*), and Mary Holland Kincaid (*Los Angeles Herald*).

8   **satanic smile:** Fowler, Will, *From a Reporter's Notebook*, Huntington Library, *Los Angeles Times* Records/Crime, Los Angeles, box 642.

8   **"like two sides of beef":** The description of the crime scene is taken from the eyewitness accounts of Underwood, Agness, *Newspaperwoman*, p. 6, and Fowler, Will, *Reporters*, pp. 74–75; also Fowler, *From a Reporter's Notebook*.

9   **119 in 1947:** See Underwood, Agness, *Newspaperwoman*, New York: Harper & Brothers, 1949, p. 119.

9   **"worst butcher murder":** Ibid., p.6.

9   **aluminum coffin with screw-clamps:** Fowler, Will, *From a Reporter's Notebook*, Huntington Library, *Los Angeles Times* Records/Crime, Los Angeles, box 642.

9   **black floor-level scales . . . "right after lunch":** Fowler, Will, *From a Reporter's Notebook*, Huntington Library, *Los Angeles Times* Records/Crime, Los Angeles, box 642.

10   **made chilling reading:** The Los Angeles Police Department has refused to permit the release of the official autopsy report.

However, authors Janice Knowlton and Michael Newton state that they obtained an "unofficial" copy of the report from a member of the Los Angeles Sheriff's Department, who copied it by hand, which is reprinted in Knowlton and Newton, *Daddy Was the Black Dahlia Killer*, Pocket Books, 1995, pp. 17–21. Extracts from the autopsy report were also read at the coroner's inquest into Short's death, annexed to Pacios, Mary, *Childhood Shadows: The Hidden Story of the Black Dahlia Murder*, AuthorHouse, 2007, p. 329. The information cited here is obtained from Knowlton and Newton's transcription, the extracts read at the coroner's inquest, and information cited in Aggie Underwood's early newspaper reports for the *Herald-Express*. There is an unsubstantiated claim in Knowlton and Newton's book, apparently from a later witness account, that a clump of grass was inserted into the vagina. One of the biggest pieces of misinformation about the autopsy report was spread by *Los Angeles Examiner* journalist Will Fowler in his book *Reporters*, which claimed the victim had an "infantile vagina" and was unable to have sex. In fact, as several men testified to the LAPD and FBI, she was physically capable of normal sexual relations, although she was usually described as "cold" (see, for example, the account of Peter Vetcher on page 71). The victim's alleged sexual "coldness" could well have been connected to the clinical condition of an inflamed Bartholin gland, which would normally make sexual relations painful.

11   **hennaed . . . bright red:** *Los Angeles Evening Herald-Express*, January 16, 1947. The *Herald-Express* noted several times that the corpse's hair had been hennaed and that there was red polish on both big toenails. The fact that the original dark strands were beginning to show was noted by the *Herald-Express* on January 17, 1947. The dead body report released by the LAPD refers to "brown hair, indication of being hennehed [sic]."

11   **butcher's or carving knife . . . razor:** Captain Donahoe of the LAPD, quoted in the *Herald-Express* on January 24, 1947.

12   **Fibers . . . scrubbed:** See LAPD follow-up report dated February 5, 1947, by F. A. Brown and H. L. Hansen.

12   **cheap scrubbing brush:** See FBI laboratory correspondence from February 1947. These reports were disclosed for the first time in unredacted form to the author in September 2015.

12   **medical training:** While there was speculation about the killer
having had some medical training or experience, this was never
stated as definitively the case, and has been much overemphasized
by some commentators.

13   **a doctor was entertained:** For example, the FBI reported
that there was "some speculation that the murderer had some
training in the dissection of bodies." See letter from R. B. Hood,
FBI Los Angeles, to FBI laboratory dated February 15, 1947, FBI
documents.

13   **"Jigsaw John" St. John:** Pacios, Mary, *Childhood Shadows*, p. 143.

13   **Two key items of information:** See (undated) report of DA
investigator Frank Jemison in the DA grand jury files: "Two secrets
have been closely guarded by a few officers in connection with
this investigation including the undersigned. They could only be
answered by the person who committed this murder." The nature
of these two key facts is discussed in later chapters. The journalist
Will Fowler claimed in his memoirs that there were three "secret
facts," but later retracted this contention.

Chapter 2: A Double Life

14   **Jimmy Richardson:** The account of the *Examiner's* role in
identifying the victim and the quoted conversations are taken from
the memoirs of the then city editor of the *Examiner*, James H.
"Jimmy" Richardson. See Richardson, James, *For the Life of Me*,
New York: G. P. Putnam's Sons, 1954, in particular pp. 296–99.

14   **Bugsy Siegel:** Ibid., pp. 69–76.

15   **eight-by-ten blowup of the bisected body:** Fowler, Will, *From
a Reporter's Notebook*, Huntington Library, *Los Angeles Times*
Records/Crime, Los Angeles, box 642.

15   **more copies than . . . bombing of Pearl Harbor:** See
interview with *Examiner* journalist Will Fowler recorded by Mary
Pacios in Pacios, Mary, *Childhood Shadows*, p. 116.

15   **V-J Day:** Fowler, Will, *From a Reporter's Notebook*, Huntington
Library *Los Angeles Times* Records/Crime, Los Angeles, box 642.

16   **Ray Richards . . . Quinn Tann:** Richardson, James, *For the Life
of Me*, p. 298; *Los Angeles Examiner*, January 17, 1947; FBI office
memorandum from Mr. Tolson to L. B. Nichols dated January 21, 1947.

16   **Russ Lapp:** See interview with *Examiner* journalist Will Fowler

recorded by Mary Pacios in Pacios, Mary, *Childhood Shadows*, p. 117.

16 **doubted . . . identification:** FBI office memorandum from Mr. Tolson to L. B. Nichols dated January 21, 1947.

16 **By 2:50 p.m.:** FBI memo dated January 16, 1947, from Mr. Tolson to L. B. Nichols.

16 **arrested . . . West Cabrillo Beach:** FBI memo dated January 16, 1947, from Mr. Tolson to L. B. Nichols; *Los Angeles Times*, January 17, 1947.

17 **Camp Cooke:** FBI memo dated January 16, 1947, from Mr. Tolson to L. B. Nichols.

17 **so sullenly beautiful:** See, for example, the recollections of *Examiner* journalist Will Fowler in an interview recorded by Mary Pacios in Pacios, Mary, *Childhood Shadows*, p. 119.

17 **Unkefer told the swarm of reporters:** Quotations from interview with Officer Unkefer in the *Los Angeles Examiner*, January 17, 1947.

17 **cut out the rose tattoo:** See also *Los Angeles Examiner*, January 17, 1947.

18 **Sid Hughes racing out:** This account and the ensuing conversation with Wain Sutton are taken from Richardson's memoir, Richardson, James, *For the Life of Me*, pp. 299–300.

18 **resurfaced with the information:** See *Los Angeles Examiner*, January 19, 1947.

19 **Mocambo heist:** See interview with *Examiner* reporter Will Fowler in Mary Pacios, Pacios, Mary, *Childhood Shadows*, p. 115.

19 **Mrs. Inez Keeling:** *Los Angeles Examiner*, January 17, 1947; *Los Angeles Herald-Express*, January 17, 1947.

20 **"teaser of men":** Memorandum dated October 28, 1949, from Frank Jemison of the DA's Office to the chief of the DA's Bureau of Investigation.

20 **"man crazy delinquent":** *Los Angeles Herald-Express*, January 17, 1947.

21 **new type of female immigrant:** For a detailed examination of female migration to Hollywood in the early twentieth century, see Hallett, Hilary A., *Go West, Young Women!: The Rise of Early Hollywood*, University of California Press, 2013.

21 **"big moment of the day":** From *A Visit to Movieland*, cited in Hallett, ibid.

22 **a pharmacist in Long Beach:** *Los Angeles Examiner*, January 18, 1947.

22 **brainchild of one of his reporters:** See Richardson, James, *For the Life of Me*, pp. 300–301.

22 **claimed it as her own:** Aggie claimed in her memoirs that the "Black Dahlia" moniker was discovered one day when she was checking with Ray Giese, homicide detective lieutenant, for any stray fact that might have been overlooked. Giese, Aggie claimed, had come up to her in the squad room and said, "This is something you might like, Agness. I've found out they called her the 'Black Dahlia' around that drug store where she hung out down in Long Beach." (See Underwood, Agness, *Newspaperwoman*, p. 7.) Richardson's version of the story, however, was supported by Chuck Cheatham, reporter on the *Long Beach Independent*. Chuck recalled that a detective told him and Bevo Means, the *Examiner* man at Long Beach, about the name when they were snooping around for an angle, and that Means had gotten the moniker into the *Examiner* first. (See interview by Mary Pacios with Gerry Ramlow, *Daily News* reporter, in Pacios, Mary, *Childhood Shadows*, pp. 112 and 114.).

23 **"class as well as homicide":** Agness Underwood, *Newspaperwoman*, p. 103.

23 **smacked him with her purse:** See Cecilia Rasmussen, "Sleuths, Scribes Give High-Profile Cases Catchy Names," *Los Angeles Times*, April 21, 2002.

23 **It was the name "Black Dahlia":** "Farewell, My Black Dahlia," in *Los Angeles Times West* magazine, March 28, 1971.

23 **"hundreds just like her":** Richardson, James, *For the Life of Me*, p. 301.

24 **offered to take her to her home:** See *Los Angeles Examiner*, January 18, 1947.

24 **lived there for a month:** See *Los Angeles Examiner*, ibid.

24 **"about six o'clock":** Richardson, James, *For the Life of Me*, p. 301. The *Herald-Express* put the time of leaving at 7:30 p.m. (*Herald-Express*, January 18, 1947).

24 **freckled man in his twenties:** See *Los Angeles Examiner*, ibid.

24 **little white pills:** Probably benzedrine, commonly used as a stimulant and pick-me-up by journalists of the time.

25 **castle at San Simeon:** See interview by Mary Pacios with Gerry Ramlow, *Daily News* reporter, in Pacios, Mary, *Childhood Shadows*, pp. 106–7.

26 **"don't try it again":** Wagner, Rob Leicester, *Red Ink, White Lies: The Rise and Fall of Los Angeles Newspapers 1920–1962*, Dragonflyer Press, 2000, pp. 215–16; confirmed by Roy Ringer in interview with journalist Rip Rense, 2003.

26 **1939 Studebaker coupe:** See LAPD Follow-up report by Hansen and Brown dated February 5, 1947.

26 **two crews of reporters and photographers:** Richardson, James, *For the Life of Me*, p. 303.

Chapter 3: The Capture

27 **"Beautiful and forgiving":** Richardson, James, *For the Life of Me*, pp. 304 and 306.

27 **boss's house in Eagle Rock:** *Herald-Express*, January 20, 1947.

28 **by one of the detectives:** Based on photographs of Manley's arrest at the Los Angeles Public Library.

28 **"I know why you're here":** Fowler, Will, *From a Reporter's Notebook*, Huntington Library, *Los Angeles Times* Records/Crime, Los Angeles, box 642.

28 **"as if you've been on a drunk":** Dialogue is reported from Underwood, Agness, *Newspaperwoman*, pp. 8–9.

28 **Harry S. Fremont:** Starr, Kevin, *Embattled Dreams: California in War and Peace 194 –50*, Oxford University Press, Kindle edition, 2002.

29 **many times he was to tell it:** Notes of the original police interviews with Robert Manley in January 1947 have not been disclosed by the LAPD. The account here is based on the exclusive interview with Manley by Agness Underwood in the *Herald-Express*, January 20, 1947; also the later interview given to the district attorney investigators during the grand jury investigation of 1949– 50 (DA, Statement of Robert M. Manley, taken at his home by investigator Frank B Jemison, at 3:30 p.m., February 1, 1950).

29 **"adjustment period":** See Richardson, James, *For the Life of Me*,

pp. 306–7; also Aggie Underwood's interview in the *Herald-Express*, January 20, 1947.

29 **"just little things":** Ibid.

30 **"cold, I would say":** Interview in *Herald-Express*, January 20, 1947. It was a recurrent theme of Elizabeth's male friends that she was sexually "cold." It was perhaps characteristic of the age that this was interpreted, by many, as a sign that she was a lesbian. There could in fact have been many reasons for such "coldness": Elizabeth might have been afraid, not attracted to some of these men, or intercourse might have been painful as a result of her inflamed Bartholin gland, the "female trouble" identified in Dr. Newbarr's autopsy report. The *Los Angeles Examiner* journalist Will Fowler contributed to much of the confusion over Elizabeth's sexuality when he wrote in his memoir, *Reporters*, that Elizabeth had "infantile sex organs" and was incapable of normal sexual relations. He later retracted this statement in a letter to the author Mary Pacios: "Regarding my telling you that Elizabeth Short had 'infantile sex organs.' That is untrue, and a ploy I used to shock all of faint stomachs and phony would-be biographers and article writers" (letter from Fowler to Pacios dated February 25, 1988; cited in Wolfe, Donald, *The Black Dahlia Files*, Appendix A, p. 340). Fowler's statements about the Dahlia investigation are consequently to be treated with extreme caution

30 **Red recalled:** *Herald-Express*, January 20, 1947.

31 **Biltmore about 6:30 p.m.:** See testimony of Robert Manley at the inquest on the death of Elizabeth Short, transcribed in *Childhood Shadows*, Appendix C, p. 317.

31 **The doorman:** The doorman, Harold Studholm, was described in a police report as being the last known person to have seen Beth Short alive (DA grand jury documents, list of persons involved in the case).

32 **of any kind:** See *Los Angeles Examiner*, January 21, 1947; *Herald-Express*, January 21, 1947.

32 **established his innocence:** *Herald-Express*, January 20, 1947.

32 **results were negative:** See LAPD documents, follow-up report dated February 5, 1947, by Hansen and Brown; also *Herald-Express*, January 20, 1947.

32 **alibi:** See *Los Angeles Examiner,* January 21, 1947: the friends were Mr. and Mrs. Don Holmes of San Diego.

32 **clear of suspicion:** *Herald-Express,* January 21, 1947.

33 **pulled off the Dahlia case:** See Underwood, Agness, *Newspaperwoman,* pp. 9–10.

34 **"die on us today!":** Fowler, Will, *Reporters,* p. 200.

34 **"Richardson would never attain":** Ibid., p. 188.

34 **"down and out":** The account is based on interviews in the *Herald-Express,* January 17 and 18, 1947; and the *Los Angeles Examiner,* January 17, 18, and 19, 1947.

35 **mistake over the bride's name:** See interview with Frenches in *Los Angeles Examiner,* January 18, 1947. According to the *Los Angeles Times* and *Herald-Express,* the newspaper article was later found in Elizabeth's handbag and referred to the name of the bride Matt was to bring home, with the name scratched out (*Los Angeles Times,* January 25, 1947; *Herald-Express,* January 25, 1947).

35 **"great deal of money for something":** *Los Angeles Examiner,* January 18, 1947.

35 **most nights:** *Los Angeles Examiner,* January 19, 1947.

35 **"act frightened":** *Herald-Express,* January 27, 1947.

35 **dyed her hair with henna:** *Herald-Express,* January 17, 1947.

36 **"well mannered":** See interview in *Los Angeles Examiner,* January 18, 1947.

36 **"trunk of the car," she said:** *Herald-Express,* January 18, 1947.

36 **American Railway Express office:** Details of the tracking down of the trunk and the conversation with Jack Donahoe taken from Richardson, James, *For the Life of Me,* p. 305.

37 **arrived at the *Examiner* offices:** *Los Angeles Examiner,* January 18, 1947. Also reference to letters in trunk obtained on January 18, in *Los Angeles Examiner,* January 19, 1947.

Chapter 4: Gilda

38 **Medford High's "Deanna Durbin":** Pacios, Mary, *Childhood Shadows,* p. 79.

38 **inference was obvious:** *Los Angeles Times,* January 19, 1947.

38 **Phoebe had insisted:** As reported from the firsthand account in Pacios, Mary, *Childhood Shadows,* p. 13.

39 **business thrived:** Ibid., pp. 12, 13–14.

39   **braided rugs to dry:** See photograph of apartment on Salem
       Street in Pacios, Mary, *Childhood Shadows*, p. 302.

39   **for Beth the movie star's life was real:** Ibid., p. 16.

40   **"manic depressive type":** Interview with Phoebe Short in *Los
       Angeles Examiner*, January 19, 1947; see also *Herald-Express*,
       January 18, 1947.

40   **"something missing":** See interview with Joe Sabia, Pacios, Mary,
       Childhood Shadows, p. 87.

40   **was a ruse:** See DA undated memo "Movements of Elizabeth
       Short prior to June 1, 1946." The account of Elizabeth Short's
       movements up to mid-1946 is taken from this and the account
       headed "Movements and Activities of Elizabeth Short, Victim," DA
       memorandum from Frank B. Jemison to Arthur L. Veitch dated
       October 28, 1949.

40   **Vallejo, California:** Ibid.

40   **merchant navy . . . handyman . . . drunk:** See DA
       memorandum by Frank Jemison summarizing background
       information on persons related to the Dahlia case.

40   **underage drinking:** DA undated memo, "Movements of Elizabeth
       Short prior to June 1, 1946." The memo refers to Elizabeth living
       with her father and a Mrs. Yankee at Vallejo (and possibly also in
       Los Angeles, although this is not confirmed) in 1942–3. Extracts
       from Cleo Short police interview taken from LAPD follow-up
       report on murder by Hansen and Brown, dated February 5, 1947.

41   **she thought they were:** Extracts from Beth's unsent letters
       published in *Los Angeles Examiner*, January 19, 1947.

41   **dashed her hopes:** See *Los Angeles Examiner*, January 19, 1947;
       Herald-Express, January 18, 1947.

42   **all of Matt's friends:** See *Los Angeles Examiner*, January 19, 1947.

42   **Tim Mehringer:** "Tim" Mehringer's real name was Sylvester
       Mehringer, and he was a lieutenant naval aviator at the Jacksonville
       naval air base in Florida. Elizabeth's photograph album included
       pictures of her with Mehringer in his naval flier's uniform. The
       DA document listing the movements of Elizabeth Short places her
       at the Colonial Inn, Riverside Avenue, Jacksonville, Florida, from
       September 1945 to January 1946. Tim Mehringer advertised for
       postwar work as a pilot in the Situations Wanted section of the
       May and June 1946 issues of *Flying* magazine, giving his address

in Jacksonville, his age as twenty-two, and his status as married. Records show that he was married to Ida Mehringer and residing at Riverside Avenue from 1946 to 1948. (See: *Jax Air News*, July 5 and August 23, 1951; *Polk's Jacksonville City Directory*, 1947–48; obituary of Sylvester Mehringer in *Mount Vernon News*, March 23, 2000.) It seems most likely that Short and Mehringer met when he was married and living at Riverside Avenue in 1945–46.

42   **Stephen Wolak:** See FBI telegram dated October 1, 1947.

42   **Joseph Gordon Fickling:** See DA untitled document, detailing background information of persons involved in the case.

43   **Chicago in July:** See DA document entitled "Movements of Elizabeth Short (After June 1, 1946)," summary timeline: Elizabeth left her mother's home in Medford on June 1, 1946, intending to meet Fickling. She stayed in Indianapolis for an undetermined time at an undetermined place, then went to Long Beach via Chicago, staying at the Washington Hotel in Long Beach from July 22 to August 3, 1946.

43   **Washington Hotel . . . provided by Fickling:** See DA document summarizing movements of Elizabeth Short: Fickling wrote in a letter to the LAPD that Elizabeth lived in the Washington Hotel, Long Beach, from July 22 to August 3, then in furnished rooms from August 3 to August 27.

43   **"seemed jealous of the sailor":** See *Los Angeles Examiner*, January 18, 1947; also *Herald-Express*, January 18, 1947.

43   **made him "crazy":** See letter from Fickling quoted in *Herald-Examiner*, January 20, 1947: "Darling, how many lips have joined with yours since ours last met? Sometimes I go crazy when I think of such things."

43   **"believe me":** Quoted in the *Los Angeles Examiner* and *Herald-Express*, January 21, 1947.

44   **"extra burden":** Quoted in the *Los Angeles Examiner*, January 21, 1947; *Herald-Express*, January 20, 1947.

Chapter 5: Dial M for Murder

45   **behind a pane of glass:** Based on accounts in the *Los Angeles Times*, *Los Angeles Examiner*, and *Herald-Express*, January 21, 1947. See also the LAPD dead body report dated January 15, 1947, which refers to "1 large mole on left shoulder."

46   **jumping from her seat:** Dialogue from the inquest into the death
of Elizabeth Short is taken from the transcript in Pacios, Mary,
Childhood Shadows, Appendix C, pp. 317–33.

47   **forty-five-minute hearing:** *Herald-Express*, January 22, 1947.

47   **where the body was found:** DA documents, report dated
November 23, 1949: "Evidence and declarations tending to connect
or disconnect Leslie Dillon to the murders of Elizabeth Short,
Jeanne French, and Gladys Kern."

47   **blocked by tall weeds:** *Herald-Express*, January 16, 1947; *Los
Angeles Times*, January 17, 1947; Pacios, Mary, *Childhood Shadows*,
p. 65.

48   **rest of his life:** The dialogue is cited from Jimmy Richardson's
memoir *For the Life of Me*, pp. 307–8. Descriptive details of the
Examiner office interior are taken from Richardson's serialized
novel *Spring Street: A Story of Los Angeles*, Times-Mirror Press,
1922; also from photographs of the office interior held in the James
Hugh Richardson collection at the University of California, Los
Angeles.

49   **lit a Lucky:** Richardson was a dried-out alcoholic and notorious
chain-smoker, his favored cigarette brand being Lucky Strikes. He
recounts his experiences with alcohol and cigarette dependency in
For the Life of Me and in his personal correspondence, presently
housed in the Department of Special Collections at the University
of California, Los Angeles.

49   **The parcel was opened:** Details of the opening of the package
at the post office and its contents are taken from DA report titled
"Summary of the Elizabeth (Beth) Short Murder Investigation."

50   **names and phone numbers:** According to newspapers such as
the *Los Angeles Examiner* and *Los Angeles Times*, the package also
contained a newspaper clipping referring to Major Matt Gordon's
marriage, with the name of the bride scratched out. However, the
itemized list of contents of the package in the DA files (see previous
note) does not include this. The police report of the incident
implies that Elizabeth's trunk at the Railway Express and the
suitcases lodged with the Greyhound bus company were tracked
down as a result of the receipt and telegram found in the package.
In fact, these had been located and inspected earlier, through
the efforts of the *Los Angeles Examiner*, as newspaper articles

dated January 18, 1947—i.e., prior to the receipt of the package—
demonstrate.

50   **previous Monday:** *Herald-Express*, January 25, 1947.

50   **must have been the killer:** See DA report titled "Summary of
the Elizabeth (Beth) Short Murder Investigation" in which the
conclusion is that the package must have come from the killer. The
fact that the package contained the receipt for Elizabeth Short's
baggage as deposited at the Greyhound bus station on January 9
is strongly supportive of the contention that it did indeed contain
the contents of her handbag, which must have been removed *after*
Elizabeth left Manley at the Biltmore, as the baggage receipt dated
January 9 could not possibly have been contained either in her
trunk previously deposited with the Railway Express Company,
or the suitcases left at the Greyhound bus depot. The style of the
message and the pains the sender took to conceal his or her identity
are difficult to reconcile with a communication from a disinterested
bystander unconnected with the case.

50   **came back negative:** A letter from the FBI to LAPD chief
Clemence Horrall dated January 29, 1947, refers to a single print
having been sent to the FBI for analysis and comparison with their
fingerprint records on January 25, i.e., the day after the package
was sent. According to the testimony of Lieutenant Harry Hansen
given during 1949 grand jury proceedings, the quality of the print
was poor, with "blurs and smudges." The *Los Angeles Times* on
January 26, 1947, gave the source of the print as the exterior of the
package and commented on the subsequent lack of reliability. (The
Los Angeles Times article refers to two prints being retrieved, but
it is clear from the FBI report that there was just one single, latent
print taken from the package.)

50   **hand that was not Short's:** Taken from the testimony of Sergeant
Finis Brown in the DA grand jury proceedings.

51   **January 26 at 6:30 p.m.:** *Herald-Express*, January 27, 1947.

51   **"Black Dahlia Avenger":** *Herald-Express*, January 27, 1947; *Los
Angeles Examiner*, January 29, 1947.

51   **"real or imagined":** *Herald-Express*, January 27, 1947.

52   **anonymous telephone call:** See *Los Angeles Times*, January 25,
1947.

52   **by the killer:** See *Los Angeles Examiner*, January 25, 1947.

53   **"gonna be dynamite!"**: *Examiner,* January 25, 1947;
Herald-Express, January 25, 1947.

53   **"embarrassing" them:** See *Los Angeles Examiner,* January 25,
1947.

Chapter 6: House of Strangers

54   **fifty-five years old:** Mark Hansen's U.S. passport application
dated 1921 gives his date of birth as July 25, 1891 (National
Archives and Records Administration [NARA], Washington D.C.;
NARA Series: *Passport Applications, January 2, 1906–March 31,
1925;* Roll #: *1771;* Volume #: *Roll 1771—Certificates: 95626-95999,
04 Nov 1921-05 Nov 1921).*

54   **Danes called it:** *Danmarks Købstæder: Aalborg* (in Danish). Dansk
Center for Byhistorie.

54   **"Treasure State":** See Spence, Clark C., *Montana: A Bicentennial History,* W. W. Norton, 1978, pp. 139–40; Malone, Michael
P., Richard B. Roeder, and William L. Lang, *Montana: A History
of Two Centuries,* revised edition, University of Washington Press,
1976, p. 232.

54   **"whistled for the dog":** Fletcher, Robert H., *Free Grass to Fences,*
New York: University Publishers, 1960, pp. 149–50.

54   **wound up in Tinseltown:** Taken from Hansen's 1921 passport
application; also DA statement of Mark Hansen dated December
16, 1949.

55   **$1.50 for dinner:** See *Los Angeles Times,* "Club Shone Brightly in
Its Heyday," October 10, 2004; Zemeckis, Leslie, *Goddess of Love
Incarnate: The Life of Stripteuse Lili St. Cyr,* Counterpoint Press, 2015.

55   **post–Pearl Harbor pay:** See *Life* magazine, January 31, 1944.

55   **Scandinavian accent:** The fact that Mark Hansen spoke with
"a very distinctive accent, he talks like a Swede or a Norwegian,"
was noted by Officer Loren K. Waggoner, formerly of the Gangster
Squad, in his testimony before the DA grand jury.

55   **toughest hoods in Hollywood:** Tereba, Tere, *Mickey Cohen: The
Life and Crimes of L.A.'s Notorious Mobster,* Kindle edition, ECW
Press, 2012, p. 74. Hansen admitted under questioning by the
district attorney's office that he had known Jimmy Utley for "about
six months" as he "came to the Florentine Gardens" (DA statement
of Mark Hansen taken December 16, 1949).

55   **bingo parlors at Venice Beach:** Tereba, Tere, *Mickey Cohen*.

55   **laid out on the table:** Reid, Ed, *Mickey Cohen: Mobster*, Pinnacle
Books 1973, pp. 188–89.

56   **abortion racket:** Mark Hansen's ex-lodger Ann Toth stated in an
interview with police that Hansen claimed to perform abortions with
pills: see DA statement of Ann Toth taken on December 13, 1949.

56   **talking to a crooked cop:** Tereba, Tere, *Mickey Cohen*.

56   **dance floor:** See DA note entitled "Information in re suspects."

56   **"dance" for the club:** NTG "spotted" the future Lili St. Cyr at
one such show in Saugus, Massachusetts. (See Zemeckis, Leslie,
Goddess of Love.)

56   **Owen "Owney" Madden:** For more on NTG and his mob
connections, see Hoefling, Larry J., *Nils Thor Granlund*,
McFarland, 2010, pp. 116 et seq.

57   **pitched up at Carlos Avenue:** See DA document entitled
"Movements and Activities of Elizabeth Short, Victim." Short left
the Brevoort Hotel, where she stayed with Gordon Fickling, on
August 27, 1946. From August 28 to September 19 she lived at the
Hawthorne Hotel, 1611 North Orange Drive, Los Angeles, with
Marjorie Graham. Short and Graham are then stated to have lived
with the musician Sid Zaid at the Figueroa Hotel from September
20 to October 1, when they moved in with Mark Hansen at his
Carlos Avenue apartment.

57   **"always in trouble beauty":** *Herald-Express*, January 18, 1947.

57   **paid it:** *Herald-Express*, January 17, 1947.

57   **all the more tantalizing:** See DA statement of Ann Toth dated
December 13, 1949.

58   **never delivered:** DA closure report dated February 20, 1951, entry
relating to Mark Hansen.

58   **"bringing her home":** DA statement of Mark Hansen dated
December 16, 1949.

58   **Guardian Arms apartments:** DA closure report dated February
20, 1951, entry relating to Marvin Margolis.

58   **when Mark Hansen was around:** DA statement of Ann Toth
dated December 13, 1949.

58   **no place to stay:** DA statement of Ann Toth dated December 13,
1949.

58   **out of his automobile:** DA statement of Ann Toth dated
December 13, 1949.

58   **back into his home:** DA statement of Mark Hansen dated
December 16, 1949.

59   **"from the time she came there":** DA statement of Ann Toth,
dated February 28, 1950.

59   **telephone bill:** DA statement of Ann Toth dated December 13,
1949.

59   **at least a month:** DA, statement of Ann Toth dated December 13,
1949.

59   **"Mark stepped in between them":** DA statement of Ann Toth
dated December 13, 1949.

59   **the fee was $1 each a night:** *Herald-Express*, January 22, 1947.

60   **"More the sophisticated type":** See *Los Angeles Examiner*,
January 18, 1947.

60   **mail . . . "copacetic":** DA statement of Ann Toth dated
December 13, 1949.

60   **crying:** DA statement of Mark Hansen dated December 16, 1949.

60   **"with her sister in Berkeley":** Quoted in *Los Angeles Examiner*,
January 18, 1947.

61   **disliked her intensely:** *Herald-Express*, January 17, 1947.

61   **must have stolen it:** DA closure report dated February 20, 1951,
entry relating to Mark Hansen.

Chapter 7: The Big Sleep

62   **purse and a single shoe:** See *Los Angeles Times*, January 25 and
26, 1947; *Herald-Express*, January 24, 1947—the day the shoe and
bag were found.

62   **identify the shoe and purse:** *Herald-Express*, January 25, 1947.
Manley's identification of the shoe and purse as those of Elizabeth
Short was subsequently, apparently, questioned by Elvera and
Dorothy French. (See *Los Angeles Examiner*, January 27, 1947;
Herald-Express, January 27, 1947; Papers of James Richardson,
UCLA special collections, Box 3, Folder 1, "Dahlia data.") However,
Robert Manley and not the Frenches was the person known to have
last seen the Dahlia, and the fact that he actually took the shoes in
his possession to have the taps repaired, and picked out the purse

partly for Elizabeth's distinctive perfume, makes his identification certainly correct.

63   **"bitter dislike":** *Herald-Express*, January 21, 1947.

63   **"Lynn Martin":** *Los Angeles Examiner*, January 29, 1947. Lynn was born in Chicago on January 25, 1931, but "always posed as 22 or over in Hollywood." Adopted at age nine by Mr. and Mrs. Fred Meyer of Long Beach, she ran away from home three times, she told Deputy District Attorney Herbert Grossman. At thirteen she had married a soldier from Texas but believed that he had since obtained a divorce. She was picked up as a delinquent by Long Beach authorities and confined to the El Retiro School for Girls for thirteen months and released in June 1945. Two weeks later, she again ran away from the Meyer home and back to Hollywood. She lived with Elizabeth for short periods in 1946.

63   **"salesman" with a rap sheet:** See DA statement of John F. Egger, February 7, 1950. "Wellington" was subsequently cleared of involvement in the murder, although he wrote a long and indignant letter that was published in the *Herald-Express*, complaining of his treatment at the hands of police and the press (*Herald-Express*, January 23, 1947; January 27, 1947).

63   **nude photographs of her:** *Los Angeles Times*, January 29, 1947.

64   **Arthur was arrested in Tucson, Arizona:** The late author and journalist John Gilmore has set forth an elaborate, unsubstantiated story that Beth was the "other" girl with Arthur James in Arizona, who managed to escape. See Gilmore papers Box 17, letter dated August 11, 1992, to Asa Bushnell; also documents relating to conviction of Arthur James, ibid. While the DA's summary of Elizabeth's movements has her in Medford and Miami in 1944, Gordon Fickling stated that he met her in Southern California in that year, before he went overseas. (See *Los Angeles Examiner*, January 18, 1947.)

64   **Joseph Dumais:** See *Los Angeles Times*, February 6 and 7, 1947; *Los Angeles Examiner*, February 7 and 12, 1947; *The Berkshire Evening Eagle*, February 10, 1947.

65   **Edward Augele:** *Long Beach Independent*, April 25, 1957.

65   **Melvin Robert Bailey:** The *Bradford Era*, March 19, 1947; *Los Angeles Examiner*, March 19, 1947.

65 **Daniel Voorhees:** *Washington Times Herald*, January 29, 1947;
    FBI memoranda and newspaper clippings dated January 29, 1947.

66 **Bill Payette to complain:** Letter from *Daily News* journalist
    Chuck Chappell *to Los Angeles Times* columnist Jack Smith dated
    January 23, 1975, Huntington Library, Jack Smith papers, folder
    "Black Dahlia," box S3.

66 **"I knew her as Libby":** Details of Christine Reynolds's confession
    and citations are taken from: the *Mirror*, November 25, 1950;
    Herald-Express, November 25, 1950; LAPD officer's memorandum
    dated November 24, 1950, Black Dahlia case; clippings in FBI and
    LAPD papers.

67 **woman of "Amazonian proportions":** *Los Angeles Times*,
    February 8, 1947.

67 **"bossy blonde":** Various supposed "sightings" of Short with
    a woman or women during the "missing week" included: at
    the Dugout Café on South Main Street on January 11; and
    at the Four-Star Grill, Hollywood Boulevard, on January 12
    (*Herald-Express*, January 21, 1947).

67 **gay women staying at the Chancellor Apartments:** DA
    statement of Mark Hansen dated December 16, 1949. On the
    other hand, Ann Toth in her interview with the DA stated that she
    went up to Beth's room at the Chancellor a couple of times and the
    girls did not look queer to her (DA statement of Ann Toth dated
    February 28, 1950).

67 **"shoved it up her fucking pussy":** LAPD officer's memorandum
    dated November 24 1950, Black Dahlia case.

68 **to "confess" to the murder:** For example, Minnie Sepulveda;
    Mrs. Emily E. Williams of Tampa, Florida, who surrendered to the
    San Diego police with the confession that "Elizabeth Short stole
    my man, so I killed her and cut her up" (*Los Angeles Examiner*,
    January 29, 1947). A Mrs. Marie Grieme of Chicago claimed that
    an acquaintance, Mildred Kolian, who "looked like a man" and
    was known as "Billie," "told me she had killed Beth Short in a
    jealous rage over Beth's association with other people" (*Los Angeles
    Examiner*, March 5, 1947).

68 **Gerry Ramlow:** Pacios, Mary, *Childhood Shadows*, p. 92.

69 **female homosexuality:** For an in-depth portrayal and analysis of

Hollywood's "sewing circle" of lesbians and attitudes toward them in the golden age of American cinema, see Madsen, Axel, *The Sewing Circle: Hollywood's Greatest Secret—Female Stars Who Loved Other Women*, Kindle edition, Open Road Distribution, 2015.

70   **Alice La Vere:** *Herald-Express*, January 22, 1947.

71   **Ben Hecht also wrote an article:** *Herald-Express*, February 1, 1947.

71   **Sergeant Peter Vetcher:** See letter from FBI field office in Pittsburgh to Los Angeles field office dated March 27, 1947, revealed for the first time to the author in unredacted form.

72   **"queer woman surgeon in the Valley":** DA closure report of Frank B. Jemison dated February 20, 1951. Curiously, the report refers to Elizabeth as having been engaged to a flier named "Quin" as opposed to the correct name, Matt Gordon.

72   **Woody Guthrie:** See Cray, Ed, *Ramblin' Man: The Life and Times of Woody Guthrie*, W. W. Norton, Kindle edition, 2012.

73   **"Princess Whitewing":** *Los Angeles Times*, January 29, 1947. The existence of Princess Whitewing was confirmed by an article in the *Pittburgh Press*, January 14, 1936, "'To loaf like Real Indian': Cherokee Princess' Dream."

73   **Mr. and Mrs. Johnson:** *Los Angeles Examiner*, January 21, 1947.

74   **mistaken identity:** *Herald-Express*, January 22, 1947.

74   **Buddy LaGore:** *Herald-Express*, January 23, 1947.

74   **Myrl McBride:** *Los Angeles Times*, January 17, 1947; *Los Angeles Herald-Express*, January 17, 1947.

75   **"a very meticulous person":** DA interview with Ann Toth dated December 13, 1949.

75   **"a make-up kit":** *Herald-Express*, January 20, 1947.

76   **the entire 123-pound corpse:** *Herald-Express*, January 21, 1947.

76   **clean up the mess:** See FBI office memorandum dated February 20, 1947 from SAC (special agent in charge) Los Angeles to FBI Director J. Edgar Hoover, revealed to the author for the first time in unredacted form. Richardson referred to "rumblings of incompetency in the police department."

76   **moniker Harry "the Hat":** See interview with Chuck Cheatham, crime reporter on the *Long Beach Independent*, in Pacios, Mary, *Childhood Shadows*, p. 73.

76   **joined the LAPD in 1926:** See Henderson, Bruce, and Sam

Summerlin, *The Supersleuths*, Macmillan, 1976, pp. 75–81; "Farewell, My Black Dahlia" in *Los Angeles Times West* magazine, March 28, 1971.

77   **Harry Watson:** From an interview with Watson recounted in Wagner, Rob Leicester, *Red Ink, White Lies*, Dragonflyer Press, 2000, p. 237. Hansen's name is spelled "Hanson'"in Wagner, but this was a common mistake, as manifested in a certificate awarded to Hansen himself by the L.A. Coroner's Office.

77   **"real strange . . . couldn't believe a word he said":** Pacios, Mary, *Childhood Shadows*, p. 104.

77   **Finis . . . the "bagman":** Author interview with Tony Valdez of Fox television. See also Pacios, Mary, *Childhood Shadows*, interview with Chuck Cheatham, former reporter on the *Long Beach Independent*, p. 72; Nielson Himmel, reporter on *Los Angeles Times*, p. 102.

78   **Ernest Jerome Hopkins had noted that the LAPD:** Hopkins, Ernest Jerome, *Our Lawless Police: A Study of the Unlawful Enforcement of the Law*, 1931, reprint, Da Capo Press, New York, 1972; Starr, Kevin, *Embattled Dreams: California in War and Peace, 1940–1950*, Oxford University Press, 2003.

78   **"police were the gangsters":** Lieberman, Paul, *Gangster Squad: Covert Cops, the Mob, and the Battle for Los Angeles*, Kindle edition, St. Martin's Griffin, 2012.

78   **commander of the LAPD Patrol Bureau:** See memorandum dated November 17, 1949, to Arthur L. Veitch, "In re Mark Hansen—Lola Titus incident," DA grand jury documents.

79   **network of paid informants:** Domanick, Joe, *To Protect and to Serve: The LAPD's Century of War in the City of Dreams*, Pocket Books, 1995, p. 101.

PART 2: DARK PASSAGE

Chapter 8: The Letter

83   **"some day have to boast about it":** De River quoted in *Life* magazine, "I Killed Her," March 24, 1947, p. 24.

83   **According to the doctor:** *Los Angeles Herald-Express*, June 17, 1947.

84   **born on the Mississippi River:** Daniel, Jacque, *The Curse of the Black Dahlia*, Digital Data Werks, 2004, p. 273.

84   **degree from Tulane University:** A detailed account of Dr. De River's training and employment history is given in King, Brian, introduction to *The Sexual Criminal: A Psychoanalytical Study*, Bloat Books, 284.

84   **celebrity Hollywood physician:** *Life* magazine, "I Killed Her," March 24, 1947, p. 24.

85   **the doctor described the type:** Ramsland, Katherine, *The Mind of a Murderer: Privileged Access to the Demons That Drive Extreme Violence*, Praeger, 2011, p. 52.

85   **clippings relating to the case:** See Daniel, Jacque, *The Curse of the Black Dahlia*, pp. 9–11; also Ramsland, Katherine, *The Mind of a Murderer*, pp. 51–2.

86   **sexual offender register:** California (1947) was followed by Arizona (1951), Nevada (1961), Ohio (1963), and Alabama (1967). By 1989, twelve U.S. states had sexual offenders registers in place. See Thomas, Terry, *The Registration and Monitoring of Sex Offenders: A Comparative Study*, Routledge, 2011, p. 38.

86   **Chloe Davis:** For a detailed discussion of the background and circumstances of the case, see Ramsland, Katherine, *The Mind of a Murderer*, Chapter 6.

87   **rival psychiatrist:** Samuel M. Marcus, cited in King, Brian, *The Sexual Criminal*, p. xxxvi.

87   **"best qualified sex psychiatrist in the country":** King, Brian, *The Sexual Criminal*, p. li.

88   **in over twenty cases:** The cases were listed by De River in proceedings before the City Council dated March 8, 1949. They included: Dyer; DeWitt Clinton Cook; Betty Hardaker; Arthur Eggers; Campbell McDonald; Spenalli; John Burton; Virginia McElhiney; Otto Steven Wilson; John Barto Case; John Honeycutt; Gieger; Peter Hernandez; Leslie Webster; Rudolph Rodriguez; Lee Burton; Raymond Latshaw; John Plannagon; Harold Hanson; and Robert Folks.

88   **children could identify them:** Thomas, Terry, *The Registration and Monitoring of Sex Offenders*, p. 37.

88   **two decades away:** See the discussion of the "age of conservatism" verses the "age of complacency" in Thomas, Terry, *The Registration and Monitoring of Sex Offenders*, pp. 37–38.

88 **receive the jury's guilty verdict:** Daniel, Jacque, *The Curse of the Black Dahlia*, p. 15.

88 **lifelong friends after the case:** Daniel, Jacque, *The Curse of the Black Dahlia*, p. 14; King, Brian, *The Sexual Criminal*.

89 **secretly at her home:** Interview with Aggie's daughter-in-law Rilla, cited by Pacios, Mary, *Childhood Shadows*, p. 114. Dr. De River also told the writer Donald Freed that he met with Aggie Underwood to discuss the case in his meetings with Freed in the 1950s, discussed in detail in Chapter 21.

89 **"Jack Sand":** DA reports, "Correspondence between Dr J Paul de River and Leslie Dillon, alias Jack Sand."

90 **lure the Dahlia killer:** Information from author's interview with Donald Freed in January 2016, referred to in detail in Chapter 21.

90 **doctor sent a response:** Letter dated November 20, 1948, from J. Paul De River to Jack Sand, DA police reports.

90 **response from "Jack Sand":** Letter dated November 27, 1948, from Jack Sand to Dr. J Paul De River, DA police reports.

90 **"Jeff '48":** The sketch was found among Dr. De River's personal possessions and is reproduced in his daughter's memoir (Daniel, Jacque, *The Curse of the Black Dahlia*, p. 177). It is also referred to in the DA grand jury testimony of private investigator Fred Witman.

91 **crisscross lacerations:** See the witness statement of Fred Witman in the DA grand jury proceedings: "This kind of rushed drawing . . . criss-cross . . ."

91 **a very "loyal lad":** Letter dated December 11, 1948, from Jack Sand to Dr. J. Paul De River, DA police reports.

91 **"Especial delivar":** Testimony of Fred Witman in the DA grand jury proceedings.

92 **term of intimacy:** Testimony of Fred Witman in the DA grand jury proceedings.

Chapter 9: The Suspect

93 **Clemence B. Horrall:** Lieberman, Paul, *Gangster Squad: Covert Cops, the Mob, and the Battle for Los Angeles*, Kindle edition, St. Martin's Griffin, 2012.

93 **forced to resign:** Buntin, John, *L.A. Noir: The Struggle for the*

Soul of America's Most Seductive City, Kindle edition, Broadway Books, 2009.

93 **Harry Raymond got into his car:** Lieberman, Paul, *Gangster Squad.*

94 **"retired" to Mexico:** Austin, John, *Hollywood's Greatest Mysteries,* SPI Books, 1994, p. 78.

95 **Lieutenant William Burns:** Lieberman, Paul, *Gangster Squad.*

95 **late in December 1948:** Date based on the testimonies of Willie Burns and Officer John J. O'Mara in the DA 1949 grand jury proceedings.

95 **as head of the Homicide detail a year back:** See interview with retired LAPD Police Captain Ed Jokisch by Larry Harnisch in the *Daily Mirror,* Voices, August 7, 2011, Part 1. Captain Kearney was transferred from Narcotics to head the Homicide detail in September 1947, when Donahoe was taken off Homicide and transferred back to Robbery.

95 **to tail Jack:** Private investigator Fred Witman, in September 1949, told Deputy DA Arthur Veitch and Chief H. L. Stanley of the DA's Bureau of Investigation about the tailing of "Jack Sand" (later discovered to be Leslie Dillon). Officer "Jones" has never been identified, although an officer named "Jones" was listed in the DA documents as being involved in the case. Witman's testimony to Veitch and Stanley effectively triggered the subsequent grand jury investigation of the handling of the Dahlia case. The undercover Miami operation was curiously left out of the testimony given by officers of both the Gangster Squad and Homicide detail before the grand jury and was not confirmed (or denied) by the DA investigators' evaluations of Witman's testimony.

96 **Leslie Duane Dillon:** See entry for Leslie D. Dillon in U.S. Social Security Death Index, Number: *445-07-6209*; Issue State: *Oklahoma*; Issue Date: *Before 1951.* Birth date is given as July 24, 1921; although in other documents date of birth is given as July 4, 1921. (See, for example, U.S. Social Security Claims and Applications Index under Leslie Duane Dillon.)

96 **father, Ray, was a metal worker:** Interview in the *Los Angeles Examiner* with Leslie Dillon's mother, Mamie, January 11, 1949.

96 **cook in a local restaurant:** See U.S. Federal Census entry under Leslie Dillon, Year: *1930*; Census Place: *Cushing, Payne,*

Oklahoma; Roll: *1925*; Page: *10B*; Enumeration District: *0007*;
Image: *104.0*; FHL microfilm: *2341659*.

96   **His aliases were many:** "Jack Sand" is the alias used by Dillon
in correspondence with Dr. De River, and Dillon himself normally
went by the name of "Jack." (See interview with Dillon's daughter
on page 233.) The alias of "Jack Diamond" is referred to by Fred
Witman. The other aliases are referred to in the U.S. Social Security
Claims and Application Index: "June 1937: Name listed as LESLIE
DUANE DILLON; Apr 1953: Name listed as JACK DILLON
MAXIM; 07 Feb 1989: Name listed as LESLIE D DILLON."
Dillon also went by the name of a friend, Woody.

97   **ballpoint pen:** See DA testimony of Fred Witman: "I
photographed an inside page [of the *True Detective* magazine
article], incomplete but where it bore a ballpoint pencil mark after
the legend, 'Be there tomorrow afternoon late. Would like to see
you. Red.'"

97   **"This is the man":** The source for the statement is Fred
Witman's testimony to Veitch and Stanley. As noted above, the
Miami undercover operation was not referred to in the grand jury
proceedings and not referenced by the DA investigators' reports,
either to confirm or deny it occurred.

98   **assigned to members of the Gangster Squad:** See DA
testimony of Officer Archie B. Case in 1949 grand jury
proceedings.

Chapter 10: Behind Locked Doors

100   **Sergeant John J. O'Mara:** See Lieberman, Paul, *The Gangster
Squad*.

101   **did not want to come to Los Angeles:** Based on the testimony
of private investigator Fred Witman in the DA grand jury
proceedings.

101   **impossible to obtain suitable rooms:** See testimony of private
investigator Fred Witman in the DA grand jury proceedings.

102   **doctor conversed with Dillon:** Details of the conversation
between Dillon and O'Mara are taken from the testimony of John J.
O'Mara in the DA grand jury proceedings (undated). The Gangster
Squad was issued with two 1940 unmarked Fords in which to
perform their assignments.

102   **Hahn's Funeral Home:** Testimony of John J. O'Mara, DA grand
jury proceedings; DA report on Leslie Dillon by Frank Jemison
(undated). Jemison's report continues that William Cowger of
Hahn's Funeral Home, Oklahoma City, stated in a letter that he
was unable to find payroll records for a "John Dillon," which was
the name Leslie Dillon told the police department he used while
working there, nor any records for a Leslie Dillon.

102   **"women, women, women":** Testimony of private investigator Fred
Witman at the DA grand jury proceedings.

102   **"soft, well-modulated voice":** Testimony of Officer Burns at the
DA grand jury proceedings.

102   **Briargate Lodge was a long:** Based on the testimony of John J.
O'Mara and private investigator Fred Witman in the DA grand jury
proceedings (undated).

102   **prowling around:** See testimony of Officer John J. O'Mara and
private investigator Fred Witman in the DA grand jury proceedings.

103   **proffered an explanation:** Testimony of Officer John J. O'Mara
in the DA grand jury proceedings.

103   **"would cut it low":** Testimony of the private investigator Fred
Witman in the DA grand jury proceedings. The account of the
events in Banning given here is taken from the sworn evidence of
Fred Witman, since Witman—as described later—was acting on
Dr. De River's instructions, and the doctor's own testimony before
the grand jury in 1949 was never transcribed.

103   **"motels, something like that":** Testimony of the private
investigator Fred Witman in the DA grand jury proceedings.

104   **"juvenile penis" . . . "frustrated fellow":** See testimony of
private investigator Fred Witman in the DA grand jury proceedings.

104   **"Shoots Out Girl's Tooth":** The article (undated) was included in
documents released to the author by the DA.

105   **two key facts:** See undated report by Frank Jemison, DA
investigator, in DA grand jury files: "A piece of flesh approximately
one pound in weight was cut from the front of the left thigh, and
there were various other small lacerations and cuts, two secrets
that have been closely guarded by a few officers in connection with
this investigation including the undersigned. They could only be
answered by the person who committed this murder. The question
is, *what did this suspect do about the pubic hairs and what did he do*

with the piece of flesh cut from the front of the left thigh?" [author's emphasis]. It is clear, therefore, that these were the two "secret facts" withheld for police questioning of suspects.

105   **rectum . . . vagina:** A memorandum from Frank Jemison to H. L. Stanley of the DA's office dated October 28, 1949, states: "The flesh cut from her left thigh weighing approximately one pound was found in her vagina and the pubic hair was found in the rectum." The private investigator Fred Witman, in his testimony to the DA's Officers Veitch and Stanley, alluded to the pubic hair being inserted into the "fundament." He also stated that Dillon knew this. Curiously, Frank Jemison's memorandum states: "There were no cigarette burns and no tattoo marks on the body." This does not correlate with the statement of Officer Mary Unkefer, who was certain that Elizabeth had a rose tattoo on the top of the left leg, whose position would correlate with the square of flesh that had been removed and inserted into the vagina. (See page 17.) Dr. De River, in an interview with the writer Donald Freed in 1953, stated categorically that a rose tattoo had been removed by the killer, and that Leslie Dillon knew what had been done with it. However, in line with his obligations of confidentiality, the doctor did not reveal to Freed or his uncle Wally Klein what that was. The interview with Donald Freed is discussed later in Chapter 21. It appears that the statement that there were "no cigarette burns or tattoo marks on the body" was made in an attempt to discredit De River, who said in his testimony to the grand jury that there were cigarette burns on the body (memorandum from Frank Jemison to H. L. Stanley, October 28, 1949). The author Steve Hodel claims to have been given a photograph from the autopsy of Elizabeth Short by the daughter of Lieutenant Harry Hansen, which shows the presence of cigarette burn marks on the body. If this is correct, then it suggests that certain crime scene photographs were improperly retained by Lieutenant Hansen—a grave irregularity.

105   **even the police did not know:** Police Chief Clemence Horrall, in a press statement of January 1949, stated that Leslie Dillon knew details about the Dahlia murder that even the police did not know. What those details likely were is discussed on page 113.

105   **going through his belongings:** Evidence of Officer John J.

O'Mara and private investigator Fred Witman in the DA grand jury proceedings.

105   **"big mouths":** Testimony of Fred Witman in the DA grand jury proceedings.

106   **"change, very quickly":** Taken from the testimony of John J. O'Mara in the DA grand jury proceedings.

106   **"knocks them out":** Testimony of Officer John J. O'Mara in the DA grand jury proceedings.

106   **obtained from some nurses:** See testimony of Officer John J. O'Mara in the DA grand jury proceedings.

106   **women's loafer-style black suede shoes:** A scaled photograph of the shoes included in the DA grand jury documents shows them to be approximately 9½ inches in length. A study measuring the size of shoe prints of male and female movie stars from the 1940s through the 1960s outside Grauman's Chinese Theatre yielded the following measurements (in inches): MALE: Bob Hope, 8¾; Henry Fonda, 8⅛; Gary Cooper, 8½; Roy Rogers, 9¼; John Wayne, 9⅜; Cary Grant, 9½; Rock Hudson, 8⅛; George Murphy, 8⅜; Gregory Peck, 7¼; Cecil B. DeMille, 9¼; Clark Gable, 8½; Steve McQueen, 8⅜; Anthony Quinn, 9⅛; Charlton Heston, 10½; Paul Newman, 9½; Frank Sinatra, 8½; Dick Van Dyke, 8¼; Sidney Poitier, 9½; Gene Kelly, 7⅜. FEMALE: Rita Hayworth, 6¼; Betty Grable, 6⅜; Anne Baxter, 7⅛; Lana Turner, 6½; Bette Davis, 5⅜; Marilyn Monroe, 5⅜; Elizabeth Taylor, 7; Deborah Kerr, 6½; Julie Andrews, 6½. Study carried out for the author at Grauman's Chinese Theatre, October 2016.

107   **"watching the street markers":** Testimony of Officer John J. O'Mara in the DA grand jury proceedings.

Chapter 11: Deadline at Dawn

108   **Except in January 1949:** The winter of 1948–9 was a record one in Los Angeles, with freezing temperatures and unaccustomed snow.

108   **Dillon opened the door:** Testimony of Officer John J. O'Mara in the DA grand jury proceedings.

109   **familiar with the area:** Testimony of Officer John J. O'Mara in the DA grand jury proceedings.

110   **"English. French":** Testimony of Fred Witman in the DA grand
       jury proceedings.

110   **"full of vitality" . . . "bouncing back":** Testimony of Officer
       John J. O'Mara in the DA grand jury proceedings. The observation
       that Dillon seemed constantly on a "high" was also made by Dr. De
       River in interview with the author Donald Freed. (See Chapter 21.)

110   **San Francisco:** Testimony of Officer John J. O'Mara in the DA
       grand jury proceedings.

111   **sailed a postcard:** King, Brian, *The Sexual Criminal*, p. xlv.

111   **reporter William Chance:** King, Brian, *The Sexual Criminal*,
       p. xlv.

112   **Dillon was taken into custody:** Testimony of Officer William
       Burns in the DA grand jury proceedings.

112   **At 2:45 p.m., he was booked:** See DA report on Leslie Duane
       Dillon by Frank Jemison (undated).

112   **Harry "the Hat" . . . Captain Kearney:** As reported in
       the testimony of Officer Harry Hansen in the DA grand jury
       proceedings.

112   **pills . . . razor blades . . . dog leash:** Testimony of witness Fred
       Witman in the DA grand jury proceedings; also testimony of J.J.
       O'Mara, ibid. A photograph of the dog leash released in the DA
       grand jury exhibits provides evidence of its condition and points
       of wear.

113   **Horrall . . . press conference:** See *Los Angeles Times*, January
       11, 1949; *Los Angeles Examiner*, January 11, 1949.

114   **"strangely reticent":** Interview with Georgia Dillon in *Los Angeles
       Examiner*, January 12, 1949.

115   **"Six feet tall":** *Los Angeles Examiner*, January 11, 1949.

116   **"knew the Dahlia, went out with her":** *Los Angeles Examiner*,
       January 12, 1949.

116   **"checked out to the ultimate":** *Los Angeles Examiner*, January
       12, 1949.

116   **"could know the things that Dillon knew":** *Los Angeles
       Examiner*, January 12, 1949.

117   **Jeff . . . the "secret details":** *Los Angeles Examiner*, January 12,
       1949.

117   **"which I told you":** *Los Angeles Examiner*, January 12, 1949.

117 **San Francisco hotel:** The San Joaquin Hotel. See DA report on Leslie Duane Dillon by Frank Jemison (undated).

117 **"he is a mythical alter ego":** *Los Angeles Examiner*, January 12, 1949.

117 **call came through:** See the testimony of Officer Harry Hansen in the DA grand jury proceedings. Hansen states that Dillon was released at 11:00 or 11:30 a.m. in the morning.

Chapter 12: Breaking Point

118 **utilities man for the movies:** *Los Angeles Examiner*, January 13, 1949.

118 **"We have insufficient evidence":** *Los Angeles Examiner*, January 13, 1949.

119 **"I have been in custody":** *Los Angeles Examiner*, January 16, 1949.

120 **lie detector and scopolamine tests:** Testimony of private investigator Fred Witman in the DA grand jury proceedings.

121 **attorney Morris Lavine:** *Los Angeles Times*, "Cathedral's Site a Legal Battleground," December 2, 1996.

122 **with her and his wife in a bar:** As reported by Officer Ahern in testimony before the DA grand jury proceedings.

122 **Jeff's story changed:** *Los Angeles Times*, January 14, 1949.

122 **2:00 to 11:00 p.m.:** *Chester Times* (Pennsylvania), January 14, 1949.

122 **friendly with Mark Hansen . . . helpful police officers:** Testimony of Officer Finis Brown in the DA grand jury proceedings.

123 **after Leslie Dillon was released:** Confirmed by Officer Ahern in testimony given in the DA grand jury proceedings; see also testimony of Fred Witman, ibid.

124 **Sara Boynoff . . . interview with Dr. De River:** *Los Angeles Daily News*, January 20, 1949.

124 **Judge Scott:** For discussion of the Chloe Davis case and the subsequent orders imposed by Judges Fox and Scott, see pages 86–87.

124 **doctor's birth name:** De River's death certificate lists his name as "Joseph Paul deRiver," his parents as "Paul M. deRiver, France," and "Helen Harper, Louisiana," and his birthday as November 6,

1894. There is, however, no recorded birth of someone with the surname "deRiver" in the year 1894. There is a record of birth of a Joseph L. Israel in New Orleans, Louisiana, on November 15, 1894. According to the certificate the parents were Mayer Israel, merchant, and wife Rose Lazard, both from New Orleans.

125 **"blindly in hiring this man":** *San Bernardino County Sun,* January 22, 1949.

125 **hearing before the City Council:** "Report of a Special Hearing of Police and Fire and Personnel Committees of the City Council of Los Angeles," March 8, 1949. Reproduced in Daniel, Jacque, *The Curse of the Black Dahlia,* pp. 135–61.

126 **letter from a William A. Miller:** Cited in King, Brian, *The Sexual Criminal,* p. liv.

126 **$100,000 claim:** *Los Angeles Times,* February 24, 1949.

127 **Arthur Brigham Rose:** Underwood, Aggie, *Newspaperwoman* (New York: Harper & Brothers, 1949), p. 178.

Chapter 13: The Lodger

128 **Case . . . Waggoner:** See testimonies of Officers Loren K. Waggoner and Archie Case at the DA grand jury proceedings.

128 **"Mayor of Watts":** Lieberman, Paul, *Gangster Squad.*

128 **Con Keller:** Lieberman, Paul, *Gangster Squad.* Keller's surname was sometimes incorrectly given as "Keeler."

128 **Ahern and Waggoner interviewed Jiggs Moore:** See testimony of Officers Ahern and Waggoner at the DA grand jury proceedings. The statements of Jiggs Moore and Mr. Carriere were filed with the LAPD but have never been released.

129 **later that year:** See testimony of Officer Ahern in the DA grand jury proceedings.

130 **Ardis Green . . . Ace Cains Nightclub:** See memorandum re: identification of photographs of Leslie Dillon by Miss Ardis Green, alias Joy Powers, DA grand jury documents.

130 **day Beth split with Gordon Fickling:** Ibid.

130 **Dillon's mother, Mamie, had mentioned:** Testimony of Officer Ahern in the DA grand jury proceedings.

131 **Hoffman . . . Lila Durant . . . Moorman:** Taken from the testimonies of Officers Waggoner, Case, and Ahern in the DA grand jury proceedings. Also the report (undated) of Officers

Waggoner and Ward filed to Sergeant A. A. Beach of the University
Division.

132 **had not reported the matter:** Report of Officers Waggoner and
Ward to Sergeant A. A. Beach of University Division, DA grand
jury proceedings.

133 **January 7 . . . 18:** From the testimony of Officer Waggoner at the
DA grand jury proceedings. Officer Ahern put the dates of arrival
as January 10 and departure as January 17.

134 **she had destroyed them:** Testimony of Officer Ahern in the DA
grand jury proceedings.

135 **Tommy Harlow:** Among the documents admitted into evidence
in the DA grand jury proceedings was a teletype from the
police department at Fort Worth, Texas. It described Harlow
as thirty-eight years old, five-foot-seven-and-a-half inches, 170
pounds, with brown hair and blue eyes. He had lived for many
years in Dallas and Fort Worth, Texas, before coming out West. On
January 3, 1949, Officers Kenard and Sawyer interviewed Mr. Sam
Rutherford and C. J. Bernard, who said Harlow had left about May
or June 1948 and was believed to be doing construction work in
Harlem City.

135 **Harlow told Officers Waggoner and Ahern:** Taken from the
testimony of Officers Waggoner and Ahern during the DA grand
jury proceedings. Additional citations from documents admitted
into evidence by Fred Witman in testimony given to Lieutenant
Frank B. Jemison and DDA Arthur L. Veitch.

135 **trailer parked outside the house:** Taken from: report of
Lieutenant Burns dated January 8, 1949; report of Burns, Greilly,
and Jones dated February 16, 1949. Both reports cited in testimony
by Fred Witman to Lieutenant Frank B. Jemison and DDA Arthur
L. Veitch in the DA grand jury proceedings. The reports have never
been released.

136 **he had worked for Tommy Harlow:** Report of Officers Burns,
Greilly, and Jones dated February 16, 1949. Cited in evidence by
Fred Witman in testimony to Lieutenant Frank B. Jemison and
DDA Arthur L. Veitch in the DA grand jury proceedings. The
report has never been released. See also the testimony of Officer
Ahern in the DA grand jury proceedings. Mrs. McCromber's
testimony established the crucial point that Dillon worked on-and-

off for Harlow, and therefore visited Los Angeles intermittently, even when he was based in San Francisco, over the latter part of December 1946 and January 1947.

137 **sleep at one of the units:** Report by Officers Ahern and Waggoner cited in evidence by Fred Witman to Lieutenant Frank B. Jemison and DDA Arthur L. Veitch in the DA grand jury proceedings. The report has never been released.

137 **Leslie Dillon was the man who had visited:** See testimony of Officer Ahern in the DA grand jury proceedings.

138 **"'This is the girl that was there'":** As recounted by Officer Waggoner in the DA grand jury proceedings.

138 **"remember things":** Further details from the important report filed with Sergeant A. A. Beach by Officers Waggoner and Ward, included in the DA grand jury proceedings documents.

138 **took a liking to Archie Case:** See testimony of Officer Ahern in the DA grand jury proceedings.

139 **Dillon looked like the man who had been sick:** Statement of James Hurst dated April 15, 1949, referred to in DA document dated November 23, 1949, and titled "Evidence and Declarations Tending to Connect or Disconnect Leslie Dillon to the Murders of Elizabeth Short, Jeanne French, and Gladys Kern."

140 **who could have been Leslie Dillon:** Statement of Burt Moorman dated March 16th, 1949, referred to in DA document dated November 23, 1949, and titled "Evidence and declarations tending to connect or disconnect Leslie Dillon to the murders of Elizabeth Short, Jeanne French, and Gladys Kern."

141 **"fellow from Batavia":** Testimony of Officer Waggoner in the DA grand jury proceedings. Also report of Officers Waggoner and Ward to Sergeant A. A. Beach of University Division, DA grand jury proceedings.

141 **"Dutch Embassy or Danish consulate":** Testimony of H. Hoffman in the DA grand jury proceedings, December 28, 1949.

142 **"have me shot or something":** See report filed by Officers Waggoner and Ward with Sergeant A. A. Beach in the DA grand jury proceedings.

143 **Clora Hoffman also recalled:** Ibid.

143 **"remember some of the things that happened":** Ibid.

144 **Occupation of Aster Motel:** Some of the witnesses (especially

the Moormans) were confused as to which cabins various guests stayed in. On this issue the account of the Hoffmans has been preferred, as they were the actual owners of the motel, and can be assumed to have been the most familiar with the cabins.

144 **"just couldn't figure it out"**: See testimony of Officer Waggoner in the DA grand jury proceedings. The "official" reason for Waggoner being taken off the Gangster detail was that his father had just become a bail bondsman.

144 **"never did learn the reason why"**: Waggoner quoted in the *Long Beach Independent*, December 2, 1949.

145 **allocation of resources . . . was so poor**: Officer Waggoner told the 1949 grand jury that he asked to be taken off the Dahlia case because there was an inadequate supply of nighttime patrol cars at the University Division.

145 **submitted a final joint report**: The very important report by Officers Waggoner and Ward addressed to Sergeant Beach of University, which is filed with the DA grand jury proceedings. The actual report is undated, but from the testimony of Garth Ward it appears to have been filed at the end of their assignment, i.e., end of July or early August 1949. The report was certainly written up after the shooting of Mark Hansen on July 15, as it makes reference to this event.

Chapter 14: Kiss Tomorrow Goodbye

146 **General William Worton**: Buntin, John, *L.A. Noir.*

148 **Brenda Allen, Hollywood's**: For a detailed account of this scandal, see Lieberman, Paul, *Gangster Squad*; also Buntin, John, *L.A. Noir.*

148 **mysteriously stalled**: Buntin, John, *L.A. Noir.*

149 **charity lotteries were raided**: *San Bernardino County Sun*, June 29, 1949.

149 **few believed he personally knew**: Buntin, John, *L.A. Noir*, footnote to Chapter 12; Woods, J. Gerald, "The Progressive and the Police: Urban Reform and the Professionalization of the Los Angeles Police," UCLA dissertation, 1973, p. 408.

149 **lie detector tests**: *Long Beach Independent*, July 1, 1949.

149 **none of the cops . . . convicted**: Buntin, John, *L.A. Noir.*

149 **Jimmy Vaus . . . wire recordings:** Lieberman, Paul, *Gangster Squad.*

150 **Thaddeus Brown:** *San Bernardino County Sun,* July 8, 1949.

Chapter 15: Panic in the Streets

151 **consequences . . . sharp and swift:** As recounted by Officers Case and Ahern in testimony before the 1949 grand jury.

152 **"change in administration":** See testimony of Officers Case and Ahern in the 1949 DA grand jury proceedings.

152 **"bad situation over there in the police department":** *Long Beach Independent,* July 1, 1949.

152 **September 13, 1949, the *Herald-Express*:** The article was picked up on the same day in later editions of local newspapers, e.g., the *Santa Cruz Sentinel.*

154 **follow-up article:** Again, this was picked up in later editions of local newspapers, e.g., *The Long Beach Independent,* September 15, 1949.

156 **several curious facts:** Even more curiously, the day before the *Examiner* article appeared, September 14, the *Los Angeles Times* reported that Thad Brown had denied that the Black Dahlia murder occurred in a motel on "S Figueroa Street." The article claimed that rooms at the motel had been reexamined by LAPD forensic chemist Ray Pinker "two months ago," because examination of the Black Dahlia file revealed that original tests had only been carried out at some of the cabins. The article clearly was referring to the motel on Flower Street and is of interest in that it suggests that tests were initially carried out at the motel prior to 1949, and again in the summer of 1949. The article also quoted Thad Brown as confirming that the motel was the *only location that had ever been identified as the place where the murder was committed.* This confirms that no location during the investigation was seriously considered a possible locus for the crime other than the Aster Motel.

157 **Thad who rushed to Hansen's bedside:** See memorandum dated November 17, 1949, to Arthur L. Veitch, "In re Mark Hansen—Lola Titus incident," DA grand jury documents.

158 **"promised to marry her, and didn't":** *San Bernardino County Sun,* September 22, 1949.

158 **"I never touched her":** *San Bernardino County Sun*, July 27, 1949.

158 **gavel came down:** Renner, Joan, *Deranged L.A. Crimes/Lola Titus, Deranged L.A. Crimes* blog.

158 **short, sad life:** Lola Olive Titus (her real name, contrary to some reports) died in November 1958 in an insane asylum. *San Bernardino County Sun*, November 15, 1958.

158 **"look into sinister reports":** *Long Beach Independent*, September 19, 1949.

159 ***Herald-Express* was more explicit:** *Herald-Express*, September 8, 1949.

PART 3: RAW DEAL

Chapter 16: Key Witness

166 **Witman in his covering letter:** Letter from Fred Witman to Arthur Lutz of the grand jury criminal complaints committee dated September 9, 1949, in the DA grand jury proceedings.

166 **given under oath:** Details of Fred Witman's background and statement taken from his testimony to Veitch and Stanley in the DA grand jury documents.

167 **dog leash:** Curiously, the dog leash was not submitted by the LAPD to the FBI for forensic examination, unlike other forensic evidence in the case, such as Mark Hansen's notebook, the letters sent to the *Examiner* newspaper, and the brush bristles found on the body. The LAPD's internal forensic report on the leash has never been released. The actual leash has supposedly, along with all the other real evidence in the case, disappeared. While this raises questions as to the possible suppression of evidence by certain LAPD officers at the time of the events in question, there is no evidence that today's LAPD has any knowledge of, or involvement in, how this happened. (See the preface of this book.)

170 **"investigation by grand jury":** *San Bernardino County Sun*, October 14, 1949.

170 **"bungling" . . . "petty chiseling":** *Santa Cruz Sentinel*, October 14, 1949.

170 **result of a secret meeting:** Memorandum from Frank Jemison dated October 28, 1949, in the DA grand jury files.

170   **Los Angeles County grand jury:** See Stoker, Charles, *Thicker'n Thieves.*

171   **Harry A. Lawson:** Taken from the recollections of Harry Lawson in the *Eagle Rock Sentinel*, March 9, 1985.

172   **Dr. Paul De River gave evidence:** Report by Frank B Jemison dated November 14, 1950, in the DA grand jury proceedings.

172   **dependent on the reports:** As pointed out in Stoker, Charles, *Thicker'n Thieves.*

172   **Hugh Farnham . . . secret mission:** See letters from Inspector Hugh Farnham, addressed to the "Chief" (referring to Thad Brown), dated October 28 and 29, 1949.

Chapter 17: The Glass Alibi

177   **fired from the Devonshire:** Testimony of Woodrow Wood as cited in the undated report on Leslie Duane Dillon by Frank Jemison, DA grand jury documents.

177   **Mrs. Shirly Anderson:** Accounts of Dillon's alibis are taken from report dated November 23, 1949, no author given, "Evidence and Declarations Tending to Connect or Disconnect Leslie Dillon to the Murders of Elizabeth Short, Jeanne French, and Gladys Kern," DA grand jury proceedings.

178   **El Cortez Hotel in San Francisco:** The police reports do not actually identify in which city the "El Cortez hotel" that Leslie Dillon checked into was located. However, given that Dillon moved there after leaving his San Francisco apartment and before moving into his mother-in-law's house in Los Angeles, it is most likely to have been the El Cortez Hotel on Geary Street, San Francisco.

178   **moved his family:** See undated report by Frank Jemison on the movements of Leslie Dillon in the DA documents.

178   **adopt the alias of "Woodrow":** A police report refers to Dillon using the alias W. Wood. (See undated DA document, "Movements and Activities of Leslie Duane Dillon.")

180   **police officers . . . took the stand:** The account of the testimonies of all LAPD officers is taken from the transcripts of their testimonies in the DA grand jury file.

182   **"he was directly concerned with this murder":** Literally in the transcript, "*It* was directly concerned . . . ," [my italics], although the meaning is clearly "he."

183   **one witness had said:** An unidentified girl who had stayed at
Mark Hansen's home on Carlos Avenue. See testimony of Willie
Burns in the DA grand jury proceedings.

184   **a few days from April 5, 1947:** DA document entitled
"Movements and Activities of Leslie Duane Dillon."

185   **"The case could have been solved":** *Long Beach Independent,*
December 2, 1949; see also testimony of Loren K. Waggoner in the
DA grand jury proceedings.

188   **seven officers who testified:** *Herald-Express,* December 1, 1949.

188   **Harry . . . stepped into the witness box:** Based on the testimony
of Lieutenant Harry Hansen at the DA grand jury proceedings.

189   **"little pet theory":** Various names have been posited for a
"medical man" who might have killed Elizabeth Short, including
those of several known abortionists. From evidence available to
date, none has been shown to be a viable suspect.

190   **"She didn't have any":** Interview in *Los Angeles Times West*
magazine, March 28, 1971.

194   **Captain Francis Kearney . . . not called to give testimony:**
If Captain Kearney was called to give testimony before the grand
jury, his testimony—like that of Officer Jones—seems to have
disappeared or to be unavailable.

195   **fully expected indictments:** Pacios, Mary, *Childhood Shadows,*
p. 112.

Chapter 18: The Verdict

196   **Harry Lawson:** *Los Angeles Examiner,* December 7, 1949.

197   **Jemison presented another report:** Document entitled
"Summary of Elizabeth (Beth) Short investigation" in the DA grand
jury files, signed by Jemison.

199   **re-interview . . . Ann Toth:** Taken from the statement of Ann
Toth interviewed by Frank Jemison and Ed Barrett on December
13, 1949, DA grand jury proceedings.

200   **interviewed Mark Hansen:** Taken from the statement of
Mark Hansen interviewed by Frank Jemison and Ed Barrett on
December 16, 1949, DA grand jury proceedings.

200   **Hansen then backtracked:** See final report of DA investigator
Frank Jemison dated February 20, 1951, DA grand jury
proceedings.

204 **retirement banquet . . . Clemence Horrall:** King, Brian, introduction to *The Sexual Criminal*, p. lx.

Chapter 19: Detour

207 **trial for incest began on December 8, 1949:** Hodel, Steve, *Black Dahlia Avenger*, Arcade, Kindle edition 2003, 2011.
207 **cross-examination of . . . Tamar:** Ibid.
208 **less than four hours' deliberation:** Ibid.
208 **People at the DA's office wanted revenge:** See George Hodel confidential telephone transcripts, ed. Steve Hodel, 2004, p. 26: "They're out to get me. Two men in the Da's [sic] office were transferred and demoted because of my trial."
208 **charges of tax evasion:** Ibid., p. 90: comments of DA investigator Walter Morgan, who is listening in on Hodel recording: "This spool and #25 following should be checked with federal income tax man in the future as Hodel's income tax is computed with this man, and it looks like they are about to 'take' Uncle for a few bucks." Also p. 91, "Spools 25 and 26 and 27 will prove very interesting to income tax investigators."
208 **allegations that he had killed his secretary:** Ibid., p. 27: "They thought there was something fishy. Anyway, now they may have figured it out. Killed her. Maybe I did kill my secretary." Hodel admits that he performed illegal abortions, "lots of them" (p. 155).
208 **accusations of being a closet Communist:** George Hodel refers several times in the recorded telephone transcripts to being investigated by the FBI. His son Steve unearthed his father's FBI file, which reveals he was being monitored for association with the Severance Club and various other leftist causes (Hodel, Steve, *Black Dahlia Avenger*).
208 **journalists . . . parked outside his front door:** George Hodel confidential telephone transcripts, ed. Steve Hodel, 2004, p. 78.
209 **convinced was hidden somewhere:** The transcript of the Hodel house bugging is full of references to the doctor's conviction that there is a bug in the house. There are repeated searches for it: banging in the basement, the opening and closing of drawers and boxes, Hodel's orders to his housekeeper, Ellen, to find the bug, the repeated turning up of the radio to drown out conversation. Further explicit references include: "Haven't been able to find it yet. Must be

around somewhere" (p. 25); "Time for research (Lots of pounding)" (p. 27); "Are there any more cops around" (p. 40); "We're tapped now again" (p. 48); "There must be something" / "There isn't anything" / "I'm pretty sure there is something" (p. 48); "He told her to never talk over the phone" (p. 52); "Did you look in the little box in there?" (p. 57); "Hodel ordered Ellen not to answer any questions over the telephone " (p. 59); various sounds of digging, hammering, and pounding in search for bug (pp. 85–86). "Don't say anything over the phone—it is tapped" (p. 95). "You're talking over a tapped line. Oh yes, it's been tapped for a long time" (p. 110). "Hodel seems to be opening and closing drawers" (p. 116). "Hodel says probably they are watching me" (p. 151). Citations from George Hodel confidential telephone transcripts, ed. Steve Hodel, 2004.

209   **two women believed the doctor had known Elizabeth Short:** They were (1) a woman named Lillian Lenorak, who had been persuaded by Hodel not to testify against him in the Tamar incest trial, and was wracked with guilt as a result; and (2) Mattie Comfort, a model who was one of the doctor's many girlfriends. It is telling that none of Elizabeth's own friends, relatives, or acquaintances ever mentioned a doctor as one of her boyfriends, or the name of George Hodel.

210   **Dr. Margaret Chung:** For an in-depth examination of the extraordinary and colorful life of Mom Chung, see Tzu-Chun Wu, Judy, *Doctor Mom Chung of the Fair-Haired Bastards: The Life of the Wartime Celebrity*, University of California Press, 2005.

Chapter 20: Fall Guy

211   **knives came out for Dr. De River:** The details of the campaign against Dr. De River are taken from King, Brian, introduction to *The Sexual Criminal*, pp. lxii–lxviii.

212   **"in retaliation":** See King, Brian, introduction to *The Sexual Criminal*.

212   **pioneering book:** See, for example, the modern criminal profiler Roy Hazelwood, who cites from and develops De River's work.

213   **Councilman Ernest E. Debs:** Cited in King, Brian, introduction to *The Sexual Criminal*, p. lxiii.

213   **suspended . . . without pay:** King, Brian, introduction to *The Sexual Criminal*, p. lxiii.

213   **before Municipal Judge Vernon W. Hunt:** Details of the trial
      are taken from King, Brian, introduction to *The Sexual Criminal*,
      pp. lxvi–lxvii.

215   **Parker . . . the top job:** See Buntin, John, *L.A. Noir: The
      Struggle for the Soul of America's Most Seductive City*, Broadway
      Books, Kindle edition, 2009.

215   **a new era:** For the transition to the Parker era generally and the
      evolution of the LAPD over this period, see Domanick, Joe, *To
      Protect and to Serve*, Pocket Books, 1995, pp. 102–3.

216   **"Lieutenant Hamilton":** Account and dialogue from Hamilton's
      visit are taken from the memoirs of De River's daughter, Jacqueline:
      Daniel, Jacque, *The Curse of the Black Dahlia*, Digital Data Werks,
      2004, pp. 1–4.

217   **Lieutenant James Hamilton:** For an in-depth investigation of
      James Hamilton, his friendship with Robert Kennedy, and his
      appearance on the scene at Marilyn Monroe's death, see Margolis,
      Jay, *Marilyn Monroe: A Case for Murder*, iUniverse LLC, Kindle
      edition, 2011.

217   **two men trespassing:** See King, Brian, introduction to *The
      Sexual Criminal*, p. lxiii.

217   **patrol car would be waiting to follow:** Daniel, Jacque, *The
      Curse of the Black Dahlia*, pp. 187–88.

218   **"We came to the conclusion":** Ibid., p. 189.

218   **"dead fish on the doorstep":** Author interview with one of Dr.
      De River's granddaughters (name withheld).

218   **to tide the family over:** Daniel, Jacque, *The Curse of the Black
      Dahlia*, p. 185.

218   **"seemed to behave differently, nervous":** Cited in Pacios,
      Mary, *Childhood Shadows*, p. 114.

218   **"The police had him, and they let him go":** Ibid., p. 114.

218   **Rilla, in a letter to Jacqueline:** Cited in Daniel, Jacque, *The
      Curse of the Black Dahlia*, introduction.

219   **"Bloody Christmas":** Cited in Wagner, Rob Leicester, *Red Ink,
      White Lies*, Dragonflyer Press, 2000, p. 240, from an interview of
      Himmel by Wagner in 1998.

220   **"In Los Angeles, where glamour":** See Radin, Edward D., *12
      Against Crime*, Bantam Books, 1951 (first published by Putnam,
      April 1950), p. 70.

Chapter 21: Voice in the Wind

222   **It was late 1953:** Details of the half dozen visits of Wally Klein and Donald Freed to De River in 1953 are taken from the author's extensive interviews with Donald Freed in Los Angeles in January and May 2016.

223   **Klein's nephew, Donald Freed:** Wally Klein was in fact the brother of Freed's stepmother, Beatrice Klein Freed.

223   **recollection . . . Ellery E. Cuff:** Freed has a clear recollection that a man from the Los Angeles Public Defender's Office was present at the interviews to lend his support to De River. This was most likely Ellery E. Cuff, who was a close friend and colleague of the doctor, and contributed a chapter to the doctor's textbook *The Sexual Criminal.*

227   **float out of the phonograph:** Willie Burns in his testimony to the grand jury stated that "all files and records relating to the case had been given over to Homicide, with exception of wax recordings which are in the Crime Laboratory." Clearly, from Donald Freed's recollection of the interviews with Dr. De River, the doctor had kept some of the recordings, or copies of them.

229   **"signature" . . . contrasted with . . . "modus operandi":** For detailed discussion of the distinction, see Douglas, John E., and Mark Olshaker, *The Anatomy of Motive,* Pocket Books, 2000; Turvey, Brent E., *Criminal Profiling: An Introduction to Behavioral Evidence Analysis,* fourth edition, Academic Press, 2011; Turvey, Brent E., and Jerry W. Chisum, *Crime Reconstruction,* second edition, Academic Press 2011. Also Keppel, Robert D., *Signature Killers,* Pocket Books, 1997. Keppel gives some examples of "signature behavior"—i.e., acts going beyond what is necessary to commit a crime, and which therefore constitute the killer's unique calling card —such as carving on the body or leaving messages in blood.

PART 4: OUT OF THE PAST

Chapter 22: The Name of the Rose

235   **Zodiac . . . BTK . . . John Reginald Christie: Zodiac:** a killer who operated in Northern California in the 1960s and '70s, whose identity remains unknown. Notorious for sending cryptic "messages" to police and the press. **BTK:** Dennis Lynn Rader, the

self-styled "Blind, Torture, Kill" murderer, who killed ten people in Sedgewick County, Kansas, between 1974 and 1991. Sent letters describing the killings to police and the press. **John Reginald Christie:** British serial killer active in the 1940s and '50s. Gave detailed testimony that led to the prosecution and conviction of a tenant of his for killings that he probably committed himself. For further case studies of serial killers and communication, see Gibson, Dirk C., *Clues from Serial Killers*, Praeger, 2004.

236 **"creative writing":** The fragments are unsigned, although, in his testimony to Veitch and Stanley, Fred Witman said they had been written by Dillon.

236 **synopses for stories:** There appears to be some confusion as to whether the fragments were found by Officer Jones in Dillon's room in Miami, or subsequently in his luggage. A police report summarizing Witman's statement refers to "fragments of letters probably found by Jones in Miami room" (DA police reports, breakdown of Witman's statement entitled "Letters and Writings").

240 **that of killing a woman:** See DA testimony of Fred Witman to Arthur Veitch and H. L. Stanley dated September 23, 1949.

241 **Keppel . . . "piquerism":** Keppel, Robert D., *Signature Killers*, Pocket Books, 1997.

241 **an intriguing photograph:** The original photograph has disappeared but it may have been among photographs now missing from the collection of the journalist John Gilmore at UCLA.

242 **case against George Hodel was notably weak:** A detailed rebuttal of Steve Hodel's claim that his father, Dr. George Hodel, was the Dahlia killer is beyond the scope of this book. One of Hodel's more bizarre contentions is that the posing of the body by the killer was an homage to the work of the Surrealist artist Man Ray, a friend of his father. The idea that the posing of the body was some form of "artwork" can be traced to the theory posited by author Mary Pacios, in her book *Childhood Shadows*, that the killer was the actor/director Orson Welles, and that the bisecting of Elizabeth's body resembled the dismembered mannequins in the "crazy house" set from the movie *The Lady from Shanghai* (Pacios, Mary, *Childhood Shadows*, p. 138). Steve Hodel did at one point convince Deputy District Attorney Stephen Kay that his father was the Dahlia killer, although it seems that Kay based his opinion

partly on treating Hodel's contentions as established fact. Steve
Hodel has subsequently written further books claiming that his
father was responsible for many other lone women killings in Los
Angeles, Chicago, and the Philippines, as well the Zodiac murders
in San Francisco.

245   **Carl Balsiger:** See closure report of Frank Jemison dated
February 20, 1951, DA grand jury files. The date of Balsiger's
overnight stay at the Yucca Street motel with Short is variously
given as December 7 and 8 in the police reports. According to
newspaper reports, Dorothy French found Elizabeth crashed out at
the Aztec on the night of December 8, 1946.

245   **Balsiger had married Jane Ellen Moyer:** See *Lincoln Journal*
(Nebraska), October 27, 1949; the *Lincoln Star*, December 28,
1949.

245   **passed a lie detector test:** See Jemison's final report, ibid.

245   **name was included in Elizabeth's address book:** See the
interview of Robert "Red" Manley carried out by Frank Jemison on
February 1, 1950, in which names from the address book are read
out to Manley. They include Carl Balsiger. Another police report
states that Balsiger's name was not in the address book but on a
piece of paper folded in with the victim's belongings, which had
been sent to the police. If this was the case, it was even less likely
that Balsiger was the killer.

247   **Tanya "Sugar" Geise:** Actress and featured dancer at the
Florentine Gardens. Married Walter Morgan of the Los Angeles
DA's Office June 7, 1945 (*Billboard*, June 23, 1945). Frank Jemison's
DA closure report, dated February 20, 1951, states that Sugar Geise
knew Mark Hansen "very well."

247   **Nieson Himmel gave an interview:** See Pacios, Mary,
Childhood Shadows, p. 103.

251   **Pamela . . . recorded a filmed interview:** Interview with
Pamela Hoffman recorded in July 2012, shortly before she died of
pancreatic cancer.

252   **tests at the Aster Motel:** Taken from document entitled
"Evidence Tending to Connect or Disconnect Leslie Dillon to the
Murders of Elizabeth Short, Jeanne French and Gladys Kern," DA
grand jury documents.

254   **made a discovery:** The photograph was originally published in a

book about the Black Dahlia case by the late actor and journalist John Gilmore, *Severed: The True Story of the Black Dahlia*, first published by Amok Books in 1994.

Chapter 23: Specter of the Rose

255   **here was a photograph:** Various writers of books and articles on the Black Dahlia case have referred to the transcript of the hearing with Fred Witman and either searched for or claimed to have seen the letter *D*, but none has actually identified and subjected to expert analysis the markings on an original autopsy photograph as discussed here. (See for example the writer and researcher Stephen Karadjis in an article in *Crime* magazine, "The Murder of the Black Dahlia: The Ultimate Cold Case" [February 3, 2014].) From the testimony of Fred Witman it is clear that there existed at one point *close-up* photographs of the pubic region showing the lacerations in detail, which must have been examined by the graphologists subsequently employed by the LAPD to analyze the markings. These close-up photographs seem to have been lost. Interestingly, the writer Steve Hodel refers to some autopsy photographs that were apparently withheld by Detective Harry Hansen. It is possible that these included the close-ups of the pubic region, showing the markings and the letter *D* with greater clarity.

255   **with the initial D:** There has been speculation that the letter *D* referred to the Italian mob boss Jack Dragna, whose home was close to the body dump site at Leimert Park. However, there is no reference to Dragna in any of the case files and no evidence to link him to Elizabeth Short.

255   **"impossible to determine":** Undated and unidentified document headed "Evidence and Declarations Tending to Connect or Disconnect Leslie Dillon to the Murders of Elizabeth Short, Jeanne French, and Gladys Kern," included in DA documents.

257   **naming . . . proprietorship:** See Graham, Loren, *The Power of Names: In Culture and in Mathematics*, Proceedings of the American Philosophical Society, vol. 157, no. 2, June 2013.

257   **Keppel, the leading expert:** See Keppel, Robert, *Signature Killers . . .*

258   **rows of books behind glass doors:** Cf. Chandler, Raymond, *The Lady in the Lake*, Alfred A. Knopf, 1943, Chapter 17.

261 **Michael Streed's report:** Report dated May 16, 2017, from Michael Streed/SketchCop Solutions to Piu Eatwell.

262 **Black Dahlia Case Internet discussion forum:** The Black Dahlia in Hollywood Discussion Forum at http://forum.theblackdahliainhollywood.com/.

Postscript

269 **"lost his marbles":** According to *Los Angeles Times* reporter Nieson Himmel. See Pacios, Mary, *Childhood Shadows*, p. 104.

BIBLIOGRAPHY

PRIMARY SOURCES

Documents relating to the Black Dahlia case, released to the author by the Los Angeles County District Attorney's Office in June 2015, in response to a Freedom of Information Act request (not catalogued).

Documents relating to the Black Dahlia case, released by the U.S. Federal Bureau of Investigation to the author for the first time in unredacted form in September 2015, in response to a Freedom of Information Act request (not catalogued).

Documents relating to the Black Dahlia case, released to the author by the Los Angeles Police Department in September 2015, in response to a legal demand under the California Public Records Act (not catalogued).

Archives of journalist and Dahlia researcher John Gilmore, UCLA Library, Department of Special Collections. Material relating to the Dahlia case and the book *Severed*.

Archives of James Hugh Richardson, UCLA Library, Department of Special Collections. Biographical material and material relating to the Dahlia case.

Archives of Agness M. Underwood, Oviatt Library, California State University, Northridge. Biographical material and material relating to the Dahlia case.

Archives of *Los Angeles Times* journalist Jack Smith, Huntington Library, San Marino, California, box S3, "Black Dahlia."

Los Angeles Times records, Huntington Library, San Marino, California, MssLat folder 7, "Crime—Los Angeles," Fowler, Will, *From a Reporter's Notebook*.

References to military records, birth, marriage, and death certificates, newspaper articles, and census records are identified in the Endnotes by appropriate source references.

SECONDARY SOURCES

Anger, Kenneth, *Hollywood Babylon*, Dell, 1975.

Austin, John, *Hollywood's Greatest Mysteries*, SPI Books, 1994.

Badal, James Jesson, *In the Wake of the Butcher: Cleveland's Torso Murders*, Kent State University Press, 2013.

Barker, John T., *Missouri Lawyer*, Dorrance, 1949.

Buntin, John, *L.A. Noir: The Struggle for the Soul of America's Most Seductive City*, Kindle edition, Broadway Books, 2009.

Burroughs, Edgar Rice, *The Girl from Hollywood*, McCauley, 1922.

Cairns, Kathleen A., *Front-Page Women Journalists, 1920–50*, University of Nebraska Press, 2003.

Carlo, Yvonne De, with Doug Warren, *Yvonne: An Autobiography*, St. Martin's Press, 1987.

Carter, Vince A., *LAPD's Rogue Cops*, Desert View Books, 1993.

Chandler, Raymond:
   The Lady in the Lake, Knopf, 1943.
   The High Window, Hamish Hamilton, 1943.
   The Little Sister, Hamish Hamilton, 1949.

Collins, Max Allan, *Angel in Black (Nathan Heller Novels)*, Thomas & Mercer, 2011.

Cray, Ed, *Ramblin' Man: The Life and Times of Woody Guthrie*, Kindle edition, W. W. Norton, 2012.

Daniel, Jacque, *The Curse of the Black Dahlia*, Digital Data Werks, 2004.

Domanick, Joe:
   To Protect and to Serve: The LAPD's Century of War in the City of Dreams, Pocket Books, 1995.
   Blue: The LAPD and the Battle to Redeem American Policing, Simon & Schuster, 2015.

Douglas, John E., and Mark Olshaker:
   The Anatomy of Motive, Pocket Books, 2000.
   The Cases That Haunt Us, Prentice Hall, 2000.

Dunne, John Gregory, *True Confessions: A Novel*, Da Capo Press 2005.

Ellroy, James:
   The Black Dahlia (L.A. Quartet), Mysterious Press, 1987.
   My Dark Places, Knopf, 1996.

Fitzgerald, F. Scott, *The Last Tycoon*, Charles Scribner's Sons, 1941.

Fowler, Will, *Reporters: Memoirs of a Young Newspaperman*, Roundtable, 1991.

Freed, Donald, ed. (with Citizens Research and Investigation Committee), *The Glasshouse Tapes*, Avon Books, 1973.

Geiger, Jeffrey E., *Camp Cooke and Vandenberg Air Force Base, 1941–1966: From Armor and Infantry Training to Space and Missile Launches*, McFarland, 2014.

Gibson, Dirk C., *Clues from Serial Killers*, Praeger, 2004.

Giesler, Jerry, with Pete Martin, *The Jerry Giesler Story*, Simon & Schuster, 1960.

Gilmore, John, *Severed: The True Story of the Black Dahlia*, Amok Books, 1994.

Graham, Loren, "The Power of Names: In Culture and in Mathematics," Proceedings of the American Philosophical Society, vol. 157, no. 2, June 2013.

Granlund, Nils T., *Blondes, Brunettes, and Bullets*, David McKay, 1957.

Guiza-Leimert, Maty, and Cynthia E. Exum, *Images of America: Leimert Park*, Arcadia, 2012.

Hallett, Hilary A., *Go West, Young Women!: The Rise of Early Hollywood*, University of California Press, 2013.

Hazelwood, Roy, and Stephen G. Michaud, *Dark Dreams: A Legendary FBI Profiler Examines Homicide and the Criminal Mind*, St. Martin's True Crime, 2002.

Henderson, Bruce, and Sam Summerlin, *The Supersleuths*, Macmillan, 1976.

Heimann, Jim, *Los Angeles: Portrait of a City*, Taschen, 2013.

Hodel, Steve:
    Black Dahlia Avenger, Kindle edition, Arcade, 2003, 2011.
    Black Dahlia Avenger II, Thoughtprint Press, 2013.
    (ed.) *Hodel-Black Dahlia Case File No. 30-1268: Official 1950 Law Enforcement Transcripts of Stake-Out and Electronic Recordings of Black Dahlia Murder Confession made by Dr. George Hill Hodel*, Thoughtprint Press, 2014.

Hoefling, Larry J., *Nils Thor Granlund*, McFarland, 2010.

Hopkins, Ernest Jerome, *Our Lawless Police: A Study of the Unlawful Enforcement of the Law*, Viking, 1931, reprinted by Da Capo Press, 1972.

Jennings, Dean, *We Only Kill Each Other: The Fascinating Life of the Man Who Inspired the Film* Bugsy, Penguin Books, 1967.

Jezek, George Ross, and Johnny Grant, *Hollywood Past & Present*, George Ross Jezek, 2002.

Keppel, Robert D., *Signature Killers*, Pocket Books, 1997.

King, Brian, *The Sexual Criminal: A Psychoanalytical Study by J. Paul De River*, Bloat Books, 2000.

Knowlton, Janice, and Michael Newton, *Daddy was the Black Dahlia Killer*, Pocket Books, 1995.

Lewis, Brad, *Mickey Cohen: The Gangster Squad and the Mob: The True Story of Vice in Los Angeles 1937–1950*, CreateSpace, 2012.

Lieberman, Paul, *Gangster Squad: Covert Cops, the Mob, and the Battle for Los Angeles*, Kindle edition, St. Martin's Griffin, 2012.

Madsen, Axel, *The Sewing Circle: Hollywood's Greatest Secret— Female Stars Who Loved Other Women*, Kindle edition, Open Road Distribution, 2015.

Malone, Michael P., Richard B. Roeder, and William L. Lang, *Montana: A History of Two Centuries*, revised edition, University of Washington Press, 1976.

Mann, William J., *Tinseltown: Murder, Morphine, and Madness at the Dawn of Hollywood*, Harper Paperbacks, 2013.

Margolis, Jay, *Marilyn Monroe: A Case for Murder*, Kindle edition, Universe, 2011.

McDougal, Dennis, *Privileged Son: Otis Chandler and the Rise and Fall of the L.A. Times Dynasty*, Da Capo Press, 2002.

McNamara, Kevin R., *The Cambridge Companion to the Literature of Los Angeles*, Cambridge University Press, 2010.

Nelson, Mark, and Sarah Hudson Bayliss, *Exquisite Corpse: Surrealism and the Black Dahlia Murder*, Bullfinch Press, 2006.

Nijman, Jan, *Miami: Mistress of the Americas*, University of Pennsylvania Press, 2013.

Noyes, Pete, *The Real L.A. Confidential*, CreateSpace, 2011.

Pacios, Mary, *Childhood Shadows: The Hidden Story of the Black Dahlia Murders*, AuthorHouse, 2007.

Pagan, Eduardo Obregon, *Murder at the Sleepy Lagoon: Zoot Suits, Race, and Riot in Wartime L.A.*, University of North Carolina Press, 2003.

Pizzitola, Louis, *Hearst Over Hollywood: Power, Passion, and Propaganda in the Movies*, Columbia University Press, 2002.

Radin, Edward D., *12 Against Crime*, Bantam Books, 1951 (first published by Putnam, April 1950).

Ramsland, Katherine, *The Mind of a Murderer: Privileged Access to the Demons That Drive Extreme Violence*, Praeger, 2011.

Reid, Ed, *Mickey Cohen: Mobster*, Pinnacle Books, 1973.

Renner, Joan, *The First with the Latest! Aggie Underwood, the Los Angeles Herald, and the Sordid Crimes of the City*, Photo Friends of the Los Angeles Public Library, 2015.

Richardson, James:
  For the Life of Me: Memoirs of a City Editor, G. P. Putnam's Sons, 1954.
  Spring Street: A Story of Los Angeles, Times-Mirror Press, 1922.

Saito, Shirley Jean, *"Aggie": The Biography of Los Angeles Newspaperwoman Agness Underwood*, MA thesis, California State University, Northridge, 1988.

Scicchitano, M. S., *Chops, Squads, Molls & Suckers: A Brief Dictionary of the Vernacular from the 1930s and 1940s*, CreateSpace, 2011.

Scott, Charles, *Black Dahlia: The Whole Story*, Charles Scott, 2014.

Special Committee to Investigate Organized Crime in Interstate Commerce ("Kefauver Committee"), Third Interim Report, Arco, 1951.

Spence, Clark C., *Montana: A Bicentennial History*, W. W. Norton, 1978.

Spinos, Juanita, *The Soul of Beth—the Luminous Black Dahlia*, Juana S. Arenas, 2014.

Starr, Kevin, *Embattled Dreams: California in War and Peace, 1940–1950*, Oxford University Press, 2003.

Stekel, Wilhelm, *Sadism and Masochism—The Psychology of Hatred and Cruelty*, vols. I and II, Grove Press, 1965.

Stoker, Sergeant Charles, *Thicker'n Thieves,* Kindle reissue, Thoughtprint Press, 2011.

Taylor, Troy, *Fallen Angel: The Tragic True Story of the Black Dahlia*, Whitechapel Productions, 2013.

Tejaratchi, Sean, and Katherine Dunn, *Death Scenes: A Homicide Detective's Scrapbook*, Feral House, 1996.

Tereba, Tere, *Mickey Cohen: The Life and Crimes of L.A.'s Notorious Mobster*, Kindle edition, ECW Press, 2012.

Thomas, Terry, *The Registration and Monitoring of Sex Offenders: A Comparative Study*, Routledge, 2011.

Townshend, Frank, *Earth*, Kimble & Bradford, 1929.

Tucker, Sophie, *Some of These Days*, Theatre Book Club, 1951.

Turnbull, Margaret, *The Close Up*, Harper & Brothers, 1918.

Turvey, Brent E.:
 Criminal Profiling: An Introduction to Behavioral Evidence Analysis, fourth edition, Academic Press, 2011.
 With Chisum, Jerry W., *Crime Reconstruction*, second edition, Academic Press, 2011.

Tzu-Chun Wu, Judy, *Doctor Mom Chung of the Fair-Haired Bastards: The Life of the Wartime Celebrity*, University of California Press, 2005.

Underwood, Agness, *Newspaperwoman*, Harper & Brothers, 1949.

Van Doren, Mamie, with Art Aveilhe, *Playing the Field*, Berkley Books, 1988.

Vaus, Jim, *Why I Quit Sydicated Crime*, Van Kampen Press, 1951.

Wagner, Rob Leicester, *Red Ink, White Lies: The Rise and Fall of Los Angeles Newspapers 1920-1962*, Dragonflyer Press, 2000.

Ware, Harlan, *Come Fill the Cup*, Random House, 1952.

Webb, Jack, *The Badge*, reissued with an introduction by James Ellroy, Arrow Books, 2005.

Wolfe, Donald H., *The Black Dahlia Files: The Mob, the Mogul, and the Murderer*, Time Warner Books, 2006.

Woods, J. Gerald, *The Progressive and the Police: Urban Reform and the Professionalization of the Los Angeles Police*, UCLA dissertation, 1973.

Zemeckis, Leslie, *Goddess of Love Incarnate: The Life of Stripteuse Lili St. Cyr*, Counterpoint Press, 2015.

A large number of newspaper reports, magazine articles, and pamphlets are also referred to in the book, identified individually in the endnotes. Local information such as descriptions of buildings, roads, and trolley cars comes from contemporary guides, maps, and photographs. Weather conditions on specific days are from the newspaper weather reports. References to feature and documentary films, along with websites, are sourced individually in the endnotes.

A NOTE ON MONEY

As the contemporary value of money is sometimes relevant to the story, in order to give the reader a rough idea of how much quoted sums were worth at the time, I have used the historic inflation calculator at Dollar Times, http://www.dollartimes.com/inflation/.

INDEX

Note: Page numbers followed by *n* indicate footnotes.